AN INKY PARADE

AN INKY PARADE

Tales for Bibliophiles

PRADEEP SEBASTIAN

hachette
INDIA

First published in 2024 by Hachette India
(Registered name: Hachette Book Publishing India Pvt. Ltd)
An Hachette UK company
www.hachetteindia.com

1

Hardback ISBN 978-93-5731-387-2
Ebook ISBN 978-93-5731-419-0

Hachette Book Publishing India Pvt. Ltd
4th & 5th Floors, Corporate Centre,
Plot No. 94, Sector 44, Gurugram 122003, India

Typeset in Sorts Mill Goudy 10.5/14
by R. Ajith Kumar, New Delhi

Printed and bound in India
by Manipal Technologies Limited

MIX
Paper from responsible sources
FSC™ C043100

For Mooch

who first showed me how to look at a book

&

Ferose

bibliophile-friend and fellow book hunter

'Books, to be interesting, must at least be second-hand.'

Christopher Sclater Millard,
in his Christmas 1919 Wildeana catalogue

'One of the many beauties of book collecting is that it is an activity that can be enjoyed, and mastered, at any level. We can all admire private libraries that are assembled with the backing of small fortunes, but just as impressive in my eyes are the collections that emerge from connoisseurship and perception deployed in the field, nudged along by serendipity and good old-fashioned luck.'

Nicholas A. Basbanes,
Foreword in *Rare Books Uncovered*

CONTENTS

PREFACE

I could have hardly dreamt that those manic visits to private circulating libraries and second-hand bookshops in Bangalore that I used to eagerly bicycle to as a fierce reader in the 1970s, would make me a bibliophile-writer and then turn me into a book collector, immersing me into the rare book world. Those little libraries have long vanished (and we don't really miss them, though we'd like some of that leafy city back) while Bengaluru's second-hand bookshops have, well, blossomed, and made bookworms out of all of us. But – and this goes for the whole country, not just my hometown – what is still lacking here are antiquarian bookshops, auction houses, serious book collectors and a functioning rare book trade.

More disappointing and even puzzling is the absence, with a few exceptions, of books on bibliophily from Indian writers. There's a lot of literary non-fiction – essays, reviews – on our bookstore shelves, but that's not exactly hardcore bibliophily. One of the sections in this book is titled 'All Kinds of Bibliophilia', and that just about describes *An Inky Parade*: writing that looks at varied aspects of book-love, bibliomania and the different stripes of book dealers, bibliophiles and book collectors out there. There is a further reading list at the end, of the best and most enjoyable memoirs of rare book dealers and collectors, and other must-read books on bibliophily.

An Inky Parade: Tales for Bibliophiles has some of my favourite previously published pieces, while several other essays have been written fresh for the book. Also in the book are: vignettes of the few Indian antiquarian bookshops and collectors, then and now; biblio spoofs and hoaxes, book crime, rare book hunting, underrated bibliomysteries, reviews of books on books, tales for bibliophiles and more of my adventures in book collecting, ending with my current focus: collecting Persian and Mughal manuscript miniatures. For those who know or have such intimacy with books and bookshops – whether ardent reader, devout bibliophile or irrepressible collector – I hope you will find something here to enjoy.

PART ONE

TALES FOR BIBLIOPHILES

'OLD-TYPE BOOKS ONLY'

I first heard of the itinerant book peddler, aka The Book Prince of Kolkata, from Madhava Rao, who had once been a reclusive and rather fussy antiquarian dealer in Bengaluru. I was grumbling to Rao one day about how seldom you see genuine antiquarian editions of any kind in our second-hand market and he said quite casually, 'Oh, there's a man from Kolkata in town hawking old books.'

I dismissed it right away. 'By old, they usually mean stuff from the forties and fifties.'

'No, no, he says most of what he has is from the eighteenth century, perhaps even older. Why don't you go and have a look?'

'Won't you be coming?' I asked, surprised. He looked up from marking prices on his books and said, 'See, I say there is no end to such things, you know.'

I knew. I hoped, though, that the end was still far away for me: that way of feeling about looking far and wide for books.

'So, where can I find him?'

'You can't. He'll find you.'

'What's that supposed to mean?'

'He's in some old hotel in the city, he won't say which. This week, he will be in Bengaluru, next week in Chennai, after that, perhaps, Hyderabad. I'll pass on your number to him and he'll get in touch if he wants you to look at his books.'

I learnt not long after that this itinerant dealer would move with his wares from city to city, staying a few months in one decrepit lodge after another, calling up second-hand booksellers and their customers to come look at his books. No one knows when he'll be in your city or where – a phone call comes out of the blue to say he's arrived and he gives you the name of a lodge in Kalasipalayam or off Avenue Road.

The call from the Book Prince came the next day, giving me the name of a lodge in Russell Market, with a forewarning: 'No new books, *only* old-type books'. The voice was surprisingly soft, even gentle. The whole thing seemed shady, so I rang up a younger, fitter bibliophile friend (who sometimes book hunts with me) to see if he'd join me. 'Should I bring along a pistol?' he asked.

'It would be unwise not to,' I replied.

'It sounds like something right out of a Holmes story – like in "The Red-Headed League",' he replied, adding, 'Perhaps we should call up some Russell Market Baker Street Irregulars to stand watch until we manage to exit safely.'

'Make the call,' I said, and hung up.

We found the lodge quickly enough; a passageway with welders tinkering and raising sparks led to a staircase with an empty reception desk. But adjoining the desk were two little rooms with their doors open, and outside one of them stood a man in a glittering gold shirt and a printed lungi, smoking. He was in his forties, thickset, with jet-black hair shiny from gel. A whiff of strong perfume drifted off him. 'Prince,' he said, smiling and gestured with his cigarette for us to enter. Oh, so his name was Prince.

We paused briefly at the landing, exchanging a quick glance with each other (for there were no Russell Market Irregulars looking out for us and my bibliophile companion only had a pen or two tucked somewhere in his shirt) and then cautiously stepped into the room. A double bed took up almost all the space inside, besides a tiny bathroom. *Where the hell are the books?* we wondered. Prince glided in, but kept the door open. 'What are you looking for?' he asked, waving his cigarette around the room. 'Anything,' I replied, slowly looking around the room and finally spotting two stacks of books in a corner, just behind the door. 'You can take the books and put them on the bed and look. I'll just be outside.' He left us alone, pacing up and down the floor, smoking and occasionally exchanging a few words with his fellow lodgers.

The books were old but none were eighteenth-century, mostly late nineteenth- and early twentieth-century, and without exception in poor condition. Several of the books seemed to have come out of the library of the same gentleman – obviously a Freemason, because most of the titles dealt with the Lodge. There was even a handwritten notebook – a record of the proceedings of a Mason meeting. Of the hundred or so books we shuffled through, only five or six were in (just about) acceptable condition. While the books weren't rare or even scarce, they were certainly not common. We were disappointed, annoyed and puzzled that such uncommon volumes had been so poorly preserved. 'Finished so quickly? Want to see more?' He had stepped back into the room, seeing we had stopped browsing. But where was more?

Under the bed, as it turned out. He flipped his bedsheet up to show books shoved underneath. 'Are all the books in more or less the same condition?' we asked. 'Same, same,' he said. There wasn't much point in browsing more. My point was doubly proven: not only are antiquarian books hard to find in our market, when they do occasionally turn up, they are ruined, many beyond the scope of restoration. Well, we thought, at least he can't ask too much for the books.

'That's too much,' I blurted out, taken completely by surprise when he quoted what seemed like a fantastic sum for the six books we had picked. I could see negotiating would get us nowhere. The Book Prince didn't really want to sell – he wanted browsers.

In the end, there wasn't any mystery to the transaction, so why all the secrecy and fuss? We had to wonder. We later figured it was his way of luring customers – book-loving fools like us. Declining his offer, we made our way out, thanking him for his time. He was quite sporting about it, saying, 'no problem'. I couldn't resist pausing at the door to turn around and say, 'You seem to know the books are valuable; why don't you take care of them?'

'Why should I take care of them? They should take care of *me*,' he snapped, glaring at us in disbelief. We forgot all about the books and could talk about nothing on our way back except The Book Prince of Kolkata and his enigmatic, hilarious answer.

BIRYANI BHAI

I was once asked to impersonate a wealthy book collector. I had to pose as a collector with deep pockets to help a friend's friend negotiate the sale of a scarce and expensive Ottoman manuscript. The irony here was lost on the others involved in this tense and strained negotiation, that I was, if anything, an impecunious collector. I was dragged into my friend's plan because even though I was a bottom-feeder in the collectors' hierarchy, I was still fairly knowledgeable. But I am getting ahead of myself and should begin with Alexander Velu, the antiquarian book dealer who initiated all this in his dogged pursuit of a beautiful eighteenth-century Turkish calligraphic manuscript.

It must have been in 2017 that Velu first heard, via the antiquarian dealer grapevine, of this fabled calligraphic manuscript that was said to be apparently lying unrecognized – languishing and perhaps even rotting away quietly – in the home of a man, a renowned cook, actually, who ran a catering service in Ambur that specialized in – what else – gourmet biryani. One or two from the antiquarian community had actually seen such a manuscript in his house with their own eyes, and even handled it, when they had called on him to ask if he would cater weddings at short notice. And on one rather odd occasion, during a *sahan saapadu* banquet – where guests sit around a large common plate and eat from it – the master chef, an amiable, proud man I will simply call Biryani Bhai, had actually removed the book from its tacky glass showcase and casually passed it around for people to handle.

Velu, an art and antiquities dealer, aghast at hearing this, decided he had to rescue this precious and rare book from the clutches of Biryani Bhai. He was a fair-minded dealer and was even willing to offer double the market price. When he finally met Biryani Bhai in Ambur under the pretext of hiring him as a caterer for a family feast, he was impressed at how carefully and delicately the cook handled the manuscript, and even more surprised at how knowledgeable he was. So those accounts of him mishandling the book and his ignorance were plain rumours, possibly started by competitor dealers to keep others away from the prize.

When Alex Velu finally laid eyes on the book, he was completely struck by its beauty and rarity. The Islamic calligraphic manuscripts more commonly found in India were nineteenth-century Kashmiri examples, mostly in the form of unbound leaves. This one was a sophisticated Ottoman beauty that looked older: twelve stitched leaves with sumptuous illumination in gold, and other rich inks. It was decorated with a rectangular gold-and-blue border, at the centre of which was a piece of exquisitely calligraphed text. How had he come by such a wonderful thing? the dealer asked the cook. 'My wife's family are partly Turkish and this has been a kind of family heirloom for generations,' Bhai answered. The dealer now realized there was no chance of acquiring it, but having come this far, asked if he would consider selling it.

'For the right price,' the cook replied, surprising Velu. Apparently, his family was in the process of moving to Istanbul, and the money would be handy in relocating. The dealer offered a sufficiently high and tempting price (which he never revealed to me, keeping the transaction confidential), which the Bhai readily accepted. They agreed to firm up the sale later in the week, with the understanding that Velu would return to Ambur after making arrangements for the payment, and then take the manuscript. As the dealer was taking his leave, the cook, perhaps to keep some convivial banter going, remarked, 'You must really value the manuscript if you are willing to pay my price.' To which Velu said, on his way out the door, 'Oh, it's not for me, Bhai. I'm a dealer, not a collector.'

'The deal is off,' said the Bhai abruptly, 'I'm sorry.' When a shocked Velu pressed him to reveal why he had changed his mind, the cook said vehemently, 'I want it to go to a collector, not a trader.' The dealer pleaded with him, pointing out that he would ensure it went into the hands of a collector who would care for it, but Biryani Bhai would not relent, and Velu returned empty-handed. After this, every other month, Alex Velu would phone the cook from Secunderabad (where he lived at that time), asking after the manuscript, and finally, after nearly a year of phone calls and letters, the Bhai said he would sell if the dealer could produce a knowledgeable manuscript collector with at least some interest in buying this calligraphed beauty. That's when Velu turned to me and asked if I would at least evince interest in it, if not outright tell the cook I was ready to buy it.

That was easy enough to do, since it seemed like such a lovely thing, going by Velu's rapturous descriptions, though there was no way I could afford it now or in the future. All I was required to do was speak to Biryani Bhai over the phone and introduce myself as a serious collector (which was true) and murmur the right things about the beauty and rarity of such a manuscript. I probably didn't do such a bad job of this, because the Bhai sounded mollified enough at the end of the call to say he'd keep an open mind about letting it go. It was only many months later, when the dealer had located an even more (I'm relieved to say) knowledgeable, deep-pocketed manuscript collector who could really afford to buy it, that the two finally completed this rare book transaction. That was the first time I realized how tricky and occasionally intriguing selling or buying a rare book could be.

BOOK-COLLECTING MIRACLES

Where would we book collectors be without our book-collecting miracles? No self-respecting collector will deny having experienced a miracle or two while pursuing an elusive rarity; a little help from the bibliophile goddess in fulfilling our quest. The first true collecting miracle I experienced was in the 1990s, when I visited a book auction house for the first time. Giri's Auction House was a little-known operation in Mysuru, run out of a large garage that I stumbled upon by chance while chaperoning some schoolchildren on a field trip. We were on our way back to Bengaluru, but not being in any rush to get back, made a leisurely stop for tiffin at a hotel that announced itself as 'deluxe'.

I wolfed down my dosa and coffee and stepped out for some fresh air. I noticed a signboard tacked by the side of a garage that said 'Giri's Book Auction House'. I dashed in to check it out and found that an auction was about to start. I hastily inspected the dozen or so book lots, each carefully numbered. Disappointingly, they were mostly old law books bound in leatherette, while the rest seemed to be badly foxed nineteenth-century books and prints referencing the British Raj. There was, however, one small lot of vintage children's books and comics, mainly Biggles, William, Billy Bunter, and Indrajal titles from the sixties, that smelled sweet the way old comics do, when you press them to your face.

I decided that if this lot came up early enough, I would bid – it did, so I jumped in. Apart from me, only two others were interested in this lot. The bidding began at ₹50 and after a quick chase, was handed over to me for ₹550. When I went to pay up in the next room where the sold lots were being held, as I forked over the amount, along with the 15 per cent buyer's premium (this is how auction houses make their profit), I discovered to my dismay as the clerk handed over my lot of books that I had bid on the wrong lot! I had misremembered the lot number and was now in possession of what looked like a bunch of heavy tomes – those damn law books!

Returns weren't accepted, so I was stuck with them, though I had half a mind to simply let the auction house keep the lot, rather than lug them all the way back to Bengaluru. However, I paid up and took the books. On the bus back, the four volumes rode with me on my lap, and it was with barely any interest that I began flipping through them. Though covered in the same faux leather as the other three, one of the volumes wasn't a law book at all, but an old Tamil Bible. The more I examined it, the more excited I got – it was the 1714 Tranquebar Bible, one of the earliest printed books in India. It was quite a find in itself, but what lay inside this volume was the real miracle. Laid loosely inside the book was an incunabulum leaf – a page from an early-printed book, probably dating back to between 1455 and 1500.

Examples of loose or disbound incunabula are not uncommon, though they can be expensive to acquire, but something about this particular leaf – a printer's device or trademark printed in red ink showing two heraldic shields suspended from a branch of a tree – looked tantalizingly familiar. (Some of you may have already guessed what I was looking at.) As soon as I reached home, I pulled out my copy of Alfred Pollard's seminal book, *An Essay on Colophons*, and hurriedly searched for the page that resembled what I had seen in the loosely laid leaf.

And there it was: a Fust and Schoeffer leaf with a colophon showing the first-ever printer's device. Peter Schoeffer had been Gutenberg's apprentice, and later, along with Johann Fust, printed the incandescently beautiful *Mainz Psalter*, which carried the first-ever printer's colophon and device. Of all the desirable early-printed leaves one could possibly find, I had hit the jackpot. Though this colophon leaf was probably from a book printed later by Schoeffer (this one was printed on paper, not vellum, and lacked the coloured Lombardic initial) it was still a splendid and priceless bibliographical rarity, rarely found as a loose leaf.

I could only presume that the owner of the Tranquebar Bible, who had managed to somehow acquire this fabulous and important manuscript leaf, must have been a Dutch missionary – and perhaps a collector – who had lived or visited India some two hundred years ago. But how it had made its way to this auction house, with the leaf intact, would remain a mystery. I recognized it for the important printed rarity it was because I had just then become interested in book history, with a focus on the origins of printing with movable type. What would have been the fate of the Tranquebar Bible and this Schoeffer leaf if someone else had won this lot? Would they eventually have recognized it, or would it just have languished under a pile of books, or simply been thrown away? I couldn't help feeling that this volume had almost been steered towards me by fate. I had, after all, not even wanted to bid for it.

Some people – especially those the collecting community

likes to cheekily refer to as 'the non-bibliographic public' – might scoff and dismiss these miracles as mere coincidence or serendipity, but the collector knows that she needs more than luck to acquire antiquarian gems. She needs what the charming bibliophile-writer Seymour Adelman once referred to as 'a little help from heaven'.

'OWN USE ONLY'

Before I turned to the profession of teaching, I worked for a brief spell at an antiquarian bookshop in Kundapur. Back then, antiquarian bookshops were rarer to find than the rare books they specialized in, so I grabbed the opportunity to work in one, even though my friends and family thought I was wasting my time. It was by chance that I even found myself there – an old school friend whose hometown was Kundapur, one day happened to step into a stationery store and found, to his amazement, that they also sold rare books. The shop – which I'll leave unnamed – had a signboard that read 'Stationery and Antiquarian Mart'! What's more, the owner, Mr R, was actually looking to hire a store assistant.

I rushed from Bengaluru to meet Mr R, a gaunt man with a closely trimmed salt-and-pepper beard in a white cotton *veshti* and bright Terylene shirt, who straightaway subjected me to a strange but oddly satisfying interview.

'You take coffee?' he asked me first, and when I said yes, he assigned me a task before excusing himself to fetch my coffee. He had picked from his bookshelves three books of varying formats – a quarto, an octavo and a duodecimo – for me to describe in cataloguing terms. R looked approvingly as I rattled off '4to, 8vo and 12mo'. He urged me to have the coffee, which was pleasantly strong and aromatic. 'One last thing,' he said, thrusting an unruled notebook and pencil towards me, 'Draw a book, showing all its parts and name them.'

Amused, I got to it, relishing putting arrows against the parts – gutter, text block, hinge, backstrip, pastedown endpapers, recto, verso, half title page, etc.

'Excellent, you're hired. Actually, what I wanted more than a bookshop assistant, was someone who can catalogue the stock correctly. Have you found a place yet? No? Well, no need to look – you can board and lodge here. We have a room on the terrace you can use; you can take your meals with us. My wife is a fine cook, but no seafood and all here, okay? We are pure vegetarians.'

I soon discovered why they say that 'the antiquarian book trade is the last resort of the Indian eccentric'. The price of each edition was marked lightly in pencil at the back of the book, but R – even when the customer was glad to pay the marked price – was reluctant to sell a book until the customer bargained with him over the price. Somehow, he managed to insert a bargain into each transaction. 'You have to give them a bargain, I say,' he would tell me after the customer had left, 'only then will they leave satisfied and come back again.' In any case, there was only the occasional customer – I was surprised anyone in town even knew the stationery store also doubled up as a rare bookshop. If a customer buying pencils or notebooks bothered to peer into that dim, dark corner of the shop, they would see a tiny cardboard sign saying 'Rare and Fine Books Inside', with an arrow pointing towards the back.

This was the larger room behind the stationery storefront, crammed from floor to ceiling with books. There was more: R never kept the best books for customers to see or browse through; all the high-end antiquarian editions were stowed away as his personal loot. I discovered this was the case when

I found a few of them mixed in with the rest on the shelves, and had begun cataloguing them. R registered this with alarm, 'Why are you cataloguing these, I say! No, no, no! Only for own use, I say, own use only, okay?'

His wife, a gentle, kind and long-suffering lady, looked like she had had enough when she discovered his modus operandi – apparently this was not the first time that book purchases were secretly being split into stock and 'own use'. It had been a long-standing quarrel between them that he must strictly buy expensive editions only for stock and not for himself. But R, unable to resist adding to his own collection, had sneaked many expensive purchases and disguised them as stock. If a customer picked one of these to buy, he would politely and cunningly find a way to discourage them. Not long after – about six weeks since I'd begun working at The Antiquarian Mart – the whole operation blew up, bringing my apprenticeship, as well as the rare book business, to a close.

Returning one day from one of his far-flung book-buying trips, R was smuggling in his loot as surreptitiously as possible, when his wife caught him red-handed. It was only later, after I had said my goodbyes to the mart, that I realized how bored R must have been with selling stationery all those years, and how turning that back room into a rare book business must have served as a longed-for escape. How slowly, over time, those incomparable editions had worked their magic on him, completely possessing him. As for me, I have always felt grateful for that short time spent in the company of those rare and fine books, and their zealous guardian. It gave me a taste for antiquarian books and initiated me into the rare book world. And while R may not have been the model bookseller, no one can say he wasn't a first-class collector.

THE SECRET BOOKSHOP

I myself simply chanced on it, this secret bookshop. Trying to cool off in the hill city of Kodaikanal one summer, I took a late afternoon walk off the beaten roads and passed a charming cottage enclosed by a beautiful garden. I would have kept on walking but the sight of a handsome antique glass-enclosed wooden bookcase sitting outside the cottage, stopped me. My generous and attentive hosts, Thomas Thanikachalam and family, had mentioned to me only that morning, how they were looking for a handsome, old bookshelf and that none were to be found in town.

I entered the garden through a 'kissing gate' (something you don't come across much anymore but this British Raj relic was once a common feature of old Indian cottages), and approached the bookcase placed outside a door with the sign, 'Browse for Bargains', but no other sign to proclaim it as a bookshop; not even a name. The glass-enclosed bargain bookshelf near the doorstep seemed to contain, to my astonishment, what looked like antiquarian books in sumptuous bindings – half-leather, marbled boards, gilt edges.

I gently tugged on the handle to open the bookcase, but it was locked. I tried peering through the glass to catch a glimpse of some of the titles on the spine and pulled back in more astonishment Dibdin's handsomely printed three-volume *The Bibliographical Decameron* – the most rousing treatise on bibliomania – was there, that too in its scarcer large paper copy edition. There were more antiquarian marvels lining the bookcase, but now my only preoccupation was to locate the owner of the bookshop, settle the price for everything in the bookcase, and then explore their bookshop more thoroughly. If such rare and precious volumes were pegged as bargains, what bibliophilic surprises lay within the premises?

Before I could knock on the door or let myself in, a man in his early seventies briskly stepped out and smiling broadly, said, 'Welcome, welcome. Please take your time to look around. I am open all afternoon.' I informed him right away that I was interested in the bargain bookcase. 'Ah, yes, of course,' he said, warming up to me further, his smile more inviting. 'What were you interested in?'

'Well, just about everything,' I replied.

'But any item in *particular*? There must be something you have your eye on?'

'The Dibdin volumes,' I said.

'Magnificent!' he cried, rubbing his hands in satisfaction.

'Let me then tell you why these copies are special,' he said. I said I was rather hoping to get them out and examine them myself. 'Surely, you will not first deprive me of a little book talk? After all, as Nodier, one of the fathers of bibliophily, said, "The next best thing to owning books is talking about them," no?'

I hesitated, and suggested, 'Well, why don't we look at them together?' His face clouded at once. 'But of course,' he said, politely but somewhat curtly; and was still frowning when he handed me a key to the bookcase. And instead of joining me, he rushed back in and shut the door with a bang.

I knew I had ticked him off (just how badly, I was to discover in a few moments) but I couldn't wait to see if those books were actually what they seemed to be. All the Dibdin volumes were in beautiful condition – none of that pervasive foxing that is common in the edition. Now, what was he asking for the set? The number pencilled in couldn't be right: ₹75. Just 75? Must be bookseller's code for some fantastic hidden price. The rest of the contents in the bookcase put me in a state of shock that I have not recovered from till today.

Elusive fine-press books from the private presses of San Serriffe, were all there – all seven of them. The bibliographer who had made them known to the world, Dr Theodore Bachaus, had a slim little volume to himself that he had even inscribed and signed to Henry Morris of the Bird and Bull Press. One couldn't ask for a more telling, highly desirable association copy. Also present in the bookcase were the highly coveted and yet derided series of 'finely' printed booklets of the Saint Ronan's Press, put out by the eccentric printer Christopher Larkspvr (Larkspur deliberately spelt in that eccentric way to throw you off).

But the one that electrified me most was *Echoes from India and Afghanistan* by John H. Watson, privately printed in Calcutta for the author in 1883. This was the edition which was widely rumoured to contain Dr Watson's manuscript signature. And indeed, there it was – on the flyleaf. There are, as most Sherlockians well know, only two or three samples of Dr Watson's signature in existence, and any of them will vouch that what I was looking at was the real thing.

When I looked for a price, there was none. 'I would like to buy everything in the bookshelf,' I declared, turning around, but I was forcefully pushed aside by the owner as he ripped off the bargain sign and hung a new one which read: 'Not for Sale.

For Private Use Only.' And then politely but firmly, he asked me to leave. I begged him to consider selling me at least one or two things, but he threatened to throw me out of the premises. I left in great dejection.

When I recounted my bibliophilic misadventure to my hosts, the Thanikachalam family, they regretted not warning me to stay away from the cottage with the bookshelf. Apparently, the owner was a book collector desperate to show off his great collection, and under this ruse of a bargain sale, lured unsuspecting bibliophiles to salivate over his books. 'But how does he come by such fantastic books?' I asked, still wide-eyed. Alas, replied my hosts, no one could tell. When I wondered aloud at what could possibly be inside the bookshop, they said with some surprise, 'Why, don't you know? They contain the bibliophilic jewels from the Comte de Fortsas auction!'*

* Please see Chapter 22 'The Booksellers of San Serriffe and Other Biblio Spoofs and Hoaxes' for more on this one-of-a-kind historic auction.

PART TWO

THE ANTIQUARIAN AT HOME

THE BANGALORE *ALICE*

I had of course heard of the 'India *Alice*' – a scruffy, monsoon-weathered copy of the classic *Alice in Wonderland* with a mysterious past, which is often referenced in antiquarian collecting and dealing circles. Apparently, it had turned up, quite extraordinarily, in some Indian bazaar in the 1950s, and an Englishman bought it and took it back to England not fully realizing what it actually was – the true first printing of *Alice in Wonderland*, the scarce 1865 copy that preceded the authorized 1866 first edition from Macmillan. Only sixteen or so copies of this 1865 *Alice* are known to exist, most of them in institutional collections. And this particular 'India' copy was even scarcer – numbering among the only dozen or so 'Hospital' copies thought to have totally disappeared. Though Warren Weaver, who eventually came to own the said copy, set the story straight in the journal *The Private Library* (Volume 6, No. 1), collectors and dealers still like to think that this copy popped up in a fruit and vegetable bazaar in North India. However, it was actually found in Bangalore, in a garage on Museum Road that had just become a second-hand bookshop.

The man who found this legendary 1865 *Alice* in Bangalore and reluctantly bought it, L.C. Kent Morgan, could only dimly recall those days in a letter he wrote to Mr Weaver:

> The bookshop was situated in a 'go-down' to the compound of a bungalow in Museum Road. It was owned by a young Indian, whose name I cannot now remember. He obviously purchased en-bloc from auction houses because they were in heaps all over the floor with no attempt to sort them out [...] I found this little shop in 1950 – and thereafter whenever I was in Bangalore I used to go and poke around to see if I could find anything of interest. It was on one of those visits that I came across Alice, priced at 1/8 rupees (about 2/3 shillings) [...] It was not long afterwards that I found the shop no longer in existence: whether the proprietor had moved elsewhere, or whether he had given up altogether I do not know.

When I first read the article by Weaver in the *Private Library* journal, I sat up straight and read it again. I had a hunch what this 'godown' might be and who the young bookseller was, and wanted to find out more. But before that, something more on the 1865 *Alice* copy: Lewis Carroll had asked Macmillan for fifty advance copies to give to friends. Its illustrator John Tenniel was unhappy with the way the illustrations had turned out and wanted a fresh print run. Macmillan obliged and then distributed and sold the official *Alice* in 1866. Carroll asked his friends to return the 1865 advance copies and donated some of these to various children's hospitals. The tiny print run from 1865 has now become the more sought-after *Alice* – the few marked as hospital copies are scarcer and more highly desired.

After Kent Morgan bought this very scarce *Alice* from this Bangalore 'godown bookshop' without realizing how valuable it was (and alas, the young Indian bookseller also missed out on its bibliographical importance and market value, letting it go for a song), he carried it back to England and placed it in his home library. In 1961, Weaver says, Morgan's attention was drawn to a notice in the paper talking about how rare and expensive the 1865 *Alice* edition was, and on seeing this, he rushed to examine his copy and found it to be that most-sought-after edition. At that time, Hodgson on Chancery Lane was the most famous book auction house, so he took it over there. The book dealer Lew Feldman of the House of El Dieff bought it for £880 – a modest sum, as pointed out by Weaver. Eventually, Mr Weaver went on to buy it from Feldman and found scratched inside it evidence that it was one of those 'Hospital *Alice*' copies donated by Carroll. Warren Weaver seems to have been the first owner of the 'India *Alice*', who was curious enough to dig out more details about the origins of this copy. He found out that Kent Morgan had owned the book originally, and wrote to him. It was Morgan who told him that it was found not in some Indian bazaar, but in a second-hand bookshop in Bangalore.

I dimly remembered that Mr K.B.K. Rao had first begun his bookshop, Select, in a garage on Museum Road. Talking to his son, Mr Murthy, and his grandson, Sanjay, of the present Select Bookshop, it was easy enough to join the dots about the godown Kent Morgan referred to – it was the Select Book Club that Mr Rao had started in the late '40s. Rao had been a frequent buyer at Cohen Auctions on St. Marks Road, coming all the way from Kurnool just to attend the auctions. Robertson, a retired Englishman and bibliophile who also attended auctions, befriended K.B.K. and invited him to use his garage in his spacious Museum Road bungalow compound. A pity that Mr Rao simply handed over a bibliographical treasure to a browsing Englishman, but how many – then or now – could really spot an 1865 *Alice* in a rubble of books and also grasp its actual worth and significance?

But how did a rare hospital copy of the 1865 *Alice* land up in Bangalore? It's possible, Weaver says, that the book had been given to a little girl (Alice Cousins), who was admitted to a London hospital and was probably the daughter of a civil servant posted to India, who (I'm guessing) went on to retire in Bangalore. When leaving the country, it was commonplace for many British families to pack off their books to auction houses such as Cohen's on St. Marks, where Mr Rao's bid must have won and he acquired the edition.

Now that its provenance has been established a little more (if not fully, for who was Alice Cousins?), I hereby, in honour of Mr K.B.K. Rao, re-christen the India *Alice* copy as 'The Bangalore *Alice*'.

THE ANTIQUARY OF BENGALURU

I was completely charmed by Madhava Rao's bookshop when I first visited. It was the very picture of an antiquarian bookshop. I should clarify here that the stock I speak of was not chock-a-block with rarities, first editions or even scarce or expensive editions. Its uniqueness and charm lay in stocking well-preserved old editions – some genuinely antiquarian, many out of print, all gathered fetchingly in one room. A room full of gilt-edged antiquarian book spines is something to behold. And then there is the smell of leather and fine paper ageing, and the rustle of tissue guards over illustrations. Rao managed to make every copy on his shelf desirable and valuable by simply preserving it carefully and presenting it well.

When I had finished slavering over the books restored and shelved with impeccable care, I exclaimed that I just had to write about his exciting antiquarian bookshop, which spanned across two rooms on the terrace of his house in Basavanagudi, Bengaluru. But with equal intensity, he forbade me to write about him or his 'East-West Bookshop'. He was content, he said, with a customer base drawn through word of mouth. 'I don't like too many people coming here,' he added. As I got ready to leave his bookshop, he suspected I might sneak a little piece on him after all and made me promise that I would not write anything.

'But then when can I write about your bookshop?' I asked, not fully believing that I had to remain quiet about what seemed like a remarkable bookshop in India – one that had turned out to be right under my nose in the city I lived.

He replied, 'When I finally close the bookshop.'

Madhava Rao, the maverick antiquarian of Bengaluru, died suddenly on a Sunday afternoon in March 2013 from cancer, which was diagnosed too late. He was seventy-eight. That morning, he went up to his terrace bookshop as usual and completed at least two book transactions over the phone (one to an itinerant book peddler who would come to his house every other week with a gunny sack of books) and then turned his attention to the daily task of restoring old books. The book peddler arrived at 3 p.m. to find that the bookseller who had called him that morning had just passed away. It was only some months before this that I had spent half a day at East-West, keenly browsing in the company of an ardent bibliophile friend. Together, we had gone over his stock with a fine-toothed comb, and though we had bought more than an armload of books each, Rao had said a little irritably at the end, 'Must you look at every book, I say?'

How could one not? There were treasures there, and hidden in plain sight, too.

All of it gone now, in a quiet deal he made with a longstanding customer, knowing the end was near. Several book dealers made discrete inquiries about the fate of the East-West stock and were told by the family that the books, along with the shelves, had been sold en bloc. They are, one hopes, with a collector now, and perhaps will be well cared for. Mostly self-taught – though more than once, he has acknowledged the role of Murthy of Select Bookshop as his mentor in the trade – Madhava Rao had an eye for recognizing an interesting or uncommon edition, pursuing it relentlessly, and then, if the copy required it, restoring it so you, his customer, could hold in your hand an antiquarian edition whose condition was more than just acceptable.

Once when I had just entered his shop, he threw open his hands to reveal a folio-sized volume torn in two halves, which he had obviously been working on. 'See, just look at this, Murthy passed this on to me last week – what does he think I am, a magician?' For the longest time in the book trade, Rao was known for being a skilled restorer of crumbling books. Perhaps he had picked up the skill for book restoration when he operated a press in the early days, or he simply had a knack like those clockmakers – for taking apart a printed book and putting it back together.

It was the small room that you first stepped into that held the antiquarian beauties; the second larger room, packed wall to wall with books, housed the newer, shinier, less-interesting books. One tiny shelf in that tiny room held much fascination for me: it was the one that housed literature, mostly late nineteenth-century and early twentieth-century editions of books by English and European authors.

Here, on Rao's little shelf, to my surprise and delight, were several rows of interesting editions in fairly desirable condition. Among other things, I found an 1894 *Gulliver's Travels*, an 1889 *Three Men in a Boat*, a deluxe 1912 *Pilgrim's Progress* and a 1905 *Essays of Elia*. I remember my bibliophile friend found a beautiful edition of *The Second Jungle Book*, with a snake embossed in gold on the cover. Most bibliophiles visiting East-West preferred the two larger Godrej glass bookcases that held history, travel, war and science books. The first two rows on these shelves, Rao's own personal favourites, had a sign that said, 'Not for Sale'. Though sometimes the bookseller himself didn't know it, other books not marked thus could also suddenly turn unbuyable. When I picked out from the shelf a first edition of *The Great Railway Bazaar*, he quietly put it back, muttering something about having to remember to keep aside books he didn't want to sell. Though I am fairly sure that the moment I desired it was the moment he decided he would rather keep it.

He started out in his early days as a collector, buying whatever looked valuable or rare to him, hoarding them for himself, and only in the late '90s, when he turned from book collector to bookseller, did he convert his personal collection into stock. Even as a struggling book dealer, he always kept a low profile, though no one could really say why. Some speculate that he had his private reasons for not advertising the bookshop. Knowing the obsessive intensity with which he conducted all his book transactions, from buying, restoring and selling, and then coming back for more fervent buying (he book-hunted in every corner of the city, ferrying his loot back in an autorickshaw), I think it was just so he could be left alone to study and play with his antiquarian loot. To savour, enjoy and take in an edition's bibliographical qualities; to work his magic on broken copies with his hands; and only after such bibliophilic ritual and intimacy, would he offer them up to fellow antiquarians for their contemplation, pleasure and possession.

KUMARS

One can only imagine it today: a set of cosy rooms in an ancestral house on a busy street in Calcutta in the '50s, resembling the finely appointed private library of a gentleman with its complex of bookcases and sitting-room furniture – that was actually an antiquarian bookshop. One could walk in for a browse and hold long conversations about rare books with its bohemian-bibliophile owner. His name was Nirmal Chandra Kumar and his bookshop was called, simply, 'Kumars'. From 1945 until his death in 1976, Kumar ran the rare bookshop from his home. The establishment took up several rooms in the house and the stock ranged widely, from fine bindings to prints to maps.

I first learnt about Kumar and his bookshop when I stumbled on a blog by his son, Aloke Kumar, on his father's bookshop and its influence on the life and work of many Bengali artists and intellectuals of his time, who were all regulars at Kumars. I was, first of all, delighted to discover there had once been such a fabulous bookshop in India – a genuine antiquarian bookshop in a country where antiquarian bookselling and buying is not an ingrained tradition. In this sense, Kumar was no doubt a maverick, and thank god for that, or Kumars would have been just one more second-hand bookshop. Eager to know more about his magnificent bookshop, I managed to contact the owner's son, Professor Aloke Kumar, to have a brief chat with him on the phone.

In his blog, 'Antiquarian of Calcutta', Aloke describes a typical photo of Nirmal Kumar: 'a stocky Bengali... he wore a white collared shirt, half-sleeved and a lungi; his formal dress was a dhoti and kurta with pump shoes. Can you imagine somebody wearing this dress and smoking a pipe or a Davidus cigar sitting in his library surrounded by books?' Kumar was probably the first Indian bookseller to publish a rare book catalogue in the long tradition of all bespoke antiquarian booksellers around the world, especially the legends Kumar had done business with, Quaritch and Maggs. The city's bibliophiles, artists, luminaries, antiquarians and bohemians – all frequented Kumars. Satyajit Ray, a regular browser here, consulted Kumar when he was making *Shatranj ke Khilari*. In a London book auction, Kumar had bid for and won a priceless scrapbook on the Mutiny.

Ray went on to pay his own little tribute to Kumar in the character of the encyclopaedic Sidhu Jyatha in the Feluda stories. The other well-known antiquary, Sir Ashutosh Mukherjee, was also a customer. When he donated thousands of rare books from his collection to the National Library, several books in that collection had come from Kumars. 'In the early 1940s,' writes Aloke Kumar, 'rare book collection was in a dismal, class-bound rut. The famous rare bookshop Cambray... was already fading, Thacker and Spink, the other well-known bookshop was alive, but there were hardly any rare books... Kumar helped to change all that. His enthusiasms included the then-unheralded British painters, Thomas and William Daniell, to be re-introduced to Calcutta once more. He bought the rare elephant folio of the plate books by T. and W. Daniell from Sotheby's to sail it to Calcutta.'

What was just as remarkable about Kumar – reading his son's reflections – was how generously and freely he gave to his customers, friends and family, even though the bookshop wasn't always a profitable business. It just about broke even most of the time, but Kumar, in the middle of his struggles to keep the bookshop afloat and care for the needs of his own family, invited his parents to come live with him. He was also apparently a gourmet and 'organized the very best of fine cooking to be presented to his friends. Sometimes such delicacies that you would only find in the pages of some rare Mughal document'.

Aloke recalls running a regular errand for his father: being sent off with books in hand to be delivered to Satyajit Ray. He also remembers how cautious everyone in the house was about handling the books, tiptoeing around the shelves, careful not to disturb them. One of the things that broke Kumar's heart, something he could never be a part of, was the sharp practice in the antiquarian trade in the late '70s, of breaking apart rare books and atlases and maps to make a bigger profit. Some of his fellow booksellers in the trade had begun to buy books with rare prints and maps, and tear them up in order to sell each print or map individually, rather than keep them intact. You made more this way than when you sold the set or the atlas as a whole.

'Kumar did not want to be a part of this and lost out,' says Aloke. 'And it was with a sense of bowing to the inevitable that Kumars mentally gave up. Nirmal Kumar died in 1976 and with his death, the literary world lost a sweet and genuinely unselfish man who freely gave of his vast knowledge and delighted in the achievements of those he influenced so profoundly.'

My interest in this unsung bookman and his cherished antiquarian bookshop is not so much for the luminaries who once buzzed around it, as much as imagining the regular traffic of ordinary bibliophiles, scholars and collectors, for whom Kumars must have been a Mecca of fine and rare books.

THE BOOKWOMAN OF SOUTH EX-II

Just when I had concluded that we probably didn't have any full-fledged antiquarian bookshops in India, I chanced on 'Memoirs of India' in Delhi. They've been trading since the mid-1980s, but are known only to a small circle of collectors in the country. Antiquarian bookshops in India seem to keep a low profile, for some reason – so low that even bibliophiles miss them. Up until the 1950s, there were apparently several Indian antiquarian bookshops; perhaps the last notable antiquarian bookshop in modern times was that of Nirmal Chandra Kumar's in Kolkata, which closed after his death in the late 1970s.

Another well-known rare bookseller, Indranath Mujumdar (better known for his publishing firm Subarnarekha), who used to trade on College Street, is also no more. It's wonderful, then, to discover that a full-on, brick-and-mortar, open bookshop (i.e., not open by appointment only) dealing in antiquarian, rare, first editions and fine books is still open for business today. Memoirs is located in South Extension-II; it's an elegant gallery with wood-panelled bookshelves. Several locked cabinets highlight the bookshop's high-end antiquarian material, which include colour plate books, rare prints and maps, fine bindings, first and signed editions, and early-printed books from India.

I was keen to see if they had interesting modern editions

and indeed, there was a small section devoted to it. Rashi Jain, one of its owners, told me she hopes to broaden this section so that a new generation of bibliophiles and collectors can find things to like and relate to in their stock. What I was drawn to more immediately on the shelf, was the green two-volume Olympia Press edition of *Lolita* – a real find, indeed! – and a first edition of *A Passage to India* (Edward Arnold and Co., London, 1924).

'We recently sold a signed Rudyard Kipling, a limited edition of his verse, to one of India's leading surgeons and his bibliophile wife; they were gifting it to someone in the family.' I had just asked Rashi who their primary customers were. 'We sell largely to institutions, embassies, industrialists, tourists and a circle of collectors. Once, we had a walk-in customer, a French tourist dressed casually in what looked like nightwear and we assumed he was there just to browse. But he bought a lot! It turned out he was the director of a leading international law firm.'

Memoirs of India was started by Rashi's grandfather, G.C. Jain, who dealt first in antiques. One day, a Parsi doctor in Mumbai, whom he bought antique furniture and decorative items from regularly, insisted that Jain buy his collection of antiquarian books as well. At that point, the Jain family wasn't interested in books, but since the Parsi collector wouldn't part with his furniture unless the books went with the deal, they took it. Once they had the books, they began looking at them more closely and found they were valuable, collected and had a market. The antique furniture business slowly turned into a trade in antiquarian books and prints and maps, as his children began sourcing material from all over the world, through auctions, dealers and private sellers.

Some of the choice antiquarian material in the bookshop: Edwin Arnold's 1908 classic on the Buddha, *The Light of Asia*; the Limited Editions Club's *Lysistrata* signed by Picasso; the Edmund Dulac illustrated edition of Fitzgerald's *Rubaiyat*; the 1883 Richard Burton Kama Shastra editions of *The Kama Sutra*. A very special book in their stock is the finely illustrated *Six Principal Ragas: With a Brief View of Hindu Music* by Sourindro Mohun Tagore, Calcutta Central Press Company, 1877. Also in stock were aquatint books by European artists in India from the eighteenth and nineteenth centuries: Solvyns, Daniell, Gould, D'Oyly, Forbes, Fraser, Zoffany and Emily Eden.

'Over a period of time', Rashi told me, 'we will be adding antique and vintage maps, engravings, lithographs and old photographic albums (by Raja Deen Dayal, Bourne & Shepherd, etc.) to our website portfolio. Memoirs of India hopes to fill the gap in the market for providing convenience, transparency and assurance in the field of rare and antique books. To reach our goal, we've created a dedicated website for rare and antiquarian books. Our extensive and detailed cataloguing assures the authenticity and accuracy of information for each book we put on sale. We also have a return policy to ensure our customers are happy with a purchase. This helps us build trust with our clients with the only website in India in accordance with international standards prescribed by ILAB (International League of Antiquarian Booksellers). We've always emphasized the importance of preserving the quality of books. To help our clients, we've started our own professional binding and restoration service with an in-house team to help with book restoration.'

Will the bookshop also accept commissions to restore books? 'Yes, absolutely, our restoration services are open to everyone. Typically, our restoration charges start from ₹2,000 onwards. We also undertake leatherbound/clothbound books for the purpose of a decorative library.'

It is unusual to find a South Asian woman in the antiquarian trade (the only other that I know of is Bibi Mohamed of Imperial Fine Books, New York) and I tell Rashi this but she makes little of it, saying Memoirs is really a family-owned-and-run business, and credits her brother, Rishabh Jain, as the one who brought the bookshop to life. I ask her to tell me a little more about her role in the bookshop. 'It has been fifteen years since I entered the enchanted world of rare, antiquarian books, and there has been no looking back. I feel blessed to be surrounded by such a wide world of literature, travelogue, art and history of a bygone era. My favourite part of my work is my interactions with my clients, where I feel happy to be able to guide and help them in building their collection and learn something new along the way. My eyes still light up whenever we acquire a new tome. I spend a lot of time going through our every new acquisition, wanting to learn everything I can about the book.'

Some of the bookshop's most enthusiastic customers in recent times, I was pleased to learn from Rashi, are young professionals who are not hesitant to spend ₹50,000 on a rare or fine book if it appeals to them. 'Young customers are quite enthusiastic about building up their collection quickly,' she said, 'and I always suggest they don't rush into it and end up buying something they don't like after a year or two. I ask them to earmark how much they want to spend every month and then decide what really appeals to them. When you start, you can't possibly collect everything, it's very important to define boundaries and budget. Instagram has been a good platform for generating the interests of young collectors. If they are based in Delhi, they usually like to visit the shop and make a selection. Our clients buy directly from the website or sometimes message us their requirements and we share the details with them over email. I've noticed that generally, clients prefer to physically inspect the books especially if they're of higher value. This gives them a complete sense of experience of handling the book in person, which a few images can never compete with.'

I point to a first edition of *Winnie the Pooh* (1926) they have, lacking the dust jacket, priced at ₹1,00,000, and tell her there is a copy online listed by a UK dealer in the same condition for ₹82,500. Would they adjust the price for an interested buyer? 'Since the market has opened up to everyone,' Rashi replied, 'it is not uncommon for customers to compare our prices with the ones online by other international sellers. The same book can have variation in pricing which are mainly based on three factors: originality, condition and completeness. A certain book's demand and availability also plays a role in a book's price fluctuation. Our prices are based on all of these conditions, which we try to update every few months. This leaves us with some scope for negotiations where we factor in all the other costs (e.g. free packing and shipping nationwide) before committing to a discount.'

Payal Patel, a regular customer at Memoirs, says this bookshop for her has been one of her must-go stops while in Delhi. 'From old historical accounts and classic novels to beautiful lithographs and artwork, there's always something to discover here. It's quite an enjoyable way to spend an afternoon, and nearly impossible to leave without a unique piece of history in my pocket.'

A BIBLIOPHILE IN BENGALURU

When the editor of *Bangalore Blue*, a nostalgic anthology of our city, invited me to write on some aspect of old Bangalore, I straightaway thought of the old circulating libraries that once dotted our landscape. My parents moved from Madras to Bangalore in 1960. My mother didn't like the hot weather and my father looked forward to going to office wearing a tie – something you couldn't accomplish easily in Madras. When we lived in Journalist's Colony, just behind Sivaji Talkies, I was a child and most things about the place are a blur now. What I mostly remember is being bundled up on Friday nights to see second shows of Tamil movies, balancing precariously on a Lambretta. In 1965, we moved to Wilson Garden, to a house on 7th Cross. On top of 7th Cross was a private circulating library called Dhanalakshmi Lending Library, and I was given some extra pocket money to get a membership and pay for reading charges.

It was – like most circulating libraries then – tiny. A single room crammed with bookshelves. As you entered, on the left was the owner-cum-librarian's desk, where Mr Anand sat – a pleasant, likeable man who was always smiling. In the evenings, the library swarmed with his friends, a bunch of very affable fellows whom I looked up to and admired. Often, long after I had finished picking the comic I wanted to borrow, I would linger inside, listening to their conversation.

There wasn't even standing space for them inside the library, so they hung out on the pavement just outside the doorstep, smoking and drinking tea. They were affectionate to all the children who frequented the library, and one of them went on to do something for me that fast-tracked my reading privileges there. On my five-rupee deposit, I was allowed to borrow only comics and that too, only one at a time.

Sunday afternoons from those times stand out sharply: the library was open for only half day, until about 2 p.m., after which I would find myself at a loose end, not wanting to dash off home right away. I would roam the streets and crosses of Wilson Garden in the mild Bangalore sun, passing barber shops from which you could always hear emanating the melancholic twang of Vividh Bharti from a radio. It felt like the whole city was napping and I was the only one awake. It was one late Sunday morning that an unexpected thing happened to me at the library, galvanizing and transforming my reading possibilities in a moment. That morning, I found that I had read and reread all the comics in the library. For the first time, I was about to go away without borrowing anything. On that Sunday, it wasn't the owner who was behind the librarian's desk but his friend, minding the shop for him.

I forget his name now, but he stopped me as I was leaving, surprised that I was going without borrowing anything. I told him I was done with all the comics. 'Then take a novel,' he said, looking a little puzzled that I hadn't picked one up already. I was about to argue with him that I only had a deposit for comics and that as a fifth-standard kid, I wasn't allowed to take adult books, but something told me to shut up and just take him up on his offer. 'What should I take?' I asked as if that was my problem. 'Have you read Chase?' he asked. I confessed to seeing several rows of his books, but only the spines, not the covers. He plucked from the shelf the title nearest to him: *A Coffin from Hong Kong*. He opened to my membership page in that folio-sized ledger book all lending libraries used in those days and jotted down the title of the book and date of issuance.

I was sure he was now going to discover I was forbidden to take a James Hadley Chase home with me; that it contravened the library's lending rules. Instead, he shut the book with a definitive thud, saying, 'Here, take, enjoy' and handed the risqué-looking paperback to me. I couldn't somehow leave without mentioning the deposit issue. And as I stood there dithering, mumbling something about the deposit, he dismissively said, 'I know, I say. So what? I'll tell Anand. How can you say you don't have anything to read when you haven't read any Chase? After you read this, you will only want his novels.' I clutched the book and ran out before he could change his mind or come to his senses.

I realized one library couldn't contain me and it became a mania with me to join as many libraries as possible. By this time, my parents had once again moved – this time to Cantonment. And though I now had access to the British Library (where most of my friends hung out, 'repairing' to Koshys or K.C. Das right after), the Max Mueller Bhavan library and the State Central Library, I chose to frequent private circulating libraries because I hankered after paperbacks. I remember a funny little library inside Johnson Market! A rather shady man called Gulabi ran it, but it was so close to my school that I could dash there during lunch breaks and browse to my heart's content.

On top of Brigade Road, a rather supercilious Anglo Indian named Lancy ran a library; he made a real fuss about lending the latest bestsellers, making members wait and wait for them, all the while brandishing the books right in front of our faces, saying he couldn't put them into circulation until he had wrapped the covers with polythene and let the gum dry. After that, it depended on his mood, or on how much he liked or disliked you; he would pretend the book wasn't quite ready to go out yet or that it had been borrowed, while all the time it would be just under his desk!

The library that endeared itself to so many Bangalore book addicts in the '80s and '90s, was Mecca Circulating, located in that little lane just off Commercial Street. (And much later, the one the owner's son, Fareed, ran in Cox Town.) A real Mecca for readers in Bangalore. It was of course Mr M, the owner, a real gentleman, who made all the difference. He was extremely polite – some would say to the point of being obsequious. But as mildly annoying as that could be, I would much rather have that than the frosty, suspicious nature of most library owners in Bangalore those days – following you around as you browsed, sniffing behind you as though to catch you at something. Mr M was tall, in his sixties, with a stained white beard and a lit cigarette perpetually dangling from a corner of his mouth. Through a haze of smoke, he addressed everyone as Mr or Miss, even if you were only a teenager.

'*Hello*, Mr Sebastian!' he would exclaim the moment I stepped into that narrow shop, a real hole in the wall if there was one. His table was at the far end of the room and he was always seen busying himself with pasting protective plastic wrappers onto his books. And the greeting would immediately be followed by (just as loudly): '*How* are you, Mr Sebastian?'

'Fine, fine, sir' was what most of us shot back, trying to

quickly turn to the bookshelves to avoid further pleasantries. But no one got away that easily.

'Good of you to drop by, Mr Sebastian.'

'Thanks, Mr M.'

'How is college, Mr Sebastian?'

'Good, good Mr M. And how's business?'

'By your grace, very good, Mr Sebastian'.

'Oh, that's good.'

'All your kindness only, Mr Sebastian, all your goodness.'

After this, no member found the nonchalance to leave without borrowing a few books and settling some – in several cases, many – old library dues.

'THOSE GLOWING MADDER-DYED REDS AND INDIGO BLUES'

Richard Kossow's Incomparable Collection of Indian Incunabula

The finest collection of rare and early-printed books from colonial India is to be found not at the British Library or even a rare book institution in India, but in a large flat in London – the private library and home of Richard Kossow, a scholarly American collector-turned-bookdealer. For almost half a century, he has been a pioneering, impassioned collector of fine and scarce books relating to India. 'Indiana' (as in 'Americana') is one of the most difficult fields to collect – the lack of bibliographies, specialist dealers and serious collectors, combined with poorly preserved copies, has made putting together a thorough, accomplished collection from the Indian subcontinent a tricky and tough bibliographical challenge.

Richard went beyond the staple, overdone focus in this field – colour-plate books, lithographs, travel accounts – to identify and assemble Indian books of bibliographical and typographical importance, several of them in colourful, beautiful native bindings. With the tenacity and devotion of the best bookmen out there, he pursued the best possible copies of early-printed Indian books from the period 1778 to 1858, many in superlative bindings. 'That I can boast of an Indian library,' he told me, 'which stands out from its peers for its breadth, interest, rarity, provenance and condition, is simply a matter of consistent application over a very long period of time.'

Graham Shaw, the influential book historian of South Asian print history, told me over email that he had seen nothing like it in all his years of looking at India's early-printed books.

> Every time I visit Richard's library, I have no idea what new wonders I will see. The door opens and your gaze is irresistibly drawn to shelf after shelf on your left lined neatly with cloth bindings in beautiful condition. The eyes flit hungrily from title to title: Tavernier's *Travels in India* in blue, Shakespear's *Wild Sports of India,* Allen's *Diary of Sinde and Afghanistan* in red with a Pathan marksman at its head, Meadows Taylor's three-decker novel *Seeta* distinctive in green, Karaka's *History of the Parsis* with Ahura Mazda in gilt, and Herklots's *On the Customs of the Moosulmans of India* with its twin minarets. Move further in and it gets better. Sit at the dining-room table and you are surrounded by fine leather bindings and gold tooling. There will now never be another opportunity to put such a collection together from scratch. The amount of early India-related material becoming available is diminishing all the time, for various reasons. Richard was in the right place, at the right moment, with the right collecting instincts. The collection is unrepeatable.

Graham, who had worked with Kossow on cataloguing this collection, called it 'a bibliographer's dream'. By doing a close bibliographical study of these books produced during the time when the British East India Company dominated the country, Kossow and Shaw are hoping to throw more light on the extent to which Indians had been involved in the making of these books as printers, designers, binders, type casters, punchcutters, papermakers and translators – something that has been shrouded so far in a kind of bibliographical haze. The British had probably supervised and designed these publications and employed European binders, but several exquisite examples in the Kossow collection appear to be the work of Indian binders – in all probability, these binders came from the same tradition of craftworkers who had once been employed by the Mughal Court to bind medieval Islamic manuscripts in those magnificent, iridescent bindings. 'I love them for their colours.' Richard enthused, 'Those glowing madder-dyed reds and indigo blues, as well as the more familiar pink-toned reds which have their origin in Islamic bindings of old, are a feast for the eye.'

In a letter to me, on Richard's urging, Graham wrote a note on what it was like to work on the Kossow collection:

> From the moment you first look at any of Richard's books, it's clear that condition has been his watchword throughout his decades of collecting. Ideally everything should be in a pristine state – as though it had come off the press and been beautifully bound only yesterday. In the context of his Indian collection, it's more than appropriate therefore that Richard should have acquired the only known copy of the Calcutta 1829 reprint of

Henry Smeathman's *An Account of the White Ants*, those voracious book-eaters!

It takes tremendous discipline and self-restraint when the opportunity arises to buy a title that you have been longing to acquire for years but you turn it down on condition grounds, knowing another copy in an acceptable state may not surface for another decade (or perhaps ever). This is a nightmare of a decision to have to take, a real collector's dilemma, especially remembering that copies in good 'original' condition have become scarcer and scarcer to find, almost to the point of invisibility. The collector always recalls with anguish the ones that got away. But patience can be rewarded. Although offered several examples in the past, it was only in 2019 that Richard finally acquired a copy of George Atkinson's supreme satire of British society in *mofussil* India, *Curry & Rice* (London 1859), insisting on the true first issue (with captions lacking to plates 36 and 37) and the detailed orange binding being in perfect condition.

Every time I visit I have no idea what new wonders I will see. What is the size of the collection? As yet, even though I've examined and catalogued over 750 titles, I have no idea. And Richard seems rather vague too, throwing out different numbers on occasion. A thousand? Fifteen hundred? Am I halfway through? Time will tell. One thing I do know is that seeing the collection 'at close quarters' has benefitted my own research significantly, setting me off in several new directions.

Richard has amassed an impressive group of early works produced by lithography, a process which acquired such prominence in South Asian printing history. Sitting on my laptop unfinished for over two decades has been a draft catalogue of India's 'lithographic incunables', but to have published it before seeing Richard's collection would have been a ghastly mistake and highly embarrassing. Apart from the many works by D'Oyly already mentioned, the collection contains John Dalrymple's *A Panoramic View of the Holy City of Benares* (Calcutta 1827); the only recorded copy of John Gantz and Sons' oddly entitled *Descriptive to a Set of Acquatinta Coloured Engravings: Illustrative of the Festivals, Wedding and Funeral Processions, andc. of the People of India* (Vepery 1834); B.D. Herald's *A Series of Nine Views around Kolapore* (London 1845); William Hunsley's *Costumes of the Madras Army* (Madras 1839–41) containing thirty-seven superb hand-coloured plates of both European and Indian soldiers; three items in Urdu issued by the Oudh Royal Press including *The Little Boy Who Stole and Told a Lie* (Lucknow 1835); Etienne Alexander Rodriguez's *Hindoo Castes* (both the Madras 1840 and the abridged London 1846 edition); and the exquisitely hand-coloured *Inscriptions on the Seikh Guns Captured by the Army of the Sutledge 1845–46* (Calcutta c. 1847). Recently Richard has also acquired the previously unrecorded *A Series of Pen Sketches of Scenery in the Island, and Presidency of Bombay* by Captain George Mackenzie, lithographed in 1842. It's tantalizing not knowing what else there is to see, but the mystery makes every visit a joy. Working on the collection as a joint enterprise with Richard himself is a privilege and a bibliographer's dream. What more can I say?

After graduating from Yale, Richard was offered a job in 1969 with a financial firm in London: 'This brought me,' he recalled in another email, 'to the heart of Europe's antiquarian book trade. The myriad of old bookshops and auction houses in London were like an Aladdin's cave of printed treasures.' And yet, his Indian journey began not at any of those bespoke antiquarian houses, but in a small bookshop in Kensington. One day, in 1972, he wandered by chance into a bookshop here and spotted a substantial quarto volume with a series of regulations for Indian courts in English and Persian. Printed in Calcutta and dated 1781, the paper and presswork were of exceptional quality. 'But at the asking price of £250 – and this was in the early '70s – from which the shop owner wouldn't budge – I thought it too dear for its content, and left it on the shelf.

'Not long after this, the lightning bolt of understanding about the importance of early Indian printing finally struck me. I used to travel to Europe often on business, where I usually managed to spend a few joyous hours in the rare bookshops of whatever city I was visiting. On one occasion I happened to be in Paris, and a bookseller there produced an extraordinary piece of Indian printing from the Vepery Press in 1779 in a contemporary binding, entitled *A Malabar and English Dictionary, wherein the Words... of the Tamulian Language... are Explained in English. By the English Missionaries of Madras.* Just the appearance of the title page, with its Tamil typography and early European design, mesmerized me.

'I couldn't take my eyes off the book or stop riffling its crisp pages full of Tamil words and English translations. For the equivalent of £55 it was mine, and I couldn't have imagined what a journey of exploration this one book was destined to take me on for the rest of my life. When I returned to London, I raced back to that bookshop in Kensington with a pounding heart to see if perchance he still had the Calcutta quarto. He did, and it's now one of the highlights in my collection.' Beautifully printed, these four compilations were amongst the first printings from the Company's Calcutta press.

Richard thinks of these early-printed books as India's 'Gutenberg experience'. He feels that even though printing from metal type had come to India as early as the sixteenth century via Christian missionaries – first, the Portuguese in Goa and later, the Danish in Tranquebar (now Tharangambadi) – the printed book as a means to spread knowledge came into its own in India in the eighteenth century, with the British and their interest in translating Indian manuscripts (on law, horticulture, medicine, chess) into English and printing them as pamphlets and books. 'I soon came to realize,' he says, 'that these books had an excitement that overwhelmed the staid, regimented publications from the later, nineteenth-century Indian presses – an excitement of typography, of paper, of binding, and of pioneer efforts to overcome immense difficulties.'

In his collection is a scarce and coveted volume of incunabular printing from India: the Tranquebar New Testament in Tamil from 1724, the first completely indigenous printing of the New Testament in any Indian language. Only seven copies are known to exist, none of them in India. His copy is unrestored, and nicely preserved. 'I found the book,' he told me, 'in a fairly unusual place, and comparatively recently in my book collecting career. It was sitting on the shelves of the travel department of Maggs Bros. Ltd., at their old premises in Berkeley Square, London. Maggs do not hold a large stock of books relating to the Indian subcontinent, but there it was about six or seven years ago, just waiting for me to discover it.'

The book I envy him for owning, though, is the first-ever fine press book from India – or at least I like to think of it that way – *A Grammar of the Bengal Language*, printed at Hooghly in Bengal in 1778 with the first finely designed Indian typeface; the work of a remarkable English civil servant named Charles Wilkins, who designed a fine Bengali metal typeface. Richard's copy is in its original Indian binding. It is a scarce book, but can occasionally be found in specialist catalogues; a copy bound in Britain was listed in 2014 for £6,000. Also in his possession is the first type specimen book issued in India, *Specimen of Printing Types in use at the Baptist Mission Press* (Calcutta, 1826).

The hunt for rare and fine Indian books took Richard all over the English countryside, visiting provincial antiquarian book dealers, paying attention to the offerings of provincial auction houses, visiting book fairs in a variety of places, and reading booksellers' catalogues from far and wide. 'Booksellers, in general, do not know how to price Indian books,' Richard said, 'as they have little awareness of their comparative importance in the history of Indian affairs and printing. I could never tell when or where the next gem would become available, but for many years they continued to surface, usually only one at a time.'

One day he came across a truly astonishing volume: a Calcutta printing of 1794 in mint condition, bound in a lustrous indigo-blue Indian goatskin binding, with gilt roll tooling around the covers and the entirety of the flat spine consisting of a repetitive pattern of fish and flowers. It was stunning, and clearly contemporary with the book's printing.

'I dubbed this unknown binding maestro the "Moghul Fish" binder, as his fish reminded me of the royal insignia used by the rulers of Oude. Years later, I found other books bound by the Moghul Fish binder in the same style, and books with copies of his distinctive roll tool used on Indian bindings in a more European style.'

Of the seven rooms in the Kossow household, all but one is filled to overflowing with specially designed bookcases, several of which are full to the brim with books on India – every one being the best-condition copy Kossow could obtain. Most of these are protected by custom-made slipcases or clam-shell boxes: one of the most stunning is a box he commissioned to hold a tall folio, the earliest known example of lithographic printing in India, titled *Heads of Families in States Independent or Protected*. The box and its inlays were created by Bill Gardner, a master leather-box maker; but the gilding was applied by a specialist gilder from Sangorski & Sutcliffe. 'You can see,' the collector pointed out to me, 'I put as much time, effort and expense into the display and preservation of early books on India as I do in obtaining the books themselves.'

His collection, Richard emphasizes, has uncovered only the first few layers of what one can glean of India's early printing – there is so much we don't know yet, he says, about the role of Indians in the bibliophilic endeavours of the British in India. While his own collection can serve as a basis for further research, he feels other collectors should jump in, so a fuller picture can emerge from multiple collections. 'This has been a fulfilling journey for almost half a century. I hope that others will feel the way I do about these books and keep on the lookout for worthy additions.'

From the months I spent getting to know Richard and his

collection, one factor rose above all others in indicating why when other collectors took only a passing fancy to colonial Indian books, Richard spent forty-five years forming a nonpareil library: he truly respects and loves them; from the first time he laid eyes on that piece of startling Vepery printing in Paris in Tamil type, he felt an immediate and deep affinity for these lovely, if neglected, books from India. Beyond bibliographical and typographical reasons, Richard is awed and tickled by what these early-printed Indian books suggest: that more than any other country it colonized, Britain was most smitten with India. And looking at Richard's books, you can't miss it.

A BIBLIOPHILE'S BIRD BOOKS

Aasheesh Pittie, a bibliophile hooked on birding since the day his father gave him Sálim Ali's *Book of Indian Birds*, was browsing through the Secunderabad Club Library one day, when the librarian, with a rather disgusted expression, told him about some very large books with 'bird pictures' that had been gathering dust on the shelves for several years. 'Believe me,' Pittie told me later, 'my heart was pounding like the steps of a pole-vaulter. I had been poring over some very large bird books in the library of the Bombay Natural History Society, and could not think of any other titles that might have found their way to the erstwhile cantonment of Secunderabad. My hunch was spot-on. When he lifted the imperial folios and set them down, there lay one of the two most valuable works of nineteenth-century ornithology. John Gould's *Birds of Asia*: not in the recommended binding of seven volumes, but in the original state of thirty-five folios. Yes, it was neither a full set, nor in fine condition, but what survived is still shockingly fabulous. Those lithographs still glow on every plate.'

This thrilling account is also instructive: the find, the recognition of what those folios were came about because Pittie was not only a bibliophile and an ornithologist, but also, in his heart, a first-rate bibliographer – though he wasn't to know that just yet. Bibliophily and birding had gone hand in hand for this businessman from Hyderabad over the years, starting with building a personal library of books on birds, to acquiring ornithological bibliographies to finally collecting antiquarian and rare bird books. And what his library had clearly revealed to him was the absence of a proper bibliography for South Asian ornithology. With still no idea of what he was going to do with it, Pittie began painstakingly maintaining a database for himself of works on the ornithology of South Asia.

'The more I pored over various bibliographic works from around the world,' Pittie told me, 'the stronger became my conviction that I had to do something similar at least for India, if not for South Asia. Those were the years when I realized the great paucity of ornithological libraries in India. Books on Indian birds published over the past three hundred years, were simply non-existent or too hard to locate. That drove me to buying and collecting them. In a way, the book was happening all the while I was filling up my bibliography.'

Pittie's staggering work, *Birds in Books: Three Hundred Years of South Asian Ornithology* (Permanent Black) was published in 2010; more recently, he has published an extension to this in the beautifully titled monograph *The Written Bird: Birds in Books 2*, available presently as a PDF on the Indian Birds website. Pittie is also the editor of the journal, *Indian BIRDS*, which can be read online (www.indianbirds.in).

I am not (yet) a birder, nor do my bibliographic interests lean to books on birds, but turning the pages of *Birds in Books*, you become swept up in the sumptuous bibliographical details of each work, fastidiously annotated, and experience the bibliographer's passion – his love for birds and his love for books coming together in one place.

'It's a terribly lonely calling,' Aasheesh replied, when I asked him what the experience of making an exhaustive bibliography had been. 'A drudge of the worst kind, and the work involved was hardly understood by anyone in libraries I've been to. Bibliography is the art of running down an original book (or work) and describing its geography by oneself. People do not understand the obsession with detail and mania for accuracy of transcription. But there's another side to it: discovering books, both rare and new, in libraries of the Bombay Natural History Society, the Asiatic Society (Mumbai) and the Asiatic Society (Kolkata), and poring over them with suppressed joy. The dirt and grime the books were kept in would blacken my computer and writing paper, and I had to carry wet-wipes to clean my hands before approaching another gem.'

Pittie's father was a philatelist of international repute and had been on the jury of major international philatelic competitions, but, says Aasheesh, 'I guess I get my bibliography genes from my mother because I haven't seen a more meticulous person than her in planning, in execution and in the art of storage and retrieval!'

Since that seminal book, Aasheesh has continued intently working on furthering South Asian bird-book bibliography. Recently, for instance, he has made available online another indispensable reference tool which he calls 'An author bibliography of South Asian ornithology: 1713–2022. Second edition (2023)' (available at https://indianbirds.in), which presently runs to 1,649 pages but could easily expand to 2,000 pages if he decides to add brief author biographies.

This ongoing work is, he writes on his website, 'an "author" bibliography of South Asian ornithology, covering over three hundred years, from 1713 up to the beginning of March 2022... to which I will add short biographies, along with a bibliography of biographies, of *all* authors listed in this work. The latter will comprise a list of references that are biographical in nature, e.g., appreciations, interviews, obituaries, etc.'

The bibliographer consulted various libraries and institutions with ornithological holdings all over India, ferreting out their archives to inform and enrich his database. He writes, 'The worst was realizing that such gems were held in libraries located in coastal cities, where the weather is paper's worst enemy and all the holdings suffer tremendously. Lack of space and/or tight budgets threaten the Kohinoors of the book world and the innumerable forgotten diamonds languishing on the shelves. I fear for their safety.'

As a collector of bird books, he has focused on rare books on ornithology. 'It was a red-letter day when I was able to pick up a rare signed edition copy of the reclusive J.A. Baker's iconic *The Peregrine*.' He also owns one of the rarest works on Indian ornithology: T.C. Jerdon's four-volume *Illustrations of Indian Ornithology* (1843–47). Other rarities in his library: a first edition of B.E. Smythies' *The Birds of Burma*, an inscribed copy of E.H. Aitken's *The Common Birds of Bombay* (Calcutta; Madras: Thacker, Spink & Co.; Higginbotham and Co.). 'My copy is inscribed by the author on the half-title page, "A happy voyage home, 19th March 1901". This must surely be the closest one can get to the publication date of this work.'

Aasheesh Pittie's new book, the evocatively titled *The Living Air: The Pleasures of Birds and Birdwatching* (Juggernaut, 2023) is bound to make birders out of all of us! It is both enjoyable and informative about birds and birdwatching. The naturalist Mark Cocker had a marvellous thing to say about *The Living Air*: 'Truth be told there are really no ordinary birds, nor ordinary life. It is all exceptional and Aasheesh Pittie is alive to this essential truth.'

Once, when I wondered aloud to Aasheesh what might have become of those stunning *Birds of Asia* Gould imperial folios if he hadn't rescued them from those dusty shelves, he replied, 'Oh, the answer to that is simple: they would probably have continued to be what they had been long used for at the club: as a convenient stool to help reach top shelves of cupboards.'

AN INKY PARADE OF TAMIL BIBLIOPHILES

A.R. Venkatachalapathy's affinity for the printed book comes from spending several hours over several days squeezed in dingy, inky letterpresses, staining his hands reading smudged proofs, gulping cup after cup of sweet tea. 'My workplace,' he writes, 'was essentially a working museum of print.' He was writing, editing, proofreading (perhaps even typesetting) and overseeing little monographs. Later, as a historian, he found himself inside musty corridors of archives; given the rare opportunity to examine antiquarian material, he came away seduced. All this and a stint as an assistant librarian at the Maraimalai Adigal Library (which he recalls as 'the single greatest education of my life') set him off in the new direction of turning book historian, a scholar of the book. His nicely titled *The Province of the Book: Scholars, Scribes and Scribblers in Colonial Tamilnadu* (Permanent Black, 2012) is not only a gift for all bibliophiles, especially the Tamil bibliophile, but a necessary book to discover, view and understand print culture in India.

An inky parade of antiquarians, bibliographers, librarians, bibliophiles, book scholars, printers, proofreaders and typesetters come alive in these pages. Interestingly, and perhaps for the first time, in a scribbler's world usually populated by Brahmins, there are sumptuous encounters with print-savvy Mudaliars and Pillais, the dominant players in the world of the Tamil printed book. They didn't pay authors very much, and their workers even less (a compositor's salary was ₹15), all standard practice, apparently. Chalapathy evokes two hilarious short stories by Pudumaipithan involving poor, struggling writers; in one, the author is on the streets his payments having bounced, and when he comes asking for his money, his publisher blackmails him into reading proof sheets! In fact, one of the delights of this book is how literary sources are often cited to nuance archival material; stories and novels reflect the world documented by letters and bibliographies.

Still, these early printers and publishers were heroic, pioneering figures, often – like Adigal's T.M. Press – setting up a private press to print their own work and staying up late into the night typesetting and proofing. Adigal began his little press in 1902 while he was still a 26-year-old Tamil pundit at Madras Christian College. He got it going for a thousand rupees. (Like him, there was also printer-publisher Thiru. Vi. Ka.) Chalapathy's own research here, both in direction and depth, is itself pioneering: for the first time, the whole history and drama (and its subtexts) of the Tamil printed book can be found in one dazzling single work that goes beyond antiquarian passion and bibliography to investigate the Tamil printed book as a cultural object, its influence and impact on Tamil authors, publishers, printers and readers.

Chapter by chapter, Chalapathy traces the evolution of the early-printed book in Tamil, and the world he makes visible is fascinating: the precolonial and colonial world of royal patronage towards the printed book, which was so hallowed that there was an *arangetram* for every new work. Chalapathy looks at the literary career of Meenakshisundaram Pillai (1815–1876) to show us how patronage worked and how it eventually declined (in the Tamil printed book, the elaborate title page comes into being now). Oddly, the next significant period in Tamil print culture isn't until the 1920s, with the rise of the novel, especially the crime and detective novel that the Tamil public heartily (even though middle-class intellectuals poured scorn on it) embraced. At last, the Tamil printed book had a vibrant market. But just between colonial patronage and the modern market, the Tamil book suffered along with its authors. Patronage had ended and the market hadn't come into being. Writers such as Subramania Bharathi and chronicler M.V. Ramanujachari suffered greatly and resorted to self-publishing.

An intriguing question that he raises is why when Tamil was the first Indian language to find print – as early as 1557 with *Thamibran Vannakam* – did printing and publishing not take off until the late nineteenth century? While Bengali and Malayalam, which had found print only two hundred years after Tamil, kicked off at once a flourishing, bespoke print culture? Why didn't Tamil make use of its two hundred-year headstart that the Tamil press in Goa, Tranquebar and Vepery had given it over other Indian languages? At least a partial reason could be that all the early pioneering efforts in the printed book were undertaken by European missionaries; there was no indigenous publishing for the first two centuries. Chalapathy identifies a turning point in Tamil printing that few book historians have pointed to: in 1812 at the College of Fort St. George (or the Madras School of Orientalism) 'for the first time, nearly 250 years after Tamil first saw print, non-missionaries and natives were involved in printing technology'; he mentions, among others, Tandavaraya Mudaliar, Kottramangalam Ramasamy Pillai and Muttusami Pillai as being involved in editing and publishing.

One of the closing chapters looks at readers and reading practices: Who read? What did they read? I wish Chalapathy had also included a chapter on Tamil book collectors: Who collected? What did they collect? Of course, all through his book, Chalapathy references the libraries of bibliophiles and the book collections of Tamil scholars (R. Muthukumaraswamy, 'arguably the most knowledgeable of Tamil bibliophiles', Maraimalai Adigal, U.V. Swaminathan Iyer, Pudumaippithan), but I still longed to read a chapter on collecting practices and how they shaped the printed book. I have to content myself with the thought that antiquarians and collectors will find a larger place in his next book. I have another little quibble too – he says that Tamil antiquarians and bibliographers are to blame for limiting Tamil book scholarship by laying more emphasis on printing than on publishing.

I didn't think it was – is – the job of the antiquarian or the bibliographer to write, a la Robert Darnton, about the printed book as a cultural object. This is a task for the cultural historian, the book historian, and I think an equal emphasis on publishing would have developed alongside if only the Tamil book historian had emerged sooner. Where would book scholarship be (and Chalapathy himself acknowledges this by naming Graham Shaw, Proilkar, Kesavan, Mylai Seeni Venkataswamy) without the antiquarian book collector and bibliographer?

CHASING A RARE INDIAN TYPE SPECIMEN BOOK

One day, I suddenly found myself on a chase to find a rare and incredible Indian type specimen book, and the extraordinary type foundry that produced it. The first reference I came across to the Gujarati Type Foundry (GTF) and its renowned type specimen book was in an unusual, intriguing essay by Jan Tholenaar, called 'Collecting Type Specimens'. Tholenaar had been a prolific and impassioned collector of rare type specimen books, and in talking about striking examples of such books in his collection, he describes a monumental production from the Gujarati Type Foundry showing an extensive range of metal typefaces and ornaments. I was astounded, excited and insatiably curious – how could I find out more about the GTF, and where, if it was even possible, could I get hold of this famous specimen book?

To understand why I felt this was such a big deal, you have to realize that all traces of India's letterpress past have now completely vanished. For me, it was eye-popping news that there had even once been a type foundry of such stature and accomplishment in India, and that it had produced a specimen book of hot metal fonts to rival any in the world. The first clue lay in Tholenaar's essay itself; he references *The Matrix*, that lush, letterpress-printed, yearly typographic journal from The Whittington Press. Apparently in *Matrix: Volume 2*, there is a little essay on GTF's unusual type specimen book. But *Matrix*, usually priced around £200, was beyond my means, and at the time I was looking for one in the secondary market, it had even become scarce.

A whole year went by without me making any progress in learning more about GTF and I was nowhere close to finding this specimen book. Then, just a month or so ago, things began to fall in place: I found not one but two sources that could tell me more about GTF and point me to their specimen book. I suddenly remembered that a wonderful dealer in fine press books in the UK I had been buying from and who had become a friend – Bill Woodbridge of Woodbridge Rare Books – had once told me he owned several issues of *Matrix* to use as a reference tool. I shot off an email asking if he might perhaps have *Matrix 2*, and if he did, would he mind terribly scanning the essay I wanted from it? Luckily, Bill did have the volume and he readily and generously sent me the essay.

Almost around the same time, I discovered completely by chance that Richard L. Hopkins, the legendary type founder and typographic scholar (who has done much, along with Paul Hayden Duensing, to revive and teach typecasting) may very possibly know more about what I was looking for. In a newsletter for the American Typecasting Fellowship that he publishes, he had written about the GTF and reviewed their specimen book. I contacted Mr Hopkins, explaining what I wanted, and though he was in the midst of a very busy work schedule, he graciously took the time to answer my queries. And he also added, quite casually and matter-of-factly, that he had a spare copy of the GTF specimen book: Would I be interested in having one?

I would be *very* interested, I answered.

The Gujarati Type Foundry was based in Bombay and had begun in 1900, and very likely shut down in the late 1980s or early '90s, when letterpress printing shops everywhere in India had begun closing down. Everyone had gone offset and it was financially a drain to keep a type foundry going. But in their heyday, they had been supplying not just Indian letterpress printers and publishers with metal typefaces and ornaments, but had been meeting the requirements of printers – private and commercial – all around the world. The chief architect of their celebrated specimen book was Manilal C. Modi, who had steered the foundry for several decades. It had taken GTF nearly eleven years to produce their illustrated type catalogue, from 1926 to 1937. And though it had a print run of ten thousand copies – to be given away or sold – few copies survive today. I count myself incredibly fortunate to be in possession of one now.

When the GTF type specimen book reached me by post, I could finally see why it had aroused so much admiration and interest. The range of matrices, typefaces, ornaments, borders and typecasting machines (for both English and Indian languages) once held by this Indian type foundry was breathtaking, and over several hundred pages, they are all shown to good effect, with many in colour. Geoffrey Osborne in his *Matrix* essay remarks that the catalogue is a 'lavish monument to typographical display and design... a reader can only stand amazed at "the industry and scholarship required in its production and origination from hand-cut steel punches".'

One aspect that amused me no end was that many well-known typefaces had been given Indian names: Clarendon is Tilak, Bodoni is Govind, Caslon Open is Ushakant, Della

Robbia is Vivekanand, Goudy Old Style is Rupam Series, etc.! I also discovered that up until the late 1980s, there were at least forty type foundries in India. And yet we know so little about India's letterpress past, its printing shops, its printers and type casters. Its history is yet to be written.

PART THREE

ADVENTURES IN BOOK COLLECTING

MISHAPS OF A COLLECTOR

Once in a rare while, an online transaction between a book dealer and a customer can go bad. Thankfully, for both seller and buyer, it doesn't happen often, but when such mishaps occur, it can leave a bad taste in the mouth about buying expensive books online. I've had my share of collecting mishaps; these things happen usually in your early days as a collector when you're still figuring out how the trade works. I'd like to recount three such mishaps here, and the lessons I learnt from them. Before I get to those, though, I must say I can still never get over how smoothly, efficiently, even magically, buying from online antiquarian dealers around the world works most of the time. There is so much trust from both sides: you pay upfront and wait the two weeks it takes for internationally shipped parcels to arrive – and when they do, you find them to be exactly what the dealer promised.

Sometimes, though, it's not what you expected or wanted. The first sour experience I had was with a bookseller in the UK. Usually they are wonderful to deal with, and when my negotiations with this particular dealer (whom I'll call Dealer A) began, it too felt secure – until the antiquarian item in question arrived. I was keen on acquiring a much sought after chromolithographic book published in the nineteenth century, titled *Illuminated Ornaments Selected from Manuscripts*, famous for its spectacular use of hand-colouring and tinting. In fact, it's often described as the most beautiful book published in the Victorian period, a high point in the use of chromolithography. A remarkable English draughtsman named Henry Shaw actually engraved the 59 or so plates in the book, and then they were painstakingly coloured individually by hand in rich, deep pigments, and in a few deluxe editions, burnished in gold.

The average cost of this book is usually around £400, but while scouring dealers listing copies of the Shaw book, I came across one provincial English dealer listing it for £200. I asked for details, and he assured me that it was indeed the same edition (William Pickering, London 1833) I was looking for. The book, a large folio and quite heavy, meant the shipping would be expensive, since it had to be by air. I paid via PayPal and waited for this volume to arrive, feeling pretty pleased at having scored a bargain. To my dismay, on opening the large, weighty parcel, I found that the plates were black and white. It was missing the only thing it was known for: colour.

It must have been some trial proof copy that did not get to the final production stage of being hand-coloured. I checked a few reference books dealing with Victorian illustrated books, and the work of Shaw and Pickering in particular, and there was no mention of copies in black and white. The book was conceived and executed with the sole purpose of showing colour chromolithography. I wrote quickly to the bookseller, adding that I wanted to return the volume – at my expense. He emailed back to say he had been unaware of these bibliographical points because someone else had catalogued it. He would have to check with his cataloguer, who was an authority on these things. The usual terms for most established dealers are that any book is returnable for any reason within a week to ten days of purchase, so strictly speaking I could return it if I did not want to keep this anomalous copy.

I soon discovered Dealer A had no intention of taking it back – for any reason. Apparently, his cataloguer swore he had seen other black-and-white copies of this Victorian masterpiece. I asked A about his seller terms listed on his third-party page (Abebooks, Biblio, Alibris, etc.) which state that books are returnable, and he flatly said he would not be honouring that since I had bought directly from him. This was a rude shock since I felt he ought to honour those standard terms, especially because the transaction had been a direct, personal one, where he profits more by not having to pay third-party fees.

Anyway, it was a lesson learnt, the moral being: if you haven't already established a relationship with a dealer, it's safer buying via a third-party book website, as they'll share some of the responsibility for a bad transaction, urge the dealer to take the purchase back, and process a refund.

My second mishap, with Dealer B, wasn't her fault; it was just a mishap, plain and simple, but nevertheless resulted in a loss for both of us. I bought a sumptuous fine press book from an American dealer priced at $250, with the proviso that I would return it in the same condition within the stipulated returns period if I ended up not liking it as much as I thought I would. The book arrived, it was in lovely condition, I handled it carefully for a few days, and decided to return it. I chose a fairly fast and expensive shipping method, and then waited for the dealer to refund the price. When I next heard from the dealer, it was a nasty email, noting that the book had been damaged in transit and she could not accept it. Had I insured it? No, I had not. I hadn't known any better then. Second costly lesson learnt: always insure anything that is worth $100 or more. We resolved it as best as we could, and I bought the book *back* from the dealer. I have since grown fond of this fine press book and am rather glad I got stuck with it; the other one, though, sits conspicuously on my shelf as a reminder of how a perfectly nice arrangement such as online rare book trading can be foiled by a few dodgy dealers.

The third transaction, with Dealer C, didn't even go through – the book dealer did not honour the sale, claiming the book had been sold, when it had not. Why had he done this? Because he had realized quickly enough that he had underpriced the book. I had heard of such things happening to other collectors but this was the first time I experienced the disappointment and sting of a bookseller holding back a sale and depriving me of a bargain. Good for him! Though, as a bookseller friend to whom I recounted this told me, while the dealer may have been within his rights to turn down the sale, he could have handled the whole thing more gracefully and honestly.

Illuminated Manuscripts in the British Museum: Miniatures, Borders, and Initials Reproduced in Gold and Colours was a four-part series of facsimiles issued by the British Museum between 1899 and 1903. Each set (of the four parts) consisted of fifteen facsimiles in a folder. These illuminated facsimiles are some of the most brilliant and beautifully accomplished plates I've ever seen, and over the years, I had managed to obtain three of the four sets. These original sets are scarce, and should not be mistaken for the later reprints that were issued as black-and-white collotype plates and are available plentifully in the market as reprints.

The four sets were also bound in book form in 1903 in an edition of just 500 copies, with sixty chromolithographed plates – and this is just as scarce. When this bound set turned up one day on ABE (it must have been a new listing, because I had been keeping my eye out for this book and had never till date spotted one in the market) with all the four parts intact, I was tempted to buy it just to get hold of the set I lacked. It was priced at around $300, and after some hesitation, I ordered it. A bit of an overkill, considering I had three of the four parts, but I still felt it was worth it – so magnificent are these plates done by William Griggs, who had found a way to add gold and colours to illuminate the plates.

Besides, it *was* underpriced. If I didn't already have most of the sets in the series, it would be a neat bargain.

A whole day went by without an email from ABE or the seller confirming the order. When the next day I still had not received an update on the order, I contacted the bookseller, with the niggling feeling that the dealer would hold back the book. Sure enough, when I heard back a little while later, it was to say: apologies, but the book had sold and he had unfortunately forgotten to inform ABE. The only online listing for his copy had been on ABE, and I had bought that copy, so his explanation was a bit off, but I left it at that. He wrote to me again to ask if he was able to locate another copy, would I still be interested and what would I be able to pay for it?

That kind of gave it away, and I wrote back to say no, I would not be interested. A week later, he relisted it on ABE for $1,100. My bookseller friend, responding to this said: a) even if he had mispriced it, he should have still honoured the sale, and b) not wanting to do that, he could have just come out and said he had mistakenly priced it too low and offered it back to me at a revised, higher price, giving me first refusal. Thinking about it some more, I should hardly be the one to get indignant over this, given all the bargains I'd got from bibliographical mistakes made by other booksellers.

What could have alerted or tipped off the dealer that it was possibly a mistake to sell the illuminated facsimile book at the price he had first listed it? I bet it was the speed of the sale. He had just listed a book above $250, and it had sold almost at once. Usually, books priced in that range linger around for a while and booksellers get suspicious if there's a flash sale for high-priced books. It occurs to them that they may have made a mistake judging its true value. Some act on it, like this dealer, and turn down the sale; others shrug it off or don't want to risk listing it for a higher price and not having a quick sale on their hands.

BUYING INTO A COLLECTION

One day, out of the blue, I received this email from Hobart Flock of Hoki-Nol Books:

> 6/28/2018 3:23 PM
> Just letting you know of a sale that we will be putting forward during the next month to loyal clients of ours (of which you are certainly one of them). We will be allowing the following discount on our ENTIRE inventory:
>
> 1-4 books: 15% off
> 5-9 books: 20% off
> 10-19 books: 30% off
> 20-29 books: 40% off
> 30+ books: 50% off
>
> We will be running this sale from now until the end of next month. Only the amount of titles/copies ordered is the trigger, so it doesn't matter if you order four $5 books and one $1,000 book, this will still qualify for a 20% discount (5-9 books: 20% off).'

I wrote back thanking Flock for thinking of me, and said I would give it some consideration. I didn't really think, however, that I could give this scheme serious consideration – 20 per cent off is something I regularly received from rare book dealers, and I could see straightaway that going for the 50 per cent off is how you'd really benefit from the loyalty scheme. This meant buying thirty or more books from a *rare bookshop* at *one go*, and though Flock had thoughtfully pointed out that you could buy, in effect, twenty-nine five-dollar books and a single $1,000 book, you wouldn't get the books you really want – that is the best fine press books Hoki-Nol had to offer – if you stuffed your bag with $5 books!

No, I couldn't afford to buy thirty fine press books in a single purchase – that would leave me with little or no funds for the rest of the year for other fine press books on my want-list, and I abandoned entertaining any idea of seizing on this 50 per cent off bonanza scheme with *nothing* in the inventory embargoed. Everything from their most expensive book in the store to the cheapest, was at half its listed price. Then, two things happened in quick succession that nudged me closer to reaching for the juiciest discount in the scheme.

The first was another email from Flock informing me that they had just bought en bloc the collection of Richard Schimmelpfeng, a notable collector of fine press books. If I was interested, he would send me a PDF of the collection now in their possession, and I could actually pick books from here to make up my list for the loyalty scheme. That kind of an offer is always a temptation for a collector (and book dealers know this better than anyone else) because you want to know what's in it – *even* when you have no intention of buying anything at that moment.

So, I said yes, please send it along. I also took the opportunity to ask Hobart Flock if he might be interested in buying books from my collection that I didn't want to hold on to – I didn't want cash, I added, but was rather thinking of trade credit I could use towards future purchases from Hoki-Nol. Not that I couldn't have used cash, but dealers are able to offer better prices for your books when you accept trade credit over cash. Flock promptly sent me the Schimmelpfeng PDF and I replied with a Word attachment that listed the books I wanted to offer for trade. It consisted of some really lovely books, a mix of high-end press books (like the deluxe edition of Whittington Press's *Chinese Ceremonial Papers*, one of the Grabhorn bibliographies and a colourful Allen Press title) as well as some scarce fine press items that I now felt didn't matter to me as much as they once did.

The Schimmelpfeng collection had me wide-eyed as I scrolled down: several fine press and book arts items that had not appeared in the market in a long while, were all part of this fine, substantial collection. Two, in particular, had me rushing an email to Flock asking they be put aside for me. I dashed this mail off without even stopping to figure out if this meant that I had now attached myself to the loyalty scheme – for if this was what I had let myself into, I had twenty-eight more books to pick! But the collection was so promising even just hastily scanning it, I must have felt assured that I would find enough there to tempt me to go all the way.

The two items that had pulled me in were the beautiful bibliography (more checklist than bibliography) Valenti Angelo had printed on his hand press in 1970 in a small edition of just fifty-five copies. Angelo had a genius for decorating books with hand illumination, and this is best seen in the books he printed himself. The checklist was not scarce – there are usually a couple of copies in the market at any given time – but it's always priced in the $850–$950 range, as was the Hoki-Nol copy, but it could now be mine for $450. The other item was a truly scarce Angelo broadside, and a much sought-after and desired hand-coloured and illuminated broadside of the Beatitudes.

I received a reply from Flock the next day, telling me the Angelo checklist had been kept aside for me, but the broadside had just sold. Of course, it was idiotic of me not to realize the R.S. PDF list had gone to several customers. At least the checklist was secured. This meant I had to race through the list, pick twenty-eight or more books and send that off to Hobart with little time to spare.

There was also some good news in that email: Flock would take all the books I had sent a list of from my collection, and give me a fair price in trade credit. I now had ammunition from an unexpected corner, and felt doubly motivated to go after not just the Schimmelpfeng collection, but the rest of the Hoki-Nol stock as well. When a private collection comes up for sale, you find things that are more than books: there's a great deal of fine press ephemera gathered by the collector over the years, as well as correspondence with fellow collectors and fine press printers.

Hoki-Nol had made small packets of the ephemera from this collection, and had priced them reasonably, and I got most of them. I didn't know the contents of these press ephemera packets, and there were too many to ask the bookshop to look into, describe and supply photos (though Flock would have been glad to do so, going by past queries I've sent to him where he has always patiently gone through things with me on the phone).

Two packets that handsomely paid off were for Stanbrook Abbey Press and the Gehenna Press, two of my big favourites; I just had a gut feeling these would be hiding at least a few nice things because both presses are known for their attractive ephemera. In the Stanbrook packet, among prospectuses and announcements, were at least three illuminated folders done on handmade paper from a very fine metal type with hand-drawn and gilded initials by Margaret Adams.

This packet had been priced $65 – and just *one* of these illuminated folders are usually priced at more in the market. Add the 50 per cent off and I got it for $32 or so. In the Gehenna packet, again among more commonly found press announcements and lists, was a small, satisfying bunch of scarce and pretty typographic things designed and printed by Leonard Baskin and Harold McGrath, that were either privately printed for friends and colleagues (bookplates, business cards, letterheads), or for Baskin's own family in the way of birthday invitations, announcements of births, wedding anniversaries and so on.

And because Baskin had done this for his own use to give to friends and family, they were done on beautiful thin, coloured handmade papers, type and ornaments exquisitely arranged by Baskin, and each little thing found in the original envelopes they were posted in, with the address written out in Baskin's hand. This packet was $45 and I paid, of course, $22.50. I've known just *one* of these privately printed Baskin items to go for $25 to $50. Hoki-Nol customers who bought these Schimmelpfeng packets must have all done very well; every packet must have held some wonderful, unexpected things.

Not long after I bought into the Schimmelpfeng collection, I had an opportunity to buy from another stellar collection, that of the renowned fine bookbinder, Gregor Campbell, who had sold a large part of his library en bloc to a bookseller I bought often from. I was given a crack at the stock before it went on the market. I didn't, however, buy thirty books, but six very choice books, every one of them scarce and beautiful. One of them was an edition of a book I had imagined would ever come up for sale, let alone being able to buy it. This was one of the twenty-six lettered copies of the deluxe issue of *For Jean Grolier and His Friends: 125 Years of Grolier Club Exhibitions and Publications, 1884–2009*.

For Jean Grolier and His Friends, according to the Grolier Club is 'the most lavish production in the club's long history of fine printing, with numerous illustrations and tip-ins'. Published in connection with the 125th anniversary of the founding of the Grolier Club, this massive work documents the hundreds of exhibitions mounted and publications issued over the years. The monumental 500 pages of text was printed letterpress on a lovely German mould-made paper, Hahnemühle, letterpress printed by Bradley Hutchinson, and designed by Jerry Kelly.

The deluxe edition was bound in quarter leather and decorated boards, and came with a portfolio of Grolier Club ephemera, both the book and portfolio contained in a slipcase. It is a truly handsome binding, especially the wine-red Morocco spine and the pretty gilt-lettered title, while the book itself is a treat for how finely printed it is, the beautiful paper, the bite of letterpress type, the tip-ins and the absorbing, informative text, part history of the club, and a handy sumptuous descriptive reference of what the Grolier had been up to from 1884 to 2009.

Before this came on the market, I had looked to acquire just the regular edition, and had been pleased to spot two copies in the market. But rather interestingly and curiously, both turned out to be 'phantom listings'. The two copies that showed on ABE weren't in stock with the dealers who had listed it. I found out the hard way: ordering a copy and being told it was no longer available. In spite of these dealers knowing they didn't have a copy, they didn't take it off their online listings. They had priced it at $400 and this phantom listing continued to show up.

I then went on to contact the two authors of the book, George Ong and Eric Holzenberg, asking if they might have a spare copy to sell of the regular edition. They didn't have one to spare, and Holzenberg told me they had 'rather gone overboard with the limitation' (279 total copies) and had regretted it, since so many more Grolier members would have liked to order a copy later.

And now this excessively rare and beautiful deluxe edition (hors commerce copy given to Gregor Campbell, who had bound the regular and the deluxe copies) was listed for just $400 – the price of the regular edition! I doubt if these lettered copies were ever even put on the market – no Grolier member would want to part with it.

When I once happened to mention to Jerry Kelly, who had designed this volume, that I had managed to get hold of the deluxe Jean Grolier, he exclaimed, 'how do you happen to have a copy of that?!'

These were some of my earliest experiences of buying from a private collection that had not yet come to the market, and getting an early – if not first or exclusive – crack at it. The whole thing was made pleasurable by having a large trade credit to use, allowing me to comfortably pick thirty items, as well as secure all the things I wanted from Hoki-Nol. To think that for days after I had got wind of the loyalty scheme, I had gone about thinking I would not take Hobart Flock up on it! None of this would be mine today if I had not taken the plunge – and what pushed me were the beauties in the Richard Schimmelpfeng collection.

(NOT) COLLECTING J.D. SALINGER

There is, in a bibliophile's life, always one galvanizing moment that defines him as a book collector and reveals to him that he is nothing if not a bookman: the pursuit to find and own first editions of one author's work that has obsessed him. I'll cut to the chase and tell you right off that I never did find that first edition – rather, I did, but it was beyond my means. But my quest to find and own that Holy Grail of first editions, J.D. Salinger's *The Catcher in the Rye*, baptized me into the intricacies of book collecting. And I found instead something that came very close to it – if not in value, at least in rarity and beauty.

It began innocently and simply enough: I wanted to find and collect as many different paperback editions of *Catcher* as I could lay my hands on. For a start, I had with me a well-thumbed copy of that '80s silver-grey Penguin from my college days, now out of print. I also had the maroon-wine-coloured paperback popular in the '90s. And then there was that rather common copy with the blank white cover that turns up ubiquitously in our bookstores.

None of them really had any value in the collector's market but they were interesting variant editions.

Taking an interest in a particular *edition* made me want to possess other editions of the book. Visiting second-hand bookshops whenever I happened to find myself in Mumbai or

Kolkata or Chennai, took on a focus, had a special purpose and added new excitement. Could this be the shop that I would find some *Catcher* edition I didn't have? Nothing interesting turned up for a couple of years. And then I got lucky – twice. On Kolkata's Free School Street, I actually found a copy of that orange-and-white Penguin from the '60s. Fairly scarce.

My true find came, unexpectedly, while indifferently browsing through the wares of a pavement book vendor in a lane behind Delhi's Connaught Place. I was almost going to leave empty-handed when I saw it. And froze. A vintage paperback of *The Catcher in the Rye*. I had only seen pictures of it in the catalogues of rare book dealers. Could it really be or was I seeing things? The 1953 Signet paperback of *Catcher* features the rarely seen illustrated cover. This was before Salinger stipulated that all his books should have bare covers with just titles.

I had bought from this vendor before and he was savvy (a steady stream of tourists buying and selling from him had told him all he needed to know about books). I had to pretend to be bored and casual when I asked to see the book, almost as though it were an afterthought. Before handing it to me, he gave the cover a more than cursory look, then glanced at me and back at the book before handing it over. It was a little tattered but there was something more: it had come apart completely and was held together by a thick rubber band.

Vintage paperbacks are collected for the cover art. If I was desperate enough to buy a book held together by a rubber band, the vendor knew he didn't have to bargain with me. I just gave him whatever he asked (plenty considering the condition, but it could well have been one of a handful left in the country) and fled from there before he snatched it back from me. Later in the hotel, looking at it leisurely, I could smell that smell old books give off; the pages were brittle and brown from foxing.

The copyright page showed it was actually a 35th printing. Very far from the 1953 first printing, but to be in possession of a *Catcher* with that famous James Avati pulp cover art, more than made up for it. The gaudy, lurid cover shows a young boy with a suitcase, red cap (worn backwards) and a scarlet scarf around his neck. Avati was a legendary pulp cover artist, best known for this illustration.

Later I would learn how to distinguish later printings from earlier imprints: the illustration was fuller, the later printings, as in my copy, were cropped with a gold border. But bringing a copy of that hard-to-find (at least in India) edition back home from a hunt was a seminal moment for me as a book collector: the collection had to be completed. I had to now look for the real thing: a hardcover first printing of *Catcher* with the true dust jacket.

Forget a first edition, forget even an early printing – in the end I spent several years hunting (crawling, really) for *just* a hardcover edition of the book. Nothing. Hardcover editions of *Catcher*, even minus the book jacket, simply don't exist in India. Today, you can find a hardcover edition of the book in our bookstores, but it's a contemporary edition. If you are a fan of the book, it's worth having just for its flaming red-and-orange jacket with a unicorn and sketchy outline of the Manhattan skyline in the background.

There's a singular difference between a first printing, first state edition and all the later ones. At the back of the book in the first state (and some early book club editions) is that photo of a young handsome Salinger that has been all over the internet and newspapers and magazines since his death. Salinger had Little, Brown remove his photo soon after publication, and ever since, the back cover has stayed blank (that's one among a few other things to look for while identifying a first printing of *Catcher*).

Trawling through online book search engines, I was quickly dissuaded from setting my eyes on a first edition: the going price for even a copy in so-so condition, was anything between $800 and $3,000. I discovered that you could find a first printing or a book club edition without a dust jacket and very possibly ex-libris for a more (very much more) modest sum. Which is what I finally did. Its market value is little but the personal value it holds for me gives it a special charge.

To own a copy from the first batch that rolled off the printing press in 1951 of *this* book, is to be given the privilege of communing daily with a copy that very possibly Salinger touched or handled or was very close to. It is for this reason that a bibliophile turns into a book collector in the first place: to chase after a copy, an edition, in the hope of finding intimacy and connection beyond the words inside a beloved book to the palpable material – cardboard, cloth, paper – of the book itself.

'WINDOWS TO THE SOUL OF THE RARE BOOK TRADE'

The catalogues of rare book dealers and auction houses have been such an important tool in my collecting and have provided so much reading excitement, that I just had to have a little chapter on them. In fact, the pleasure and utility of rare books and manuscripts catalogues can only be fully known to collectors and dealers. Before I turned collector, I would flip through them indifferently and chuck them away. Now I wait for a new catalogue to come in the post or as PDFs on email from booksellers who specialize in my collecting interests.

I drop everything else I am doing and immediately scan the contents of the newly arrived catalogue – and only after I have satisfied myself that there's nothing there that requires urgent attention, will I settle down to do anything else.

In his *Essays and Papers* (Scolar Press, 1977), the scholar-collector Tim Munby nicely summed up the place that catalogues have traditionally had in a collector's life: 'To receive one at breakfast, to skim through it with one's porridge, possibly leaving the table to dictate a telegram if circumstances demanded it, to note complacently how the books one bought for modest sums in the past have risen in price – these are among the highest pleasures of life.'

That other great scholar-collector of Victorian Yellowbacks, Michael Sadlier, wrote in *Passages from the Autobiography of a Bibliomaniac*, 'I shall never forget the arrival by post of the first slim Bellew catalogue. After tearing through the catalogue's eight pages, I felt so breathless that I had to sit for minutes before I was... capable of going through the whole thing item by item... I made pencil crosses, I drafted a long telegram. Then I commended my cause to Providence and went through the catalogue all over again.'

Lessing J. Rosenwald, a wealthy and formidable collector, who could have bought rarities at any asking price, was himself unable to resist looking for a bargain within the pages of a just-arrived catalogue. In his 1976 memoir, *Recollections of a Collector*, he confessed, 'There is no more delightful pleasure for a bibliomaniac than to satisfy his avocation on his day of rest by perusing his accumulation of sales catalogues... one always has the hope (seldom realized) that somewhere buried in such a miscellany is an item may be overlooked by the more astute dealers and the more catholic collectors.'

Catalogues, as collectors can tell you, are not all about pleasure; there's pain involved, too. Perusing a just-arrived catalogue, you know there's some risk involved; a bit of tension as you run your eyes over the listing. What you're afraid of seeing there is a book listed for half the price you paid for your copy, and worse still, remembering how well pleased you were then that your copy had been the most reasonably priced. What could make this better, or make up for it a bit, is spotting in the same catalogue at least a book or two listed at much higher prices than you'd paid for them not too very long ago.

There's also the regret you experience when noting how

so many books with high prices in this recent catalogue had once been available at more moderate prices, and you stupidly didn't buy them then. Munby captured this accurately again when he wrote, 'The excitement of receiving new catalogues is perhaps matched only by the peculiar heartache of reading or rereading old ones, which has all the pain and some of the pleasure of visiting old love letters – pleasure and regret about what we did and what we did not do.'

A.N.L. Munby once produced a single copy of a handwritten catalogue of his eighteenth-century books for his friend Harold Foster – when they were just Cambridge undergraduates! Munby wanted money to collect other things, so he asked Foster if he would be interested in buying his choice collection of books painstakingly put together from book-hunting trips to David's Bookshop and other dusty antiquarian places, and his friend expressed keen interest. Munby then wrote out a catalogue, replete with asking prices, footnotes and little asides.

The greatest pleasure to be found in book catalogues, though, is not in price comparison but in the bibliographical description for each entry written by the bookseller. These make for some of the richest, most rewarding reading for both collector and dealer. Accurate and fulsome details about not just the edition but about this particular listed copy, followed by an absorbing, knowledgeable note on either the printer or the press or background details on the book's production.

And it's not anymore just confined to printed catalogues; you see the same richly described entry for each book in the ABE inventories of these very dealers and bookshops – which is why I've found it so instructive as well as so much fun to browse AbeBooks. Pull up a fine press book you are considering/exploring buying, or are simply curious to learn more about, and ABE will list as many copies as there are of the title. Then read the bibliographical book description put in there by each dealer. Some will be just adequate, some will be lengthy, one or two will even have some wit to them, others will strike a more personal note by including their own opinion of the edition.

Roy Vernon Sowers, antiquarian bookseller and curmudgeon, would include in his catalogues at least one book from his personal collection that was not for sale. No amount of money, he would say, could tempt him to sell it. All collectors and dealers, he felt, ought to realize that some books come without a price tag.

One of the tips an older bookdealer will offer a younger rare bookdealer preparing to issue her first catalogue, is to keep the entries for the books priced between $25 to $75 short and sweet, and to spend more time on researching and writing longer bibliographical descriptions for the higher-priced books. The higher the price, the more substantial (if not longer) the entry. Sound advice, I am sure, and yet I have been quite charmed and moved by famous dealers who've taken a different approach.

The renowned scholar bookseller E.P. Goldschmidt, we are told, once spent over two weeks writing a catalogue entry on an armorial bookplate that he was intending to price at £20. Christopher De Hamel at Sotheby's is known to have slogged over entries, with closely argued texts, for auction items with low estimates. The late and remarkable Ian Jackson was happier writing long bibliographical descriptions for $5 items in his inventory, than for his high-end antiquarian stock. He once wrote a five-page description for a pamphlet he was giving away for free.

'Bookshops open and close. Booksellers retire, change professions, and pass on. What remains, other than memories and reputations, are their catalogues, the lasting tangible record of a bookseller's creativity and expertise – a remembrance, a talisman...' These remarks are by John R. Payne, from his preface to *Great Catalogues by Master Booksellers*. It brings together 140 bookseller catalogues that Payne, a bibliographer, has found remarkable and useful over the years as an index of rare and fine books. 'Catalogues,' he goes on to say, 'are the windows to the soul of the rare book trade.'

Along with all the usual antiquarian bookdealer suspects – Quaritch, Rosenbach, Harrington, Sotherans, Maggs, Rota, Eberstadt, Kraus, Reese – there are quite a few nice surprises: the spoof catalogue from Caveat Book Shop, and that sumptuous catalogue of books about books from the Alida Roochvarg collection, that Oak Knoll brought together. Payne has thoughtfully included the introductory essays and prefaces that accompanied these catalogues, making his book a useful tool for collectors and dealers, finally giving bookseller catalogues their due.

A fond pastime for me when I can't seem to be able to get anything read is turning to old catalogues, and while away time there. These aren't the contemporary catalogues that I've received over the years, but catalogues from bookshops from the past that specialized in fine press and the book arts. Some of my favourites are the catalogues (now scarce) issued by Chiswick Book Shop, Philip Duschnes Rare Books and Dawson's Book Shop from the 1930s to the 1990s. All three bookshops had specialized in the arts of the book.

I am often amazed at the prices listed here for books from the famous presses, as well as the prices for some iconic press books. I've paid more for shipping than the price of some of these books as sold then!

One day, I sat down with a stack of catalogues from Chiswick and Duschnes, and made a list of the prices fine press rarities sold for then. I offer a few of them here to my fellow fine press book collectors (and anyone sufficiently curious) so you can look at them with the same mixture of glee and envy as I did. One of the absurdities I noticed here are books that don't matter today at all, either in terms of price or reputation, being priced higher than most of the high-spot fine press books listed alongside them in the same catalogue.

For instance, from Philip C. Duschnes's catalogue 9, put out probably around the mid-1930s: Doves Press books are uniformly priced \$5, while first editions of Christopher Morley that no one cares for anymore and which can be had for \$5 today, are priced at \$10 and \$20. Scarcer Edward Newton pamphlets were \$30 and above, while Eragny Press books were routinely listed for \$7.50! Today, you can get a Newton for the same \$30 asked then, while even the most unadorned Eragny Press book commands a price of \$800, going up to \$15,000 for their more luscious productions.

Ashendene Press books ranged between \$25 and \$30, with the *Bibliography* listed at \$57.50. Kelmscott Press books also varied from \$20 to \$45 for the more attractive books. The Bruce Rogers-T.E. Lawrence Homer's *Odyssey* was \$62 (today it's \$5,000 and over). The great Eric Gill *Gospel* from Golden Cockerel: \$35. Leonard Baskin's *Cancellersca Bastarda Displayed*: \$60. John Fass's *Hammer Creek Press Type Specimen Book*: \$25. Eric Gill proofs, suitable for framing: \$1 each. Most of Golden Cockerel for \$6.

At the same time, in the same catalogue, books from the

Limited Editions Club are $10 and 20! And Nonesuch Press for the same – at published prices. These today haven't gone up very much more than what they cost then – while *Gothic Architecture* from the Kelmscott Press listed here for $7.50 is worth $1,500 today. Chiswick's catalogue 75 titled 'Printing and Calligraphy', lists the *Fra Luca* of Bruce Rogers-Stanley Morison-Grolier Club at $17.50, while Will Ransom's *Private Presses and their Books* is $35. Today, *Fra Luca* is a $2,000 book and Ransom's widely referenced history of modern fine presses can be got for $15.

The 'pocket cathedral', the Kelmscott *Chaucer* on paper: $1,000. Today it's a $50,000 book.

Here are prices for some of Bruce Roger's big books:

- Geoffroy Tory: $10
- 'Pierrot of the Minute': $30
- Letters of T.E. Shaw to BR: $20
- Magnum Opus: Oxford Folio Bible in two volumes: $265
- *The Construction of the Roman Alphabet*: $10
- A fragile masterpiece, *The Centaur*, 1915; BR's first showing of Centaur type: $125 (today: $4,000)
- Bruce Rogers's *The Song of Roland:* $250

Now, wait for it: illuminated manuscript leaves starting at $3.50 for leaves with illuminated initials, and $15 for leaves with one or two illuminated miniature paintings. Duschnes even notes that these are 'mounted and ready for framing'.

Exquisite illuminated/calligraphed Koran leaves for $2.

An entire book of hours for $300.

The Haggadah on vellum by Arthur Szyk, 1939 (said to be 'the most beautiful book in the world'): $1,150.

Horae Beatae Mariae Virginis, a fifteenth-century book of

hours with 87 vellum leaves, 18 large and small miniatures: $2,000. Today, just one leaf from here with a small miniature would cost more than the book at the time.

Persian manuscript with many miniatures in gold and colours: $800.

A French Psalter: $250.

A jewelled Sangorski & Sutcliffe binding for *Rubaiyat*: $1,000.

An entire notebook of Eric Gill's drawings for $750 – today possibly between $15,000 to 25,000.

A calligraphic manuscript from Graily Hewitt of a Morris poem: $250.

1905 calligraphic manuscript by Alberto Sangorski of *Rubaiyat* in gold, red, blue and many colours with elaborate designs. About 41 initials in gold and silver: $500.

Thirty-nine items of John Fass. A collection of marbled papers (unfinished) includes several title pages, Christmas cards, proofs, invitations and cards, some printed for Valenti Angelo – the associations are rich, various turtles by Angelo and DePol: $50.

By 1980, all the prices go up, looking almost like today's prices. Most of the Allen Press are $400, the Allen Press bibliography is $1,750. A presentation copy of Hammer's *Holderin* to Fritz and Annie Kredel is $3,500. Valenti Angelo's *Checklist* is $700 (with a presentation to John Fass!). But there are some juicy bargains, too: a brown levant Morocco of Zapf's *Typographic Variations* with a large Z in red as an onlay on the cover for $300; for about $75 there are leaves and proofs of Herman Zapf's *Feder und Stichel* on Japanese paper! A large, archival collection of John DePol items for $1750, consisting of 90 wood engravings signed, annotated or in proofs, and

94 unsigned prints; twenty-six leaves from the Kelmscott *Chaucer* from the collection of Sydney Cockerell, with a letter from him asking the addressee to come see his collection of Kelmscottiana for $3,500.

To that excellent English bookman, John Carter, should go the last word on the subject. In a chapter titled 'Bibliography and the Book Trade', he did a grand summing-up of what a bookseller's catalogue is that should stir the heart of every dealer and collector:

> On that bibliophile Parnassus where Poggio and Edward Johnston discuss the set of capitals and lower case in a manuscript, where Aldus exchanges notes with William Morris on the merits of Jenson's roman, where de Thou laments his anachronisms with Roger Payne, where Grolier and Roxburghe and Heber have kept comfortable seats for Lenox and Beradli and Gordon Duff – in that select company, all of whom know how much they owed to their booksellers, the verdict might well be that the most important, most pervasive, and most enduring contribution made to bibliographical studies by the antiquarian trade were to be found in the pages of booksellers... the most natural medium of expression, namely, in his catalogue.

COLLECTING THE LEAF BOOK

The pleasure of a leaf book lies in the thrill of possessing a rare, beautiful or famous original specimen page from an important book, pleasingly mounted or tipped into a (usually slender) volume, attractively bound, containing a finely printed scholarly essay on the significance of the leaf (and the book it comes from). If owning an ephemeron like this doesn't excite you, then the leaf book is not for you since in essence, *this is the excitement of a leaf book.*

The other pleasure – and one not to be scoffed at – that a leaf book extends to a collector is to be able to own (at least) a fragment from an illuminated manuscript or an early-printed book that one could never dream of owning, since it would be well beyond one's purse. I have been drawn to pursuing and collecting leaf books ever since I found out such a fine thing existed for collectors to own. I suppose for the book collector, the leaf book is the equivalent of those holy relics that pilgrims go in search of to bring back home.

There are all kinds of leaf books: for instance, the many press bibliographies I own of modern fine presses, contain leaves from the books they printed tipped into the book, or a book in my possession like *On Collecting William Morris*, which has a tipped-in leaf from the Kelmscott Press, though the text has nothing to do with that leaf in particular – these are counted as leaf books too, and have been included in the checklist of *Disbound and Disbursed: The Leaf Book Considered*, put out by the Caxton Club in 2005.

But perhaps the 'purest' form of the leaf book is when a famous specimen leaf is sold accompanied by just an essay on the beauty and typographical merits of the leaf. The most famous of these, of course, is *A Noble Fragment*, issued by the antiquarian firm of Gabriel Wells in 1921, which included an original leaf from a Gutenberg Bible, with an essay by collector Edward Newton extolling its historical importance and giving the collector an opportunity to own a piece of the most important book printed with movable type in Europe. The specimen leaf, nicely spruced up in a Morocco binding, was sold then for a pittance; today, it would sell for an estimated hammer price of $85, 000 to $1,25,000.

In *Disbound and Disbursed*, Christopher De Hamel points to the Gutenberg leaves Scribners sold in the 1950s at $350 each (with some special leaves such as those of 'The Sermon on the Mount' being priced higher), and remarks that if someone then had the wisdom to buy even a dozen copies of these leaves, 'one could retire in great comfort'.

The classic leaf book has usually contained a leaf from the most iconic books printed in the fifteenth and sixteenth centuries, venerating the printers behind it: a Fust and Schoeffer leaf, a Jenson leaf, an Aldine leaf or in one case, a leaf from *Hypnerotomachia Poliphili* – a grand catch by any leaf book standards – a Caxton leaf, and so on.

A note in a catalogue from Bromer Booksellers nicely sums up the appeal and importance and the value of the leaf book:

> A product of the intersection of scholarship, fine printing, and connoisseurship, the leaf book has become, in many

cases, the de facto means of accessing certain incunabula. Take, for example, the book produced by the Caxton Club in 1905 to honour its namesake, with a leaf from an incomplete copy of William Caxton's 1477 edition of *The Canterbury Tales*. The only complete copy to come up for sale in the last twenty-five years was in 1998; it contained leaves supplied from other copies, and the last text leaf was a facsimile. Nevertheless, it sold for $4.2 million. Likewise, with a more recent book containing a leaf from the 1462 Fust and Schoeffer Bible, of which the last complete copy sold in 2002 for roughly half a million dollars.

These books not only provide entry into an exclusive strata of collecting, they also advance scholarship on the printers of these works and the society that influenced them. Very often, we gain bibliographical insight into these works, as many will include a census of recorded copies. And finally, the books themselves have been produced by some of the best fine presses of the 20th century-Grabhorn Press, Plantin Press, John Henry Nash, and even Arion Press, to name but a few.

The modern leaf book has engaged me more – partly because I can't afford the classic leaf books! Of the modern leaf books I own, perhaps the most important in my collection is *Pages from Presses* (2006) from the Whittington Press. This is a grand, fun and scholarly leaf book by David Butcher on the five classic British presses: Kelmscott, Doves, Ashendene, Eragny, Vale and Essex House, with a leaf from each press tipped in. In its deluxe edition – which I don't possess – the bound leaves are more and include a Doves leaf on vellum, plus it comes with an additional portfolio of leaves. (In this way, I was at last able to own a leaf from the Eragny Press.)

When Whittington's printer John Randle and fine press scholar Butcher spotted disbound copies of books from these great presses for sale, they saw an opportunity to do a fine and useful leaf book. They were further encouraged when they were able to locate vellum leaves from the Doves Press, many with Edward Johnston's initials. The scarcest leaves they were able to locate to include in the book, are a few Doves leaves gilded in gold by Graily Hewitt. For Butcher, the loss of some of these damaged or imperfect copies was worth harvesting if it meant it brought a collector closer to examining paper and typography from these great presses at length.

The price of the book is worth it for the absorbing, concise and pleasurable essays on each press by Butcher, and for the lovely Czech handmade paper they are printed on. I'm so glad, looking back now, that I bought the book and didn't swap it with another collector – which I nearly came close to doing. A nicely priced copy of the regular edition was available a few years ago from a UK dealer, but because it was a heavy, folio-sized book, he quoted, quite understandably, a fairly high shipping charge.

This made me hesitate – usually when the shipping is high, I decline – but this time, I went through with the purchase, and I've never seen another copy of *Pages from Presses* come up for sale since.

De Hamel notes that there is an interesting, largely unnoticed 'pre-history' to the leaf book: the homegrown leaf book from as early as the fifteenth and sixteenth centuries. As a palaeographer and Sotheby's cataloguer of illuminated manuscripts, he has seen several examples of fifteenth- and sixteenth-century manuscripts showing miniatures that seem to have been cut out from thirteenth- and fourteenth-century manuscripts and pasted in to make the present book more beautiful or appealing. The same has been seen in early-printed books, where woodcuts from older books would be cut out and stuck into seventeenth- and eighteenth-century books to enhance the volume.

The other factor in this pre-history is more charming: the modern or contemporary homegrown leaf book! That is, today's amateur collector picking a volume from her collection and extra-illustrating it by pasting in fine examples of handpainted initials and decorations or illuminated miniatures or wood engravings, to enrich the volume at hand. I myself have done this in a small way to two items in my collection – let me hasten to add that the 'extra illustration' I used here was not torn out from another volume, but they were all issued loose, in a disbound fashion.

One of the most attractive (though common) leaf books I own is *French Illuminated Manuscripts*, 1958, from the Grabhorn Press, with an original leaf from a fourteenth-century book of hours tipped into it. Printed as beautifully as the best of the Grabhorn Press books, my copy contains a small leaf with many illuminated initials on both sides of the leaf, as well as intricate floral borders in the margins. In addition, the book also has an illuminated miniature drawn by Mary Grabhorn of the Anointing of Mary, that was handpainted in blue and colours, and then blocked in gold.

Most book dealers who list a copy of this leaf book never fail to mention how garish and unbecoming the gold blocking feels in this otherwise fine book. Even if I do see their point, I confess to rather enjoying the bright, shiny gold in this modern-day miniature. I was lucky in that my book of hours leaf seems to have more illumination in it than other leaves I have seen in other copies of this leaf book. (And lucky, too, for what I paid for it – having bought it for half its usual listed price from a Grabhorn collector who wasn't looking to get more for it.) But I digress.

After having the book in my possession for a few weeks, I noticed that the Grabhorn brothers, Edwin and Robert, had (as par for them) generously included several front and back endpapers of this lovely English handmade paper (possibly also to pad up this slim book), and this gave me an idea.

Over the years, I've bought single leaves/fragments of illuminated manuscripts, with at least five of them being from a book of hours. All of them, not quite incidentally, French – they are the easiest to get in the rare book market: English and German illuminated leaves are the real catch, being scarce. Why not add these leaves to the book, one to each page? I had a professional binder tip them onto each endpaper leaf, interleaving them. And now my copy of *French illuminated Manuscripts* is gloriously adorned and affords fine examples to illustrate or amplify what the author of this monograph, H.C. Schulz, has to say about what characterizes French schools of illumination and illuminators.

The other bit of extra illustration I did was simpler: a portfolio of John DePol's wood engravings had been assembled together at Oak Knoll Books with DePol and Henry Morris collaborating. DePol must have had a large stock or surplus of his engravings printed directly from the block, and it seemed fitting to put them together into sets housed in an attractive clamshell box accompanied by an introduction and a note printed by Morris for the occasion. To this, DePol added another touch: he signed – if he had not originally done so – each of these engravings tipped onto a card stock paper.

The sets are largely a gamble – there's a lot of middling illustrations printed without impression on smooth machine-made paper, while a few of them are lovely examples of DePol's work on more laid papers with more noticeable impression. The luckiest owners of this portfolio, to my mind, are those who have a set that includes his wood engraving of Bruce Rogers – a scarce DePol print which alone, when found listed separately, is priced as high as half the cost of the entire portfolio. The BR engraving was not in my set. (Though Rob Fleck at Oak Knoll looked high and low for me through every set they had in stock to see if one was included in it.)

I bought the BR engraving separately from another bookseller and added it to the box. It then occurred to me that I had several of DePol's masterful engravings as single broadsides – his portrait of William Morris and Gutenberg, engravings of hand presses, keepsakes for the typophiles and so on, all of them on handmade paper with a fine impression to them – and that I should add them to the portfolio. And so I did, and now I enjoy looking at my richly illustrated portfolio each time I thumb through it again, or show it to fellow DePol collectors.

What a difference these additions make to the set; earlier, when I would take the box out to look through the engravings again, I would usually close the box with a sigh that it wasn't as nice as it *could* have been, knowing how much more else DePol had to offer – and now that those fine examples are *in* there; the work of this master engraver is – at least in *my* portfolio – better represented.

Are leaf books still being produced? Yes, very much so. The

two most recent ones have been *Letters from the 15th Century: On the Origins of the Kelmscott Chaucer Typeface* from Pirages Fine Books and Manuscripts, and *The Kelmscott and Doves Presses: A Leaf Book with Original Calligraphy by Martin Jackson* from Heavenly Monkey (HM) Press. Most interestingly, Rollin Milroy, proprietor and printer of HM, while putting his leaf book together, came to an interesting conclusion regarding these leaves.

In a blog post on the HM website, he notes:

> Last month, I spent a few hours on a rainy Sunday sorting the Kelmscott *Golden Legend* and Doves Bible leaves to be included in the next book. Looking at an unbound or broken book is different than flipping through a bound copy: some aspects of the printing and setting stand out in ways they wouldn't otherwise. For example, the Kelmscott printing isn't actually that great – the inking is inconsistent, tending toward too much. The Bible is much more consistent in its printing, but one thing that struck me is Cobden-Sanderson's type doesn't really suit a book the size of his Bible (large quarto). In the essay by Pollard included in the new book, he comments on the type's readability: "... I must confess to being unable to read more than twenty or thirty pages in the Doves Press type without feeling perceptibly chilled". The Bible pages are dense, the lines are long, and the text is already somewhat impenetrable. The type is perfect for the octavo format employed for most Doves books, but on a Bible page I started noticing qualities of the majuscules that looked odd. The H in particular sticks out, like a sort taken from the wrong type case.

I think what pleased Rollin most about making this leaf book is the opportunity to feature Martin Jackson's calligraphy in the book – printed in the regular issue, and hand-done in the deluxe. Here is part of his note on printing and edition details for the book: 'The text is set in Centaur and Martin's calligraphy is printed, in red, from polymer plates. The Arches paper was dampened for printing. The edition is fifty-five copies: five (I-V) hors de commerce; thirty (21-50, the 'Printed' issue) with Martin's calligraphy printed, in red, from polymer plates; and twenty (1-20, the 'Written' issue) with all of the calligraphy actually written in by him, plus a gilded flourish on the title page and essay opening.'

The prospectus for *Letters from the 15th Century* describes the impetus for making yet another leaf book on the Kelmscott Chaucer:

> 'This is a unique leaf book in the way that it combines three elements: a significant private press production involving people at the top of their craft, a scholarly commentary that contributes to a further understanding of the history of printing, and—most important—five leaves: one from the Kelmscott Press "Works" of Geoffrey Chaucer and four from books issued by German printers at work in the 1470s.
>
> The story of the production is heavy on serendipity: in the winter of 2012, after purchasing a very incomplete copy of the Kelmscott Chaucer at auction, we considered the possibility of producing a leaf book, but because the Chaucer—universally considered to be one of the most beautiful books ever printed—had been written about

> by so many different people in so many different ways, we didn't know what aspect was left for us to explore. The one topic we fastened on as thus far inadequately examined is the origin of the work's typeface.
>
> We soon learned that Morris, who is known to have owned more than 500 incunables, most admired—and was, consequently, most likely to have been influenced in his typographic design by—Peter Schoeffer of Mainz, Johann Mentelin of Strassburg, Günther Zainer of Augsburg, and Anton Koberger of Nuremberg. Over the course of the years succeeding the purchase of the defective Chaucer, we were fortunate beyond all expectations to acquire incomplete books from each of these four eminent printers. As a result, the present leaf book will allow the reader not only to read in the accompanying essay about the influence on Morris of his typographic forebears, but also to compare with his or her own eyes the resemblances between the Kelmscott leaf and the leaves from four centuries earlier.'

The most recent leaf book I bought is the one I am most pleased to have. It is a very special copy of a book I already owned – *On Collecting William Morris: A Memoir* – and about which I have written in *The Book Beautiful: A Memoir of Collecting Rare and Fine Books*. Printed in 2007 as a private press book in a small edition of 150 copies by The Printery, a fine press operated by Kay Michael Kramer, this account of collecting Kelmscott Press books by Jack Walsdorf had three editions, with the rarest and most desirable being the first fifteen copies bound in quarter leather with a gilt spine and decorated paste paper sides. It came in a slipcase with an original leaf from the 1895 Kelmscott edition of *Child Christopher and Goldilind the Fair* tipped into the book. The second copy I acquired in June 2023 was a fortunate find: one of six copies from the fifteen reserved for the author, with his signature at the colophon, and the tipped-in Kelmscott leaf bearing a particularly beautiful and large decorated initial designed by Morris. Walsdorf is a collector I've long admired and it was thrilling to possess a copy that once belonged in his private collection.

RANJITSINHJI'S 9,000 ELEPHANTS VISIT SERENDIPITY BOOKS

Ian Jackson, the highly erudite and witty antiquarian who died suddenly on 18 February 2018, contributed some of the most unusual, droll and entertaining essays and books one can find in the literature of contemporary bibliophily. I'm saddened at the thought that we won't now see more of his sly, original antiquarian musings. One of the earliest things he did that amused me much was a trilogy of 'guide' books that explains why a once-magnificent bookshop called Serendipity wilfully conducted its business in a quixotic, puzzling fashion. Jackson did this by examining why Serendipity's equally singular owner, Peter B. Howard, ran it in the eccentric, totalitarian and generous way he did.

The three volumes, all illustrated, were titled: *The Key to Serendipity: How to Buy Books from Peter B. Howard*, *The Key to Serendipity: How to Find Books In Spite of Peter B. Howard*, and *Ranjitsinhji's 9,000 Elephants Visit Serendipity Books.* The last in the trilogy, about maharaja and cricketer Ranjitsinhji's elephants visiting this bookshop, was written for Jackson's little son, and tells the story in pictures and text of how Ranjit's elephants go on a rampage to Serendipity Books, and on arriving, are surprised to find they needn't have bothered at all – the bookshop looked like a herd of elephants had already been through the premises!

I came very late to the legend of Peter B. Howard and his one-of-a-kind bookshop. Around the time I began learning of him, there were already four monographs privately printed as tributes to Peter and Serendipity. On blogs and websites, there were accounts from his longtime customers and colleagues about their experience of being in this cavernous bookshop in Berkeley, California. One thing that ran through most of the accounts was the kind of compassionate and brilliant curmudgeon he was, and his unpredictable dealings with customers and those in the trade.

Once, a customer foolishly asked Howard if there was any rhyme or reason to the way he shelved the books, and Peter is said to have arched his eyebrows and replied: 'Yes, my rhyme, my reason!' You had to be careful about what kind of questions you asked Peter. The wrong one meant you would be ignored. If the books you'd brought to his desk to purchase met with his approval, he would light up and ask *you* questions. Howard died in 2011, but had started dealing in literary manuscripts as early as the late '60s, quickly becoming a towering figure in modern rare bookselling. I'd like to mention a serendipitous little find I made connecting Jackson and Howard, that also turned out to be a lucky bargain.

One day, in August 2014, I was looking for a letterpress keepsake tribute to Howard and located a copy at R&M Gerber Books. Or at least I thought I had until the proprietor, Richard Gerber, informed me it was the trade edition. Just before he rang off, he said, offhandedly, 'I think I might even have one or two of these keepsakes signed by him.' At my end of the receiver, I whistled silently – anything signed by Peter

Howard would be fantastic to have but I already knew that something like that would be beyond what I could afford, since it was bound to be scarce.

I would be delighted to get hold of a signed copy, I said, not daring to ask him how much it was for. He said he would email me once he had found them. After ringing off, I began searching for Peter Howard–signed items in the market – there were none. The only thing closest to it was a copy of *The Key to Serendipity*, with this bookseller description: 'Written on the front free endpaper of this copy is the single word, "mine"—denoting Peter B. Howard's personal ownership of this particular volume, in the late legendary bookseller's own hand.' The price was predictably high. 'That's that,' I thought. Surely, Mr Gerber's copy wouldn't be something I could hope to buy. A little later in the day, there was mail from Gerber Books.

He had found them: two volumes of Jackson's *A Key to Serendipity*, both signed and dated by Howard on the title page, and he would let them go for a price that suited me. Bless him. I sent a cheque right away, telling him I wanted only one of the two signed copies. Gerber told me later that Peter had actually signed this copy for him at a book fair. (At the first chance I got, I had the copy re-inscribed to me by Jackson!) 'Peter was really a great bookman,' reminisced Gerber to me. 'I will always remember his generosity, great stories, and the old Porsche always parked beside the shop.' And I will always associate Peter Howard's generosity with Richard Gerber's own generosity towards me – he could so easily have marked up the price for this signed copy or not parted with it at all, but he let me have it so that I, too, could have a small share – late as I had come to it – in the legend of Peter B. Howard, the sui generis bookseller.

PART FOUR

ALL KINDS OF BIBLIOPHILIA

THE SCRUFFY INCUNABULIST

The antiquarian book trade has embraced a parade of memorable characters, none to my mind more delightful than the book collector Solomon Pottesman, the incunabulist and self-taught bibliographer. He was also known to the trade as Potty or Inky for his love of incunables. He haunted every auction house in London every day of the year for his entire life, looking for them. He didn't work and probably lived on some modest inheritance that allowed him to buy incunabula, which means he seldom bought anything printed after 1500. He knew every auction price and record going back decades and many felt with such a retentive memory he would have made a formidable antiquarian dealer himself, but while Potty sold some books now and then, his passion was his own amazing library of incunables – which meant he bought more than he sold.

I've delighted in his sharp, even severe, collecting focus that made him disdain anything printed after 1700. Whether he bought anything or not, he was often in auction houses (seated in his own favourite chair right up front) and was forced to hear and see what others were buying. Once, and this really cracks me up, someone bought the *Kelmscott Chaucer* and Potty whispered to him, 'Well, I suppose it's okay, if you get rid of it *quickly*.'

Alan G. Thomas, in his marvellous and affectionate

portrait of Solomon Pottesman in *The Book Collector* (Winter, 1979) says Potty could have become a leading antiquarian dealer, but he sacrificed it for his grand passion of building his own library. Apparently, Potty could tell you not only which reference book you needed to consult but also the shelf number where it was located in the British Museum Reading Room. But once he had finished telling you about the book, there was no more need for research. He could tell you prices and provenance without looking at a catalogue. He knew the bibliographical importance of most books.

The other (lesser-known) portrait of Solomon Pottesman is by Fred Snelling from his book, *Rare Books and Rarer People,* and it is largely uncharitable, viewing Pottesman as an annoying, persistent figure in the auction rooms causing everyone a great deal of inconvenience. Snelling worked as a clerk at Hodgson's Auction House and frequently dealt with Pottesman at the end of an auction, when winners queued up to pay for their bids and collect the goods. Pottesman, Snelling writes, took forever to write out a cheque, slowing down the process of winding up sales. Though he made out cheques often, it would still be like the first time he was writing one. If Snelling asked him to hurry up, Pottesman would mumble something about not wanting to make any errors in the cheque. After that was done, Pottesman would proceed to pack and parcel the books himself. For this purpose, he always had on him brown paper and string. He would painstakingly wrap them, unwilling to be hurried, and finally ask to see the cheque again to make sure it had been made out correctly.

One day, Snelling says, he got fed up with Pottesman holding up his work and began shouting at him. Shocked and hurt, the incunabulist left saying he wouldn't stand to be treated that way. Snelling adds that he felt terrible later on about the scolding, and for the rest of his Pottesman sketch, tries to make up by telling us why Inky was a truly great bookman. Pottesman could often be seen at book fairs with various brown paper parcels dangling from his hands, tied to his wrists with a string. He was terrified he would leave them behind in a taxi, and so attached the parcels to himself. His most valuable books were in bank vaults because he feared flooding in his house; to protect the books in the house from possible over-flooding from the bathroom, he had the water pipe to his toilet disconnected, using a bucket to flush instead.

What remains with you is Thomas's gentle, skilful portrait, taking you to the very end of his friend's life, as he lay in hospital, with Alan making visits to cheer him with catalogues and choice early-printed books. Pottesman had remained a bachelor, and on most national holidays when everything was closed, especially the one day in the year when even his beloved British Museum (where his string-tied parcels held up the line at security) was shut, he found himself alone. On such days, Thomas would invite him to have supper with his family, but Potty would always back away, making excuses.

He was a gifted pianist but very few people knew that, writes Thomas; he loved the cinema and sometimes saw the same film every night for a week. He was relentless in his book quests, and on any given day, could be found in one bookshop or the other, hoping for more incunabula to turn up. Once, during those last days when he was ailing, Alan went to the hospital taking with him the catalogue of the auction he had just been to, and pointed out the book (printed in 1459 by Fust and Schoeffer) he had just bought. Potty asked him if he knew why it was so important and Alan, thinking to himself that he wouldn't pay £12,000 for it if he didn't know why, pretended not to know. 'You ignoramus,' Potty said and held forth with his old bibliographical finesse, perhaps for the last time. He died, not long after.

'With the death of Solomon Pottesman... the world of antiquarian books has lost one of its most learned and eccentric figures,' wrote Thomas, '... it is a tribute to the warmth of his unforgettable character... to his almost childlike sincerity and integrity... that those who knew him best, those who suffered the most frequently, are those who miss him most and mourn him most deeply today.'

THE BOOKSELLERS OF SAN SERRIFFE AND OTHER BIBLIO SPOOFS AND HOAXES

The distinguished antiquarian bookseller Bernard Rosenthal issued a catalogue in 1990 that seemed to list some rather odd – some would even say fishy – items. One entry, priced at only six dollars, was described as: 'Quintclaim, 1352, a document in Latin. Matted, in a Perspex envelope, in a frame, in a half Morocco box, in a fitted case, in a solander trunk, in a dresser profusely gilt, enclosed in a small Norwegian farm. Written in a Veriaude script, somewhere between the typical miniscule of Lue Nautique Fringe and that of a Nutaisse Frutcaque. It is very rare.'

And then followed a photo of the document showing a squiggly manuscript hand which remarkably enough resembled English, and read simply as: 'Happy Birthday Barney.'

One or two more items in the catalogue of such side-splitting dubiousness. 'Two single leaves, one larger than the other, both worn. Bound by Eve (not in Adams)' and the jig was up: it was a spoof catalogue. A biblio spoof. It had been the work of Christopher de Hamel, the renowned manuscript scholar paying tribute to the antiquarian bookseller, Bernard

Rosenthal, by spoofing his first famous catalogue from 1954 that had listed great rarities.

There has been an entertaining – if lowkey – tradition of biblio spoofs in the annals of antiquarian book dealing and collecting that I relish and collect avidly. And some of them can be very scarce. The Rosenthal-de Hamel spoof catalogue was issued in only four copies, impossible to obtain. What I have is the facsimile issued in 2010 by Ian Jackson to celebrate this famous bookseller's 90th birthday.

Finding a copy of the next biblio spoof, of which there was only the one original edition, involved vigorous pursuit and patience before I unearthed it – the Caveat Bookshop catalogue spoof done in 1946 by bookman Francis Farquhar. Among the many choice items, there is a resplendent Ashendene Press folio titled *To Hell with Dante*. A biblio spoof is not to be confused with a literary spoof - of which there are perhaps too many – where a famous author's style (or plot) is parodied. The biblio spoof revolves around the world of printing, bookshops, libraries, bookselling and collecting. They also differ from biblio hoaxes.

A modest example of a biblio hoax, for instance, is *The Mainz Diary* from 1940. This slender letterpress pamphlet reproduced a diary left by Gutenberg's wife, telling of how after her husband had gone to bed unable to solve the final step in printing with movable type, she had figured out a way and had got up in the middle of the night and printed the first page of the Gutenberg Bible on her own. The diary was done so skilfully, dropping scholarly details here and there, that some people who bought the monograph thought it was recounting real events. It was the mischief of private press printer Arthur Rushmore of the Golden Hind Press.

The most celebrated book-collecting hoax is the Comte de Fortsas Sale. Unlike the other spoofs and hoaxes I have been describing, this actually took place in 1840 in the provincial town of Binche in Belgium. The Fortsas Sale has had so many retellings in various private press publications, from the two editions with text by Walter Klinefelter done by The Press of the Woolly Whale (the first done for the Carteret Club), and the two editions by the Press of Ward Schori (one was a miniature), and by the Bird and Bull Press with the text by the collector Lessing J. Rosenwald. Only recently did I uncover one more, a most marvellous take on the whole affair by Tim Hawley of the Contre Coup Press, that reverses everything and leaves you blindsided. I'll save this for the end.

The events that all these finely printed books narrate, begin with Comte de Fortsas, a rich man obsessed with collecting only unique copies – if he heard of another collector having the same copy, he would chuck his own out. He had faithfully followed Brunet's bibliography and when it said there that a book was rare, he purchased it without fail. But soon, Fortsas realized that these had become common books. He decided to follow his own nose, taste, instinct, and went after books Brunet had not listed.

He would go after the only extant copy of a book. If he found out after some years that there was another copy somewhere, described in a catalogue or bibliography, he would remove the book from his collection, either giving it away or destroying it. Such was his bibliomania. When Techner's bibliography came out, much was lost. Many books the Comte had thought unique, had counterparts! A large portion of his collection had to be thrown out and he was left, finally, just before his death, with fifty-two books.

But what books! Every title, 'a newly discovered constellation in his bibliographic firmament'! No other copy of these books existed. His heir, a greedy young man, decided to auction them and had a catalogue made. This was sent out to all the great collectors and dealers and librarians of the day in Europe. 10 August 1840 was the date set for the auction in his hometown of Binche.

Imagine, says Klinefelter, one of these elect bibliophiles receiving this catalogue in the post; how his evening would proceed: you are the collector now retiring for the night. You have decided the evening will be a quiet, restful one where, after a nice supper, you will sit down in your library with a vintage wine and leisurely look through the catalogues that have come in the mail before you begin the book you have set aside for reading that night.

As you flip and thrum through the catalogues, you already know nothing there will engage you – rare and scarce appear so many times in the books described in most catalogues, that they fail to stir you. You spot the rather thin Fortsas catalogue and decide to skim through it – a minute or two and you will drop it from boredom. The cover does not inspire any confidence. And then you read about Comte's obsession for the only copy known and you sit up. As you read through the descriptions of each book, you cannot believe your eyes – true rarities! Rarities upon rarities! You are now in a complete bibliomaniac frenzy.

Gone is the quiet evening you looked forward to. You must have many books therein. All you can think about is plotting to get to Binche and carrying away the titles you desire. There will be rivals and your thoughts now are only to outbid them. You go to bed but you cannot sleep. You wake up and look through the catalogue again to make sure you aren't dreaming.

More catalogues were demanded, but none more were sent. When some took the trouble to travel to Binche for it, Hoyois the printer said 'Out of print' to these already-overwrought bibliomaniacs. The bids began pouring in. The question on everyone's lips was, 'Are you going to Binche on 10 August?' Those envious began to claim they already had half the books in their library – why this would be a shameful lie would come out only after 10 August.

Highly reputed book dealers were sure some of these copies were there somewhere in their inventories, gathering dust – but alas, a thorough search yielded none. Truly, these copies were unique, it would seem. On the 10th, they began arriving, the giants of the book world from all over, especially Paris. It is said that Nodier, Brunet and Techner arrived in the same stagecoach. As the visitors began enquiring where the town hall was, they were told there was no such hall; similarly, enquiries about the Comte drew blank stares, 'Who the devil is Comte de Fortsas?' they asked. The visitors decided the townspeople were ignorant; what was the world coming to if they could not remember a nobleman and a distinguished bibliomaniac who had died only last September?

The townspeople began to be amused by all these strange people wandering in the town and then amusement turned to fear. Was there an anarchist plot afoot? The police chief was informed. As he was making enquiries, another set of individuals began appearing in town, distributing notices – what was officially called an 'Avis', it said that the auction had been cancelled, doubtless collectors would be disappointed but the town of Binche had taken it upon itself to buy the whole lot for the public library, so that Fortsas's books stayed in the village.

Crushed and outraged, these bibliophiles went looking for the public library (if they could not bid and buy them, they wanted to feast their eyes on these rarities) but no such place was found. It soon became clear the whole thing was a hoax – there was no library, no books, no Comte. Some took it in their stride and others boasted they knew all along, some later said they had never come to Binche, and a few, just a few, had suspected from the start it was a literary joke, 'a masterpiece of bibliographic deception'.

What was remarkable about it was not the prank itself, but the scholarship it was carried out with: each fictious book in the catalogue was meant to appeal to the tastes of particular collectors – so that they would salivate over it and get ready to outbid their rivals. Never had so many giants in the rare book world been taken in on such a grand scale – from bibliophiles, they had turned bibliomaniacs, and at the end of the journey, bibliofools or biblioboobies. Who had been responsible for this biblio hoax?

One journalist had even guessed the identity of the man, and had – on the day the sale had to happen, 10 August– published an article as if the sale had taken place, giving an elaborate account of the fictious auction. The man was Renier Chalon, a retired major in the army and someone known for his pranks; a man deeply read in literature. Chalon, along with two other associates, had conceived the idea for the catalogue, and had prepared for it by finding out the weaknesses of all these bookmen, who had had submitted to their queries without realizing what it was going to be used for. Each collector's focus was found out and a book that they could not resist was invented. The three or four people who had not been taken in, were Nodier, Techner and Pollain.

Techner had written to Hoyois saying, 'the books and the notes were curious – are you not up to something? M. Nodier thinks the catalogues of rarities unknown to bibliophiles a jolly facetious joke.' But torn between his doubts, he placed bids anyway so he won't lose out on the sale! Voisin wrote to Hoyois before he made the trip to Binche, asking if this was a biblio hoax of a very learned and witty nature. Pollain wrote an article quoted by Klinefelter, even naming Chalon. 'One knows', he wrote, 'what effect the magic words, *unique copy* (original emphasis), produce in the bibliomaniac.'

Some even profited from it: one of them realized that in a few years, the Fortsas catalogue would be of interest, and collected every copy possible and was proved right – he was able to sell them at an unusually high sum (since then even facsimiles and reprints of the catalogue have become very scarce, the early reprints even rarer, with only rare book institutions possessing a copy). The Bird and Bull Press edition of The Fortas Sale has, in a pocket at the back, a reproduction of the Avis, the announcement that the auction had been cancelled. This was made from the original Avis in the collection of Rosenwald.

I come now to the edition that turns all this on its head, the work of Tim Hawley at Contre Coup Press: *True narrative of the Early Life and Cruel Abduction of M. Jean-Népomucène-August Pichauld, Comte de Fortsas. With an exposé of the supposed Fortsas Hoax* (1982). The pamphlet 'describes, as genuine, the origin of the Fortsas collection of unique books, usually considered imaginary'.

The handwritten manuscript was discovered among the personal effects of Thomas J. Wise, the bibliographer and forger, in 1982. It is in French, written in a shaky hand. Wise himself had obtained it in 1932 and stowed it away secretly.

Apparently, it was first discovered in Middle Hill, the mansion of Thomas Phillipps, the vellomaniac, clutched in the hands of a skeleton uncovered in the basement of the servant's quarters. In the manuscript, Wise had written in his hand a cryptic, chilling note: '... must be stopped!'

The manuscript itself is written in first person, narrated by Jean-Nepomucene-August Pichauld, born in the Chateau de Fortsas, which is near the town of Binche. 'My earliest memories,' he records, 'are of hiding in my father's library, watching him catalogue the vast collection of manuscripts and rare early-printed books that had been handed down through my family over the centuries. Even as a child, the vellum leaves of ancient tomes stirred an ineffable feeling of joy in my breast. My father was generous in allowing me to handle the precious volumes, and would tell me tales of the scribes and early printers.'

His father suddenly dies when the boy is twelve – elephant folio atlases fall on Papa and kill him. The young Comte assumes responsibilities at Fortsas, but with it, comes a horror of books, so he seals the library. Soon, he undertakes the dissolution of the library. 'I sent off wagonloads of rare incunabula, edition princeps, medieval manuscripts, Aldus's, Caxton, Jensons, and books of hours to the dealers in Paris and Brussels. Finally, the endless shelves in the library stood as mute and barren...'

As he grows up, though, the old feelings of bibliomania return, but with an originality that is striking: he would collect only unique copies. And began buying them in the hundreds, pitying other collectors at auctions who were buying books that anyone with money could buy. He alone was amassing, on the other hand, books that had become so excessively rare that only one copy now remained in the world, and he had secured it – as he would for all the other rarities that were described as 'only known copy'.

But as bibliographies came to be published, it became evident that many of the books Jean had thought unique, singular, were scattered across libraries and collections in Europe. He gets rid of them, keeping only the copies that have no mates anywhere. So far so good – in the main, the events seem to be unfolding as they have in all the Fortsas accounts. Then comes this: 'Throughout this period of my collecting I tried to remain unknown to the book collecting world, making my purchases through agents from whom I kept my identity secret. I became friends with only one other collector, M. Renier Chalon, the president of the Society des Bibliophiles Belges at Mons. I was forced to let him into my confidence because of his ability to locate items for my collection. However, I pledged him to secrecy about my existence.'

After his wife dies, and more bibliographies reveal many books in his collection not to be so unique after all, he keeps just fifty-two, and ropes in Chalon and Hoyois to make the catalogue. However, he has Chalon put in the information that the collector who had formed this unique library was now dead. He makes sure a copy of the catalogue was sent to 'that laughable group, The Roxburghe Club' with that fool Dibdin raving on about the joys of collecting. He wanted to show them what a true collector can accomplish. 'Alas,' says, Jean Fortsas, 'this would spell my downfall.'

On purpose, he picks Binche, the kind of provincial locale that will annoy those dealers and collectors accustomed to Paris and London and Berlin. However, on 2 August 1840, as he sat before the fireplace contemplating the grand auction to come, he is kidnapped by some masked men who put him on a ship, and when they reach ashore, bundle him into a trunk.

When Fortsas is let out of the trunk, deprived of water and food, he sees that he is in the alcove of a house. An hour later, 'an Englishman of noble deportment' addresses him. The gist of their exchange is that the English gent (whom Hawley purposely does not name, for he wants the reader to catch on that it could be none other than Sir Thos. Phillipps, Esquire) has gone to all this trouble in order to secure Fortsas's books all for himself. You see, it was his friend and fellow collector at the Roxburghe Club who had lent him a copy of the catalogue. He simply could not tolerate having to bid for them with so many rivals on his back.

'What of the auction?' asked Fortsas weakly. 'That has been taken care of,' says the English nobleman, and shows him the Avis, the notice of the auction cancellation. 'But Chalon would not stand for it,' cries out Fortas, 'he will expose the fraud.'

'Don't worry about Chalon,' says the collector, 'he has been bribed with rarities from my collection and will instead scapegoat himself as the perpetrator of the hoax catalogue that brought all the bookmen. And he will deny the existence of one Comte de Fortsas.'

The Englishman takes leave of the Comte, who realizes he is going to be entombed within the walls of this alcove. His last line, 'My only hope is that...', stops midsentence.

Coming back to biblio spoofs, a favourite of many remains *The Private Presses of San Serriffe* (1980) written by one Dr Theodore Bachaus, who introduces us to the dubious private presses found on this little island country of San Serriffe in the Indian Ocean. Many were taken in, not for a moment doubting there was somewhere a country called San Serriffe famous for its private presses whose capital just happened to be called Bodoni and where the chief of police went by the name of Claude Garamondo.

This witty and imaginative spoof was only one of several concocted by the noted fine press printer Henry Morris of the Bird and Bull Press. He had been inspired to think of this when he had come across an April Fool's joke in 1977 by *The Guardian* newspaper in a special supplement featuring a little-known country called 'The Republic of San Serriffe'. Morris, in the guise of the irrepressible Dr Bachaus, went on to create grander fine press productions such as *The Booksellers of San Serriffe*, with several tipped-in illustrations and three full-page wood engravings of these partly real, partly mythical bookshops. A bookseller catalogue entry for this lavish fine press spoof sums it up wittily:

> Those of you who were impressed by Dr. Bachaus' earlier book on the Private Presses of San Serriffe will be absolutely shattered by this in-depth survey of the booksellers of San Serriffe. The book has an historical introduction by Dr. Bachaus, which is followed by chapters on Hobart Flock of Hoki-Nol Books (hmm!), Ki-flongian Booksellers, Ltd., Grandiloquent Bookshop, Cloacina Books, St. Luke's Paper Mill and Bookshop, Contre Kook Mail Order Books, and Exterminator Books. The book is accompanied by a letter from Dr. Bachaus to the purchaser talking about the book, and enclosing four commemorative stamps from the Republic of San Serriffe inserted in an envelope with a canceled stamp.

One more offering from Dr Bachaus aka Henry Morris must be noted for its Indian connection – to be specific, Puducherry, then Pondicherry: *The World's Worst Marbled Papers*. In 1978, Morris got a call from a man from California, saying he represented a firm called Mere Cie Ink, that made handmade papers in Pondicherry. They were going to set up a mill for handmade paper and had been told Henry Morris knew a lot about these things. He said he was an amateur and that they should consult a paper engineer or chemist.

Just before he rang off, the man said that they had at Mere Cie several reams of marbled paper which they were discontinuing and if he would be interested in them if offered at a low price. HM had just been complaining how expensive marbled paper from France was: $2. 75 per sheet of 19 x 25 inches. Mere Cie would sell him 1,000 sheets for 60 cents per sheet. Additionally, these marbled sheets were made from 100 per cent pure rag paper. A bargain like this, thought HM, comes once in a lifetime.

He asked for samples and when they arrived, he was disappointed. Some swishing of garish colour had been made from an oil base, with no pattern, an there were air bubbles in the paper. This was the most unprofessional paper he had seen but he still could not resist the bargain, thinking he would use the good sheets that were not as garish and had some pattern. He ordered 1,000 sheets, which arrived in a large wooden crate. He was shocked on opening it – they looked more dreadful than the samples. All of it. Nothing to do about it, since he had ordered them after seeing the samples. He paid for them, but told Mere Cie that they were really bad and that he could not use them. He intended to get them to the garbage.

Some weeks later, publisher Thomas Taylor dropped in

to see the papers, having heard of this mishap and one look at them, he burst out in uncontrollable laughter saying these were 'the worst marbled paper ever made', and that he should think of putting them in a book and calling it just that.

Epiphany struck HM: that's exactly what he would do with it – make a book. But what if the California firm that represented Mere Cie sued him for defamation? So, he came up with publishing it as a book from San Serriffe, with an introduction by his old friend Theodore Bachaus. He told booksellers they must not connect him with the book, opened an account under San Serriffe and when the last cheque was deposited, closed the account and vanished into the night.

He braced himself in the coming weeks for some backlash from Mere Cie, expecting a phone call or a letter, pulling him up for this stunt. But nothing happened for weeks and he relaxed. Then he got a letter out of the blue from the bookbinder David Bourbeau, who said he had bought the book and found the whole 'in-joke' hilarious, saying he was 'glad there is a true wit among us'. He narrated what had happened: a rep from Mere Cie had come selling the same marbled paper to him, and Bourbeau had said it was awful and he did not want it. The rep said another printer had also said the same, though he had still gone ahead and bought some reams of it. Bourbeau asked, 'Do you know what he did with it?' And then showed him the book. The man's reaction was one of amusement. He had enjoyed the joke himself.

Later, the main man from the California firm corresponded with him, saying they found the whole thing pretty hilarious and had no intention to sue. But they still had several reams of it, just in case he knew anyone who would want some...

My personal favourite among biblio spoofs, though, is the

kind that stays subtle and doesn't give it away – or at least has you thinking 'there's something a little off about this narrative but I can't think what'. The most successful example in this category of the understated biblio spoof is 'Christopher Larkspvr (the v keeps you distracted) and the Saint Ronan's Press', published in 2006 in the journal *The Private Library*, about a fascinating author-printer of little talent who persuades some of the finest presses in the world to print his mediocre work. At the end is a full bibliography of these imaginary books, with title pages and typographic pastiches, printed by the likes of the Coddlemere Abbey Press (which stands in for the much-admired Stanbrook Abbey Press).

'Christopher Larkspvr' is a beautifully done bibliographical spoof where even if you figure out your leg is being pulled, you feel the author's pleasure in the way he works it all out, as he goes about carefully building his clever, knowing, witty details. At the end, you can't help wishing that Larkspvr and his press were real. Now, *that's* the formula for the perfect biblio spoof. But who is author of this bibliography? That remains a mystery, though in the footnotes to the spoof, there probably lurks a clue.

One more favourite hoax remains to be told – this one is actually contemporaneous since all the characters in the account are with us today. *The Anatomy of a Literary Hoax* by Sidney Berger, printed by Henry Morris at the Bird and Bull Press in 1994 on Frankfort paper, in an edition of copies. About fifty copies were hardbound, while the rest were in wrappers.

A bibliographical prank more than a hoax, it never ceases to amuse, fascinate and delight me. At the end, *Nagashizuki: The Japanese Craft of Hand Papermaking* (1979), a fine press book that Morris had once printed at his Bird and Bull Press, is a list of resources the author of the book, Timothy Barrett, had consulted. One of the entries there, *The Invention of Paper* (1971) by Daniel Wilcox, turned out to be non-existent – no such book, no such author. How and why had that title got in there? Surely, a scholar like Barrett would not make up something like that?

It turned out that Barrett had never included such a title in his resources list, and hadn't even known it had crept in there. Until he was alerted to it by... Henry Morris; it was he who had slipped it in purposely. Morris confessed this to Barrett only years later, when they were doing the second book on papermaking together. Morris said he had done it to see if paper historians were paying attention to such bibliographical lists, and his suspicions had proved right – they weren't, since not a single scholar had made an issue of the fake book. Barrett was understandably upset with Morris, as he felt the prank had sullied a serious, important study of papermaking.

At some point, Timothy Barrett mentioned it to Sidney E. Berger, who had worked closely with Henry Morris on various book projects, and was a friend of the printer's as well. Berger came up with a plan for Barrett to get even with Morris: they would get a printer to actually make up a title page for that same book. It would read: Daniel Wilcox's *The Invention of Paper: A History and Handbook* (London: Crosby Lockwood and Son, 1875).

Berger wrote a casual letter to Morris, talking of this and that, and then in a kind of by-the-way fashion, said he had happened to be looking at *Nagashizuki*, and had spotted a typo in the Resources List: the printing date for that Wilcox book should have been 1875, not 1971. He got a speedy reply from an astonished Morris, asking for a scan of the 1875 title page.

Berger had it ready to go, knowing this is what Henry would want to see first.

Morris was bewildered and completely taken in (unusual for a prankster like him, but I suspect no one, not even he, could think that someone would go to such lengths as to typeset a false title page). He now confessed of his prank to Berger and said the tables had been turned on him – a scholarly book on paper that he had thought did *not* exist, a book title that he had borrowed from a Sesame Street Children's Educational booklet, seemed to have an actual existence. He told Berger he now had dealers in Britain searching high and low to unearth this Wilcox book.

Barrett and Berger let Morris keep looking for the book for a whole year before they let him in on it. Berger says, 'I wrote Henry another long letter in which I embedded a paragraph which said something like "Oh, by the way, I am sure you figured out that the Wilcox book was a hoax." The rest of the letter was small talk.' Morris realized what had happened, cursed Berger and Barrett, but then laughed along with them.

Morris had an appreciation for things like this and said he would print the book if Sidney wanted to tell the story. At the end of *An Anatomy of a Literary Hoax*, Morris notes: 'I still think Sid's joke was wonderful. I admire the careful planning and attention to detail that made it all so believable. I was entirely taken in and searching all over England for a copy of that 1875 edition. A masterful hoax by an expert.'

'A MOST DESIRABLE ASSOCIATION'

There is not just one kind of association copy, says John Sparrow, the scholar-collector who spent a lifetime assembling them. The first kind of association copy he points to is the most impersonal – a book you find or acquire carrying the bookplate or seal of a famous collector. Even if the volume is shabby, this mark is a kind of cache – in Sparrow's own collection, for example, are some books with the library stamp of Richard Heber – 'Bibliotheca Heberiana' – and 'to possess one of those books gives me a pleasure that I find it difficult to define', writes Sparrow in *Association copies: An essay with examples drawn from the author's own collection* (Jonathan Hill 1978), a finely printed letterpress pamphlet. Such a copy, he says, is akin to meeting someone known to come from a good family, even if that person had no agreeable qualities of his own!

Sparrow then goes on to describe the varied forms association copies can take. Some books in his collection, again of no distinction, give him pleasure because they are not only from a famous collector but have been made a thing of beauty by a fine binding made just for the book by the collector or by a famous binder. He owns a copy, for instance, of a 1610 volume bound in red Morocco for Jacques Auguste de Thou (a revered sixteenth-century book collector) with his arms and monogram. Further, another 1555 octavo with de Thou's arms and monogram in citron Morocco – this one additionally bearing the Heber book stamp! (When I first read this, I had to envy whoever owned this very copy now, with its storied association having passed through the hands of Heber, de Thou and Sparrow! This is the sweet nature of association copies).

He is quick to note that these volumes please him more aesthetically – for the beauty of their bindings, rather than their provenance. Sparrow is hard to please – some of us would be thrilled to bits to have a copy that belonged to de Thou and Heber, even if it was in pieces, let alone in a fine binding. We will see how fastidious Sparrow is in how he holds to what makes for great association copies – the above don't greatly please him as much as the distinction he goes on to make with examples from his own collection.

Pleasure in a book's historic provenance invokes snobbishness, and pleasure taken in a book with personal association invites charges of sentimentality because the pleasure or satisfaction in such a copy has nothing to do with its intrinsic merit, be it literary merit or even physical beauty. The satisfaction comes from some emotional association that is very personal: akin to the thrill a non-collector would feel towards a sacred object. Sparrow has his own sacred objects among manuscripts and books, and is not impervious to its thrills. About books as relics, he says, 'I am moved by such things, and am not ashamed of being moved; every book collector is, I suspect, at heart a sacramentalist.' Still, Sparrow is after something else: association copies that are humbler in origin from his collection. He identifies three types: 'Autograph Association', 'Appropriate Association' and 'Instructive Association'.

He dismisses the most common and obvious example of 'autograph association' – a book signed by the author, as in a limited, signed modern edition. There is no true association here. It's just an autograph. As an example, from his library, the copies of *A Shropshire Lad* and of *Last Poems* that A.E. Houseman signed for friends. A bare signature is no different from a library stamp or bookplate, according to Sparrow.

He also dismisses a copy made distinct by the signature not of the author but of its distinguished *owner:* his copy, for instance, of Edmund Gosse's *Life of Donne* (1899) carries the signature of Henry James. He reveres James but finding or happening upon his signature in a book does not excite or thrill him – it just shows that James had once owned the book. Who knows if he even read it? All such books with signatures of famous people mean little and it does not count for the genuine personal association copy.

He has an Aldine 1524 edition with some Latin scribbling that could denote it belonged to Erasmus. But what did the book mean to Erasmus? What if it had meant nothing at all? (So strict is Sparrow.) Once at an auction, he had won a copy of a 1604 volume that had some ownership scribbles in the flyleaf that showed the copy was once owned by Ben Jonson. It gave him a personal thrill that was more sentimental, but not really of rich personal association.

'I derive a similar mixed pleasure from a book that I discovered wasting its sweetness unrecognized on the shelves of a country bookshop,' writes Sparrow. A book printed in 1601 in Venice that bore the motto and signature of John Donne upon its title page! Imagine such a find; but Sparrow is simply indifferent to it. He speaks of another 'personal find' that filled him with pleasure. 'Let me now mention one more book that passed through his (Donne's) hands and now is mine. It was the first expensive book I ever bought: the first edition of Donne's first publication, *Pseudo Martyr* (1690)'. Sparrow goes on to describe this particular copy. It bore a handwritten motto, '*Ex Dono Authoris*' (Given to me by the Author or Presented by the Author), not in Donne's hand, of course, but in the hand, as it turned out, of his close friend, Rowland Woodward. Donne had presented it to Rowland.

The excitement in this copy came many years later, when he was browsing in those Paris bookstalls on the quays. 'There is little nowadays to be found in those once happy hunting grounds, and it was without much expectation that I plucked out a small octavo.' Sparrow was about to put it back when he peeped into the flyleaf and found it had belonged to Rowland Woodward. And also on the flyleaf was a shelf mark that indicated that this volume had stood only four places away from *Pseudo Martyr* in Woodward's library. He bought it and placed it next to the *Pseudo* in his library – he has now only to find the three intervening volumes.

An example of a wrong association copy for him would be Bernard Shaw's copy of Keats's *Poems* – this would be a distressing object for him; a case of misplaced autograph. For him, the right association copy was one given to him by John Carter, *The Golden Treasury*, edited by Mathew Arnold, a selection from the poems of Wordsworth. The book itself is common but is lifted out of the ranks of the ordinary by an inscription in the flyleaf: 'Rob. Browning from M.A.' – 'the whole complex of association could hardly be more appropriate'.

Perhaps only what would have been richer is if it had been presented to Tennyson. Another rich association copy in his collection is *Poems and Ballads*, 1866, with an inscription in the poet's hand: 'To W.M. Rossetti from his friend, A.C. Swinburne'. 'Could there be,' asks Sparrow, 'a more desirable association for this particular book?' Perhaps the one that gives him the most pleasure is a copy of a first edition from the Cuala Press, 1914 of W.B. Yeats's *Responsibilities.* On the title page is this in the poet's hand: 'Maude Gonne from W.B. Yeats, June 1914'. He found this for 30 shillings in a Charing Cross Road bookshop, one rainy Sunday afternoon.

Some copies are 'instructive' association copies – they reveal something about the book or the author, usually in margin notes by the author or notes by a contemporary owner of significance. In 1936, when Blackwell's was disposing off books from the library of Houseman, he, like so many, bought many books. Houseman would usually not write his name in books, or have a bookplate or stamp or even annotate (except rarely) his books. Blackwell's had placed a slip into many of these volumes on sale denoting: 'From the lib of A E Houseman'. One such book, Palgrave's *Golden Treasury*, Houseman had actually drawn straight lines – with a ruler – across poems he did not like or approve of in the collection! Certainly, very revealing of what poets or poems Houseman enjoyed and did not.

'A most desirable association copy,' concludes John Sparrow, 'would have all three: personal association, appropriate association, and instructive association.' But even he can't find one in his library that fulfils all three marks of what would be the most priceless association copy for a collector to possess.

ADVENTURES IN MINIBIBLIOMANIA

The first miniature book I bought was called, appropriately enough, *My Adventures in Minibibliomania*. It was the story of how Katherine Rickards, a collector, assembled a large and fine collection of miniature books. I was happy to discover that my collecting focus of the book arts extended even to miniature books. I bought *My Adventures in Minibibliomania* from Karen Nyman, one of the foremost dealers specializing in miniature books today. Nyman had been a collector before she turned dealer.

She had started out collecting regular-sized antiquarian books, with a focus on beautiful bindings. Perhaps it was her affinity for fine structure in the physical book that turned her to miniature books (where the best of them require great skill and artistry to make, since they are usually no more than 3 to 4 inches in height and width), which she began collecting in June 2005.

'I bought and read all the reference books,' Karen told me, 'and by October I was buying miniature books in large quantities from a well-known collector who was selling his collection. He sold me books at a fair price and taught me a lot and mentored me and I created my first e-catalogue in April 2006. It consisted entirely of books I had bought from him.' That collector was none other than Robert E. Massmann, a legend in the world of miniature books. Massmann had not only been a collector but also the author and creator of dozens of notable miniature books.

'Bob (Massmann) lived in Connecticut,' Nyman continued, 'and I had met him at my first MBS Conclave. He was selling some of his vast collection at the Book Fair. I asked if I could visit him one day and buy more. I went to his home and bought hundreds of books and I continued buying from Bob for several years. He was a wonderful man and seemed to know *everything* about miniature books.' The MBS Conclave Nyman mentions is an annual gathering of the members of the Miniature Book Society, an event where members can look forward to books swaps, fairs, auctions and talks revolving around miniature bookmaking. The conclave has been a very important part of her life. 'Since the first MBS Conclave I attended in 2005,' she notes, 'I have never missed one! I learn a lot, see a lot of interesting books, and am surrounded by good people who share my passion. And they are so much *fun*.'

I have always wondered where and how specialist dealers like Nyman find their stock. We all have some idea of where and how antiquarian dealers of regular-sized books go looking to add stock, but how do you replenish miniature books? 'As I became known,' said Nyman, 'people started contacting me when they wanted to sell their collection. Also, I visited bookstores everywhere, looking for miniatures. And I started buying on eBay.'

I've also been curious about how one shelves miniature books – especially a dealer with a large and fine stock like her. It turns out that Nyman has a library with specially built bookshelves that are six feet wide and eight feet tall, but with – and this was key – *shallow shelving* just four inches deep! She also stores miniatures in drawers, wall cabinets and antique clock cases. Karen has seen nearly every kind of miniature book that's out there (and they *are* innumerable, and not just the one kind most of us think) – but what was her favourite kind, what did she collect herself, and what are rarities collectors should look for?

'For me, letterpress books and well-crafted books with interesting content are worth collecting. I am also drawn to many religious books, particularly old ones. And children's books – because they are so charming. Book-sets interest me, too: like the Aunt Laura series. Some personal favourites are *ABC's for Book Lovers, Book of Hours,* and *Rudolph the Red-Nosed Reindeer.* I am most drawn to the work of Barbara Raheb who writes out her text in a calligraphic hand, and in a book size that is just 1–3/8 inches in height, is able to engrave illustrations that are hand-coloured.'

As for rarities collectors look for, Nyman says it all depends on what field of miniatures a collector is interested in. But two or three that she is usually on the lookout for are *Noel* by Achille J. St. Onge and *Galileo a Madama Christina di Lorena* by The Salmin Brothers. She once sold a copy of *Galileo* (which is 'one of the smallest books printed from movable type') that had been on consignment with her, and since then has even managed to acquire a copy for herself.

Nyman has been the recipient of the Miniature Society's two most distinguished awards, the Norman W. Forgue Award for 'outstanding contribution to the world of miniature books' and the Glasgow Cup, which goes to 'a member who has shown a special dedication' to the society. Her website, Karen Nyman Miniature Books, puts out new catalogues regularly and lists acquisitions under various miniature categories. Though with no plans presently to publish or create a miniature book of her own, she continues to be very focused about collecting and selling miniatures for 'their beauty and the skill it takes to produce them.'

That first miniature I bought from her, about Katherine Rickard's adventures in collecting miniature books, supplied me with my first introduction to the world of miniature book collecting. Rickard began collecting in the 1970s, and by the early 1980s, she had 500 miniatures. 'I went,' she says, 'quite quickly from minibibliophile to minibibliomaniac!' She recalls a private collector she had been steadily buying from, one day telling her, 'I don't have anything more for an advanced collector like you.' She realized only then that she had become a miniature collector of note.

Today there are wealthier, more important and scholarly woman book collectors of miniatures, such as Patricia J. Pistner, but Katherine's is a story of a collector with limited funds foregoing everything else to make a collection possible. She's also the only miniature collector that I can think of who has provided us with a book-length account of collecting these 'biblio-midgets'.

Collecting is what she wanted to do with her life, Katherine decided early on, and worked very hard at it, advertising for the books she wanted that had eluded her (pre-Internet collecting meant both collector and dealer had to get their want-lists out in print), ordering every catalogue and combing through bookshops. Later, she discovered there were actually antiquarian bookdealers whose specialization was selling fine miniature books such as Dawsons, Bromers and Lorsons.

She also learnt that she could buy directly from the printer or the press that was making the miniatures: Robert Massmann, Hillside Press, Ward Schori, Norman Forgue, Black Cat Press,

Achille Onge books, etc. Dawson's, she loved, and found the people she dealt with fun. Helen and Glenn Dawson were very, very nice, she writes, always answering letters and taking calls. Her favourite dealer from whom she ordered the most, she notes that they issued around ninety lists, each having thirty to fifty books, and over the years, she bought at least ten or fifteen from each list, sometimes the entire list.

In 1991, looking at Dawson invoices, she figures she must have bought about 600 miniatures from them. She would wait expectantly for each list to arrive, and the moment she got hold of the list, would scan it rapidly and phone in her orders, rather than order them over mail. Others were getting to the book faster via phone, and once, she learnt a costly lesson when out of the thirty-five books she wanted from a Dawson's list, only five were available. She had sent her order via the post; others had called the bookshop.

From the Lorsons, she figures she must have bought about 170, including from their first list from 1980. Jim and Joan Lorson would send her a bunch of books on approval, and would just ask her to return what she didn't want. She would take what she wanted and return the rest, and include with the books a cheque for what she had bought. Bromers did the same – sent her books on approval and later invoiced her for what she kept. She had never known anything like it. Book people are so nice, she notes. She bought many of the fine miniatures the Bromers published, several in their deluxe editions.

(Incidentally, the second miniature *I bought* was from Joan Lorson. *Printers on Morris* in the deluxe issue, but at a slightly reduced price because it lacked the extra Moser wood engraving of William Morris). I would occasionally speak to Joan Lorson on the phone, and she would talk to me about those heady days of bookselling when her husband was alive. She missed him dearly. Jim Lorson had been a legend in book arts selling.

By 1992, Katherine had 5,000 miniature books. She would travel anywhere if it meant finding a miniature rarity, or keeping up correspondence extensively in order to acquire the books she wanted. For just one book, she would travel hundreds of miles. One of her first (of many) rare book hunts happened in 1982, when she went looking for a copy of *Catalogue of the library of miniature books collected by Percy Edwin Spielmann*.

This was an important reference tool in the miniature book field that is not as difficult to find today as it was in those pre-Internet days – I see currently about six copies listed online, but Katherine had to go to a lot of trouble to locate a copy for sale. She advertised for it, and incredibly enough, a collector answered to say he had it, but would only lend it to her to read; he wanted it back by a certain date. Such trust and generosity, notes Rickard, takes your breath away.

She wrote to Norman Forgue, but he did not have a copy to spare. Anne Bromer of Bromer Booksellers called about something, and she asked after it, and Mrs Bromer said no copy had been seen in five years and she had a waitlist of fifty people!

Katherine wanted it so bad, she could taste it!

Forgue called to say he had a personal copy but did not want to part with it. They went back and forth for some time, making witty exchanges, Forgue calling her a temptress. Finally, he said, ok, it's yours if you are crazy enough to pay the price I want for it. She didn't hesitate. Rickard was doubly pleased with her purchase when a few days later a letter came from Louis Bondy, saying copies of the Spielmann catalogue were impossible to find; even though he had been co-author, he could not get hold of one now.

She ordered 10,000 mini bookplates and got special bookcases made to house her collection. By now, Katherine had come to a point where, if a dealer was going out of business and selling all, they would contact her first, and usually, she would buy their entire stock en bloc.

She had become very interested in the books published by Doris Varner Welsh, but found it difficult to get hold of her miniatures. Finally, she found an address for her press, and wrote. She got a warm letter back, and managed to buy a few more titles. Meanwhile, she discovered Doris had been working on a history of miniature books; the manuscript was ready, but Welsh had not proceeded further with publication.

Katherine sprung to action and worked on it with her, and it was published. Later, with Katherine urging her, Doris wrote her biography, *A Lady and Her Books*. Welsh had many rarities that she had always said no to selling, but when she died in 1991, she left all her books to Katherine. But Rickard had to pay thousands of dollars before receiving the books because of an overestimate by a non-book lawyer as inheritance tax, plus pay Doris's expenses as she had no other assets, and finally the lawyer's fees.

When the trunk of books came, she made notes as she unwrapped them. For four hours, she looked: scarce treasures emerged one after another.

Finally, Katherine Rickard sold her collection to various collectors and dealers. Bromers bought back many of their books.

My first experience as a collector 'pre-ordering' a fine press miniature was buying Anne C. Bromer's *XI LXIVMOS: Memoirs of a Bibliomidget*. I pre-ordered it in 2015, and copies for sale were ready to ship by January 2016. An absorbing and lively account of a miniature book publisher, this is a beautifully designed and printed miniature from the hand of Rollin Milroy, fine press printer at Heavenly Monkey Press. It tells the background story of the making of 11 high-end miniature books Anne and David Bromer produced from 1977 to 1989, with a bibliographical description for each.

When Anne and David Bromer began their bookselling career in the 1960s, they were at once 'drawn to beautiful books distinguished by design, illustration, typography, letterpress printing, handmade paper and fine binding'. They had an unmistakable allure to them, the handling of which was a sensual experience. This aesthetic became the stock in trade of Bromer from the instance of their first catalogue in 1968, to the present.

In the '70s, they became drawn to the miniature book, when they found themselves in possession of a six-point Goudy type, and thought it might be charming to use in a miniature volume. They wanted to fuse their interest in private press books and in a 64mo volume to make 'the book beautiful'. All their books from the first, were printed to the highest standards of fine press printing, using the finest designers, illustrators, printers, calligraphers and binders. They were issued in regular and deluxe editions.

Their second books, *Poems of Life of Emily Dickinson*, was described by Stanley Marcus, a famous miniature book collector, as one of the most perfectly printed miniatures of the twentieth century. On handmade paper in beautiful type, with wide margins, perfectly set, and nine coloured illustrations. In the deluxe, these were done with hand-applied water colours and the initials illuminated in gold, and signed by the printer and calligrapher.

The above is everything that will go into a finely printed book in a regular size, so these were private press books in their own right. These miniatures were adhering more to the fine press tradition than even regular-sized letterpress books! One day, Henry Morris of Bird and Bull Press wrote to Anne Bromer, saying he had a little text – a sentimental tribute to his Meihle Vertical press on which he had printed all his books so far – and thought the subject might make a nice miniature book.

No. V-109. The Biography of a Printing Press was printed on his own handmade paper, and he made the purple paste paper covers as well. With the text was a checklist of B&B books. (Later, Morris would print *You Can Judge a Book by Its Cover*, a very sumptuous miniature). The Ashendene Miniature remains their most important publication. St. John Hornby of the Ashendene Press had made eight copies of Horace's *Carmina Saphicca* for Queen Mary's dollhouse. One copy was given to her, and the rest to family members.

When a copy came up for auction, the Bromers successfully bid for the Bridwell (which has a large Ashendene archive and holding) for the hammer price of $22,000, a record price for a miniature in the twentieth century. The idea followed to reprint it as a miniature. Michael Hornby, the printer's son, wrote the introduction, and Bridwell let them print it on the Ashendene Albion, last used in 1935. 150 copies were printed using the original plates.

They did two miniature projects with artist Edward Gorey and three miniatures were done as calligraphed manuscripts. What the Bromers point to in the memoir is that by using the best and most tasteful material and careful craftmanship, fine letterpress books can be produced on a miniature palette.

PHILIP R. BISHOP

Collecting Mosher in Depth

Though I've written often about accomplished book collectors, I'd never really had the privilege of actually knowing one personally until I began corresponding with Philip R. Bishop, the distinguished scholar-collector of the Mosher Press books. I first heard from him in 2015 when he wrote to generously acknowledge an essay of his I had mentioned in my column, talking of an astounding rare book find he had made, a vellum copy of a Mosher limited edition. I don't collect Mosher Press books myself, but I was familiar with this gifted designer-publisher and his finely printed books because Norman Strouse, a bibliophile hero of mine, had been an ardent Mosher Press collector, and it was gratifying to hear from Bishop, who had known Strouse well. Strouse had been the greatest collector of Mosher books until Bishop came along and took that devotion to greater and newer heights: becoming the foremost collector *and scholar* of Mosher in the world.

Bishop has written the definitive bio-bibliography of Mosher (*Thomas Bird Mosher – Pirate Prince of Publishers*) and continues to fervently research and produce numerous groundbreaking essays on the Mosher Press and its extraordinary creator. In my reply to Bishop, I said: 'One of the things that drew me so much to Strouse was that he seemed to be one of the few collectors willing to talk and write about his collecting experiences, and with such great enthusiasm, too. So many collectors seem to shy away from enunciating the details of a hunt or a transaction. I hope you will do another book, this time a more personal account of collecting and dealing in Mosher.' I also asked him if he wouldn't mind telling me more about Strouse and him.

When he wrote back, I was excited to read, 'I am working on several books, one of which will be my book-collecting memoirs that currently number somewhere around 750 typed pages (including my 90 essays done for the Delaware Bibliophiles). More important is *The Collected Letters of Thomas Bird Mosher,* a work which I'm well into, but which will require a couple more years, I'm sure. 2016 will be a pivotal year for me to continue the work of compiling more TBM letters, which presently number around 525.' Bishop also obligingly filled me in about his longstanding biblio-relationship to Strouse.

> We began our "relationship" as me, the humble novice collector and he, the man who most personified the term "Mosher collector". I'd write to him about my discoveries and new acquisitions, and he'd encourage me to continue. At some point, our correspondence evolved to more of a collector-to-collector discussion, and I know he could sense my passion in the collection of all things related to Thomas Bird Mosher and the Mosher Press.
>
> And now that Strouse is no more, it has been my great honour and privilege to carry on the legacy. I first assembled a collection that rivalled the great collection of Norman Strouse and then surpassed it (although I like

to think of our collections as two gems used in making up a crown). One of my goals was to collect more of the Mosher books printed on real vellum than Norman had succeeded in doing. I have. Another was to rival the manuscript material in Norman's collection. I have. The reality of the Bishop Collection is that it's the largest and finest ever assembled.

Bishop began collecting the Mosher Press in the mid 1980s – he found them first at a neighbourhood bookshop he frequented, called 'The Book Haven'. Once he had developed a taste for these typographically handsome books, he looked further afield for more from the press.

Having assembled over the years a monumental collection from the press, he began focusing on other sub-collections related to the press, of which the richest and most beautiful are his Mosher books in exemplary fine bindings and the editions printed on real vellum. The Bishop Collection of Thomas Bird Mosher and The Mosher Books now consists of around 4,500 items. Included in this overall tally are: thousands of *The Mosher Books* imprints in various states, including many association copies, trial publisher's bindings, hand-edited copies, or other unusual copies. 562 handbound leather books in richly tooled bindings, forty-eight hand-illuminated copies of Mosher's imprints. Hundreds of his more limited/numbered books printed on Japan vellum, and forty-four of *The Mosher Books* printed on real vellum.

When he was recently inducted into the Grolier Club, he exhibited – along with other new Grolier members – three Mosher Press books he had handpicked from his collection. Accompanying his July exhibit this year was a collector's statement that described him as: 'Smitten. Driven. Narrowly focused. Unrelenting monomania.'

Indeed, Phil is the best and finest example today of a collector collecting in depth. In his own words:

> Collectors tend to adopt certain rules or parameters for their book collecting. I have a number of such rules which include not only the subject matter, but also rules about acceptable condition. Such rules function as guidelines to keep the collector focused on what the boundaries of the collection entail. They also function to keep the collector focused on what he or she is trying to accomplish. Sure, it's just fine to assemble all sorts of books one falls in love with, but if it's a collection, then there should be a rhyme and reason why one selection is made over another. If you have unlimited funds, by all means buy to your heart's content. It doesn't matter if you have little or no focus other than acquiring subject only to one's whims or interest du jour. Many an interesting assemblage of wonderful books have been amassed in such a broad or in some cases haphazard way. That's well and good, but it is not necessarily a collection. You're a buyer, not a collector. To be a collector requires a different tact, a limiting of focus and pursuit over the long haul. The idea is to come up with a collection which hangs around a subject or concentration, and in doing so takes on heightened meaning and scholarly value.

Anyone wanting to know more about Thomas Bird Mosher and his carefully printed limited editions or read more of Philip Bishop's research and essays on collecting the

Mosher Press, need only turn to the ultimate reference to all things Mosher: Bishop's scholarly and entertaining website (www.thomasbirdmosher.net) on the press and its publisher. For me, discovering the bibliophilic writings of Bishop has been so satisfying because here, at last, is another impassioned collector writing about collecting in colourful and scholarly detail – and in the process, generously sharing his research and his collection with scholars and fellow collectors. His accomplishment in collecting Mosher in depth is singular and profound; his ardour, his scholarship and his devotion are a model for all bibliophiles, and a challenging and joyful inspiration.

I was thrilled to learn recently that Phil had generously posted on his website something I had said to him about his recent acquisition. One of the most beautiful books in my collection is *American Bookbindings in the Library of Henry William Poor* (George D. Smith, printed by The Marion Press, 1903) by Henri Pène du Bois. It is, as one catalogue description has it, 'A stunning example of color reproduction, containing thirty-nine covers of fine bindings in vibrant and true colors and shimmering gold.' Phil now owns possibly the most beautiful copy of this book in private hands – for years he pursued a finely bound copy of *American Bookbindings in the Library of Henry William Poor* that had a connection to Mosher, and finally, triumphantly, snagged it. Here is a description of this fine binding and its binder from the collector:

> A striking and magnificent mosaic morocco binding heavily onlaid and gilt-stamped by Alfred William Launder, Bradstreet's finest binder, who bound for major collectors such as William Loring Andrews, Robert Hoe,

Henry William Poor, and J. Pierpont Morgan in the early 1900's. Richly adorned with multiple large sections of onlaid morocco including a central beige pattern and intricate maroon strap work. Gilt stamped and tooled fillet borders and winding vines terminating in prominent solid hearts on the beige morocco. Single gilt fillet ruling along all board edges. Spine with five raised bands, six compartments decorated to match the cover designs. Wide dentelles with six fillet concentric rectilinear edge motifs of different composition, signed on front dentelle in gilt pallet, 'Bradstreet's'. Marbled pastedowns and end-sheets. Top edges gilt. Original cloth covers bound-in at end. Copy #160 of 200 copies on handmade paper. This copy signed by Henry W. Poor.

Phil sent me an email with a link to his fascinating, detailed post on how he acquired this copy, accompanied by a magnificent photograph of the binding. I was spellbound by the sight of the fine binding, and excitedly wrote a note to him. The next thing I know, my comment was added as a tailpiece to the tale of the Launder find:

No one else in the bibliosphere – and I mean no one – but you, Phil, could have done justice to this 'treasured book' and its technically masterful binding. As the book's former owner, Jeff Stikeman, said when letting go of this copy to you, 'It's going to the best place'. And it will now, after having wandered for over a century, stay put here in the Bishop-Mosher collection, having at last found not just a fitting, worthy home but companionship, too, as it shares shelf space with your row of gorgeous Mosher books in fine decorated bindings.

THE BLOODLESS BIBLIOMYSTERY

In retrospect, I must admit that my novel – *The Book Hunters of Katpadi* – would have been better served with 'a bibliographical romance' for a subtitle than 'a bibliomystery'. Readers expected murder, mayhem, a detective, pursuit, fisticuffs and a crackling denouement at the end, and instead got a bloodless bibliomystery. To be sure, *Book Hunters* is a mystery with a crime in it, heroines and villains, but the only detective work is of a bibliographic kind, and the unmasking at the end probably feels like a postscript.

There is, however, a small and quiet tradition of the bloodless bibliomystery in the mystery genre that mostly goes unnoticed because it is so lowkey as far as plot and action are concerned, preoccupied as it is with bibliographic shenanigans. Before I look at a few that have become classics in the field, I must say something about why I chose to make my novel one of these bloodless bibliomysteries.

'This craze for rare books breeds crime,' quips a character in Carolyn Wells's 'The Shakespeare Title-Page Mystery'. And so it does – but what kind of crime? Murder? Mutilation? Serial killing? If we are to believe most bibliomysteries, it would be all of the above – however, in the real world of antiquarian dealing and collecting, there is no murder or mayhem; the darkest, most heinous crime is usually theft, or deception and deceit in one form or another. But killing someone over a rare book? *No* – doesn't happen. Even in that lone instance a few years ago of an English antiquities dealer (in, among other things, *Harry Potter* first editions) being brutally stabbed in an altercation, it seemed unlikely that the motive had anything to do with rare books.

Bibliomysteries persist in depicting the world of rare books as murderous and dark, while the opposite is true: it is made of up genial, decent, gentle, ethical men and women – whether collectors, librarians, or booksellers – who are probably not beyond possessing a foible or two, which could be anything from being ill-tempered to being vain or greedy. Or just coming off as too garrulous, show-offy or boring. But they are not going to, for example, enter your house on some false pretence to chop your arm off because they suspect you to be a forger. That's how *The Forgers*, one of the more successful entries in the genre opens: 'They never found his hands'.

The book is partly set in the world of contemporary rare book dealers, antiquarian book fairs and modern first editions. At least a couple of scenes in the book reference the New York Antiquarian Book Fair (though Morrow refers to the fair only as the show at the Park Avenue Armory) and I can't recall another contemporary bibliomystery that features the NY Antiquarian Book Fair. By featuring fictional book-dealer characters that trade and show and sell here, *The Forgers* gives you a peek into high-end rare book dealing, specializing in buying up entire private collections of all kinds of literary material, from author letters to inscribed copies to association copies.

Bradford Morrow, the author, knows this world well, having once been a book dealer in modern firsts himself. 'I thought to myself,' he said once in an interview to fellow novelist Karen Russell, 'what would a ruthless forger most want to deprive a rival of having? Pens, nibs, inks, antique papers, subterranean connections in the rare book world? No, his hands, of course. So it began with that single image and all the narrative possibilities and challenges it offered. The rare book community, a collective of brilliant eccentrics among whom murderers don't generally mingle, is one I have been a part of for my whole adult life – first as a dealer, later as a collector – so most of my research was already done by the time I wrote that sentence and those that came after.'

Well, all the more reason why Morrow should have known better than to depict the rare book world as murderous. This portrayal of the antiquarian book world as being capable of such psychotic behaviour I have always found unconvincing and silly, even in the best of bibliomysteries, and that includes John Dunning's popular Cliff Janeway series of an ex-cop turned rare book dealer.

And so when I set out to write my little bibliomystery, *The Book Hunters of Katpadi*, I wanted to show a world of professional dealers and accomplished collectors who were, in the main, fair-minded, though not beyond the wiles and temptations of bibliomania. Another annoying feature of contemporary bibliomysteries I wanted to address is how little bibliophily there is in most of them. They promise a plot about rare books and collectors but they all turn out to be conventional mysteries with the *de rigueur* body count, time-wasting investigation, list of suspects, red herrings, et al. There is no 'biblio' in these bibliomysteries! In *The Book Hunters of Katpadi*, I wanted to put the biblio back in the genre – if as a formula, most bibliomysteries were 75 per cent mystery and 25 per cent biblio; I made my novel 25 per cent mystery and 75 per cent biblio. The mystery is slight, just a sliver of the plot, while bookish matters bloom and overtake the story (some might say choke the plot).

I wanted the bibliophilia in my novel to be intense, unrelenting and mounting with each new chapter, with my characters wanting to be known solely by or through their love of books as objects. Bibliophile readers of the book, particularly, I had hoped, would get a deeper sense of my heroines, two intrepid bookwomen, who desired to be known by what they felt, thought and said about the art of the finely printed book, as well as by their actions on behalf of rare books, which are mainly bibliographic in nature.

But writing a bloodless bibliomystery infused with rampant bibliomania was not my only task: I had to invent from scratch, from the ground up, a fairly convincing antiquarian book world that is non-existent in India. Since we've always lacked an ingrained tradition of antiquarian trading and collecting in this country, the characters that people this novel, as well as the props and toys they play with, are not just fiction, they are pure fantasy. And because it is all so fantastical, I had to fuse it with the larger, truer and more historical tradition of bibliophily in the West. The chapters in the book that feel to some readers as veering off from the plot are the sections invoking this real, continuing and bespoke tradition of bibliophily in the rest of the world, with its famous book collectors, respected scholar-dealers, private printers and celebrated rare bookshops.

One of the most successful bibliomysteries out there, *The Name of the Rose*, had plenty of erudite digressions on medieval monasticism and theology, but no one then seemed to mind that it came in the way of the narrative because a reader could sense it was tangentially, if not intrinsically, important to the atmosphere and background of the novel. In the same roundabout way, the long digressive chapters on bibliophilic history in *The Book Hunters* impassion the narrative – or at least, they ought to. *The Book Hunters*, admittedly, is an experiment. How far I've succeeded in pulling this off, only readers of the book will know or can tell.

It would have been easy enough to pace the story briskly or stick to the main plot, but I was after something else: to introduce the world of the book arts – in all its myriad aspects – to the Indian reader, whether it's a young reader just discovering books or a die-hard bibliophile. I suppose more than a proper bibliomystery, what I ended up writing was a romance – a romance of bibliophily.

The Nijmegen Proof is the great classic in this category of the realistic bibliomystery – before I get to this little beauty, I want to mention one other that is fairly satisfying: *Knock or Ring* by Michael Nelson, written in 1957, which is a sharp, witty and knowledgeable biblio-novel on the shady but prevalent practice of big-name, powerful booksellers forming a secret ring to control the prices of rare books at an auction. The way it works is simple: the ring, usually made up of the top rare book dealers in the field, agree to not bid against each other in an auction. Instead, each of them bid on different lots, and usually the other bidders in the room – made of either collectors or librarians or booksellers with less clout – know better than to go up against the ring, allowing the bidder from the ring to make low bids and have it knocked down to him for a fraction of the price it would have realized if the bidding had been honest and vigorous.

Later, the ring will meet and hold a private auction amongst themselves (which they call a 'knockout') and divide the loot between them. In *Knock or Ring*, a hapless, failed antiquarian dealer finds himself unexpectedly tangling with the ring when he happens to bid for a very rare book that the ring is desperate to snag. All the fun and suspense in the book is from watching this reluctant hero take on the mighty London Ring. Will he beat them at their own game, or fail again? I'll let you find out for yourself. If you are fed up, like I am, with gumshoe bibliomysteries and crave something more bibliophilic, then *Knock or Ring* is just what you want.

One of the worst-kept secrets among bibliomystery connoisseurs is what a cool but tough little masterpiece *The Nijmegen Proof* is – and yet, strangely, this slim 150-page biblio-novel published in 1988, set in the antiquarian book trade, continues to be unsung, unnoticed and even unread. Perhaps this is because it is never very apparent what is going on in the book – you may even have to read every other page a few times over in order to follow the story. There is a further complication to it: almost every character in the book is based on some real person, but given a fictional name. They are drawn from the world of rare book trading across both sides of the Atlantic – the UK and the US – and the book features an array of characters that usually make up the trade: low-end and high-end book dealers, special collection librarians, very moneyed collectors, book runners and auctioneers.

If you are well entrenched in the trade, you can apparently identify who's who in the book. Barney Rosenthal, the famous manuscript dealer, owned a copy of this novel filled with his annotations pointing out who all these characters and events are based on. (How I would love to get my hands on *that* annotated copy!) Its author is S. Barkworth, but that's a pseudonym for Arthur Freeman, a highly respected scholar-dealer who is already an 'insider's insider'. I can only imagine how much fun he must have had conceiving and writing this bibliomystery meant to entertain his colleagues in the antiquarian trade. It is not only a whodunnit but also a 'whoisit'.

One of the oddly mesmerizing aspects of this novel is its matter-of-fact, unsentimental attitude to rare books and its hardened, satirical view of high-end dealers and librarians. The characters go through their routine of wheeling and dealing in a jaded, weary way, as if rare books were just another commodity they had to trade in. At first, as a reader, you feel a bit put off at such nonchalance, but gradually it becomes more appealing and entertaining and funny, adding authenticity to the rarefied atmosphere they live and work in. 'Rare books,' as one high-end dealer in the novel defines it simply, 'are books which cost money.' *The Nijmegen Proof* is so dismissive of its own plot that even a much-touted auction in the climax fizzles out!

When the book opens, we realize that all these people in the rare book trade have suddenly been alerted to an innocuous-sounding item in an auction catalogue, a hidden fragment or proof that could actually turn out to be the first-ever specimen of printing from movable type in the West, dated 1441, thereby predating Gutenberg's 1445 Bible. An antiquities dealer called Pooney (shades of Moses Shapira in the real world) who stumbles upon this proof, is met with scorn by his colleagues in the trade, who label it a forgery. Humiliated, he kills himself. His landlord, to recover unpaid rent, seizes his things and auctions them off along with the Nijmegen (pronounced *Nymegen*) fragments, not knowing its uniqueness.

However, when the proof comes up for bidding and the

auctioneer asks for a thousand pounds, he is greeted by stony silence and is forced to finally scale it down to a disgraceful bid. Irritated, the auctioneer snaps, 'Well, ten pounds?' And old Bogue, who was no one to trifle with, waved lazily and murmured, with a roll of his eyes, 'And why not?' The room exploded in laughter; no one bid against Bogue, and the auctioneer angrily banged down his ivory gavel.' One of the dealers in the story tells us that this bit of biblio-myth has since become a catchphrase in the trade: 'I may add that our people still quote, "And why not?" in comparable situations – it is a bookseller's tag.'

Now, as it goes up for auction a second time, real-life rare books dealers and librarian disguised as fictitious characters chase the proof, as they cross and double-cross each other. I think I've been able to guess that the novel's rather reluctant hero, a scholar-dealer called Lieblich, is probably E.P. Goldschmidt; the renowned dealer, F.F. Teutsch; the New York dealer has to be the legendary H.P. Kraus, and Fackerly's, the bookshop, is probably Quaritch or Maggs – though I could easily be wrong on all scores. I'm sure somebody else in the trade will be pointing to someone else. The colophon for the book says 'limited to 650 copies' but the print run must have been larger (it is abundantly, easily and cheaply available) and all copies are signed as S. Barkworth, a fictitious signature. (Or is it? One can never tell with this book). One of the jacket blurbs for the novel is by Arthur Freeman himself, who says, 'Absolutely wonderful. I really admire it.' And why not? It *is* quite wonderful.

LONDON'S FABLED BOOK RUNNERS

Two legends in the London antiquarian book trade who continue to fascinate me, are Driff and Stone, London's famous book runners. (Martin Stone has been profiled a few times, Driff less so). Their knowledge and eye for rare books, uncommon editions and where they could be lying hidden and undiscovered and underpriced, is legendary. Their book finds would later be sold to collectors or dealers at their true market price. Buy cheap, sell high. Stone and Driff have figured as central characters in Iain Sinclair's *White Chappell, Scarlet Tracings,* feverishly combing through the bookshops of London for rare book treasures. However, there has also been some mystery surrounding Driff – he suddenly disappeared. Vanished. Without a trace.

Occasionally, there were rumours in the book trade that he had been sighted for a minute somewhere before he vanished again; or that he had vanished to India! Driff was – and probably still is – a vegetarian with a love for Indian food. On his long book-hunting trips all over Britain, he would just as single-mindedly search for Indian restaurants to feast on a veg. thali as for obscure bookshops. For many years, Driff published his own idiosyncratic, opinionated guide called *Driff's Guide to All The Secondhand and Antiquarian Bookshops in Britain*, which upset many booksellers for the way it dismissed even the most famous bookshops as being of little interest to the true book hunter. ('A corset may be what this shop most resembles. The parts that show will be very attractive but those that don't will be under considerable pressure.' [*Driff's*, 1986]).

Sinclair described this pocket-sized guide as 'Swiftian in savagery'. If a bookshop got even a mildly approving write-up in the guide, the owner would be ecstatic and say, 'Driff gave me a good mention' or 'Driff let me off lightly'. Driff liked to also be known variously as Dryfeld, Driffield, Drif, or Dryfield. The photograph of Driff used in his guides was that of Raymond Carver(!) because Driff felt he looked exactly like Carver (or was it Driff, posing as Carver?). He once started a free bookshop: anyone could come in and take what they wanted. It didn't last long.

When browsing in bookshops and if asked by the owner what he was looking for, he would honestly answer: 'I am looking for a £1,000 book priced at less than a £100.'

Stone and Driff have made alluring book finds for various collectors and book dealers in their time. Iain Sinclair has written on Driff, and the legendary bookseller Peter Howard of Serendipity Books has a booklet on Stone (which also has a limited edition with a portfolio of photographs of Stone done over the period of a year) recounting this book scout's memorable finds. In turn, Stone wrote a marvellous tribute to Howard, starting with a description of his first sight of the cavernous Serendipity Books:

> In the dream landscape of every bibliophile, there is a vast shop, seemingly chaotic, constantly churning and changing. If the moment is right, almost any book may be found there... Serendipity Books... is no dream; at its helm is Peter B. Howard, substantially human, quixotic, fired-up and endlessly entertaining. I first met Peter at the Olympia Bookfair in the late 1970s; he had a table of

> James Joyce in absolutely marvelous condition, many of them inscribed. I stood there hypnotized... Peter peered down at me with avuncular concern. "Stay well away from Joyce," he said. "He's a nightmare to buy and sell." He said he'd like to see my books and I gave him my address and phone number.

Stone moved to Paris because that is where all the good books are, and died in 2016. A finely printed letterpress book was produced as a tribute titled *The Remarkable Martin Stone.* It is uncommon to see accounts of or about antiquarian dealers and collectors getting such lush typographic treatment. Such accounts are usually done as trade editions – very functional affairs, where the text is the focus. Ah, but *The Remarkable Martin Stone*, essays on the fabled blues guitarist-turned-London-book-runner, is printed in a small edition of 150 copies on Hahnemuhle Ingres paper, composed in Monotype Bell with a frontispiece engraving of this legendary book scout in a fetching binding of patterned Japanese cloth.

And each copy is signed by the printer, binder and artist. The book is published by Booktryst, edited by Stephen J. Gertz and designed and printed by the accomplished scholar-printer Alastair Johnston at his Poltroon Press. The engraving of Stone is by Frances Butler, and is bound by John DeMerritt. Gertz's introduction to Stone is followed by essays by those who knew this maverick as guitarist or bookrunner, and sometimes as both.

But what of the reclusive, mysterious and wonderful Driff? Has he resurfaced in London, and stalking bookshops? Or is he here in India, still (if he was here at all)? Or is he perhaps, as Sinclair once reported, haunting Brick Lane once more for dal soup, papadoms, onion bhaji, vegetable curry and black coffee?

ROSY AND LILLY

Few accounts of antiquarian book selling and collecting are as absorbing as Joel Silver's *Dr. Rosenbach and Mr. Lilly: Book Collecting in a Golden Age*. Fewer are even as finely focused, narrating a story of the rare book transactions between one impassioned collector and one renowned antiquarian dealer, set against the backdrop of modern book collecting in its golden age. In the 1920s, J.K. Lilly, a pharmaceutical industrialist with a passionate interest in rare books, began buying most of his books from A.S.W. Rosenbach, who had become America's most famous antiquarian book dealer. Both men 'sought great examples of great books.'

It isn't an emotional or subjective account, and yet you can feel, thrumming just underneath, the book collector's thrill and the passion of the bookseller. 'Book collecting came naturally to Lilly,' writes Silver. 'He possessed an eye for quality and detail, and a taste for the extensive minutiae that mark the highest levels of any collecting field.' He always bought cautiously, studying a dealer catalogue for a long time, comparing it with other copies when he could, and then taking the plunge.

But he was yet to deal with America's most famous antiquarian book dealer, the scholarly Dr Rosenbach, who seemed always to be able to offer the best copies of the rarest books. Lilly had been reading Rosenbach's well-written catalogues with great bibliophilic pleasure, but as Silver notes, they couldn't take the place of actually meeting Rosenbach, which Lilly did in January 1929 because catalogues 'couldn't carry the same combination of charm, knowledge, anecdote, and uniquely expressed confidence in the importance of the books as could Rosenbach's in-person performance.'

The young book collector couldn't help buying some nice editions before he left, so persuasive was the doctor. Later, Dr R wrote him asking, 'Have you a first *Robinson Crusoe*? We have just received a superb copy.' Lilly wrote to him asking for more details, wanting assurance, and R cabled saying: 'No copy like the above has been sold at auction in 75 years. It is the rarest of all the greatest books to find in perfect condition. This is probably the finest copy in existence... I am very glad to quote you the special price of $16,850. If we stocked this, it would sell for 18,500, but I am giving you the first offer of it.'

Some of the other expensive and remarkable rarities he went on to purchase from Rosenbach include a *Canterbury Tales* printed by Caxton, *Pride and Prejudice* in original boards, a polychrome Grolier binding, Gower's *Confessio Amantis* and Francis Bacon's *Essays* from 1598.

Published first in a bewitching-looking limited edition of 140 copies by the Bird and Bull Press, *Dr. Rosenbach and Mr. Lilly* also has a trade edition by Oak Knoll Press that keeps the original typographical design by Henry Morris, the woodcuts and the deluxe illustrations, adding a new preface.

One reason why his book succeeds so brilliantly when most other antiquarian accounts have faltered, is for how much the author trims out. Instead of another thickly detailed survey of book-collecting practices, or one more definitive biography of either Lilly or Rosenbach, Silver turns in an elegant, precise, carefully detailed and expertly executed tale of antiquarian book collecting, buying and selling.

Why is this book so much fun for the bibliophile? Why does it excite and thrill so much? I think the enjoyment comes from the minutiae of book transactions that Silver knowledgably and engagingly describes in evocative prose: first reading about an individual copy in a catalogue or a bookseller's description, the suspended waiting while you decide, and then the rush from deciding you definitely want it no matter the cost, making the purchase, and finally getting the book in the mail or having the book dealer hand it to you.

The ritual is repeated with each new buy and the bibliographical pleasure derived is not from just the buyer-collector's emotion, but the emotion of the bookseller, who acquires the hard-to-acquire copy, describes the book, prices it and then offers it to an individual collector who he knows might want it. Written from deep inside the world of antiquarian rare books, *Dr. Rosenbach and Mr. Lilly* is a scholarly yet literary account of one memorable book collector and one unforgettable bookseller that is destined to become a modern classic in the literature of antiquarian book collecting and dealing.

COLIN FRANKLIN, SCHOLAR-COLLECTOR, RARE BOOK DEALER

I have nearly everything the scholar-collector and dealer Colin Franklin has written – from those published as trade editions to those done as private press books. But since *Letters to my Granddaughter on Book Collecting* had been privately printed for the author, it remained elusive. No copies could be found with anyone. It had been done in a small edition, some on pure vellum, some on handmade paper, and the rest on regular paper. I sent out feelers to every UK bookdealer, but no one could turn up a copy. I even wrote to the printer, Paul Nash of Strawberry Press. No luck there, too. I wanted the book very badly, but it looked like even for the love of money, one could not be found. One dealer suggested I write to Colin Franklin himself, and ask if he has perhaps one copy to spare. I balked at this. I didn't have the courage to bother him, lest he think me a pest. Then one day, out of the blue, Paul Nash the printer wrote to say he had one copy now – Colin Franklin had returned a copy printed on regular paper to put up for sale; did I still want to buy it? I grabbed it gratefully (astonished at my luck) before either changed their minds.

The book is charmingly illustrated by Phillida Gili, though the letters themselves are not as interesting as they could have been. Still, I was happy to acquire a copy at last. My favourite Franklin book is *Bookselling, A Memoir*, printed in a tiny edition by Bob Baris at his press on Scroll Road. Baris printed this on his iron hand press, on dampened Twinrocker paper. The presswork is immaculate – the design, the type, the title label – perfection itself. I often show this little gem as a reason to print books not only on letterpress, but on a handpress on dampened handmade paper. It is elegant, austere, crisp.

Franklin reminiscences about his beginnings as a collector and how that led him to become a dealer. As a schoolboy, he would cycle to all those famous antiquarian bookshops – Maggs, Quartich, Chatto and Windus – to look at their fine press books. When he decided to turn antiquarian bookseller, he began with his own books for stock. He had been a distinguished collector of early-printed books and private press books, as well as the author of *The Private Presses*, a much read and consulted account of the private press movement. One of the first things he did soon after was to travel to New York to meet the impresario dealer, Lew David Feldman, who had shown interest in his vellum Kelmscott set. While Feldman was considering, Colin headed to an antiquarian book fair in LA, and showed his 'Catalogue One' still in galleys to fellow booksellers, all of whom complimented him. Not one book sold, he said, but Feldman seemed to show promise in buying his beloved Kelmscotts.

'Never worry if you sell something too cheaply, they'll always come back for more,' Mark Cohen of Marks and Co. told him, one day. At Culham, where Colin and his wife Charlotte lived, a barn was converted into his bookshop. And there, visitors from all over the world would come to see the books. He would listen to the transistor all day loudly when by himself. 'One can only learn their (books') mystery by owning them, experiencing, and viewing them by lamplight in one's chair, not remotely or under the discipline of any library,' he notes in the memoir.

Catalogue One is what he called his first offering, and not wanting to be stereotyped as a dealer only in private press books, he gave it the title: 'Fine and Rare Books Before Kelmscott'. Another austerely beautiful book Baris did for Franklin is *The Triple Crown* – the text is a talk Franklin gave at the Bridwell Library when they acquired a vellum copy of the Doves Press Bible – all five volumes. Perhaps the only known copy, this one Emery Walker's own copy, is in a special binding. Franklin says only three copies on vellum were printed by Sanderson, none for sale – one for the printer, one for Walker and one just in sheets. Both the bound copies, at the time of his talk, had not been found.

Franklin takes the opportunity to congratulate Bridwell for pulling off a coup by acquiring the 'Triple Crown' in English fine press printing: vellum copies of the Kelmscott *Chaucer*, inscribed by Morris to Edward Burne-Jones, the Doves Bible, the only known vellum copy, and the Ashendene Dante, in a binding by Douglas Cockerell. In 2012, he published *Obsessions and Confessions of a Book Life*, printed in a larger print run this time as a trade edition from Oak Knoll Press.

A memoir of antiquarian bookselling in the England of the '60s and '70s, of which a rare book dealer could say, 'those were the days', for it was a time when you could buy Kelmscott Press books for sixty or hundred pounds, or snap up for six thousand pounds a whole Kelmscott set (lacking the *Chaucer*) in vellum inscribed by Morris and Burne-Jones to A.C. Swinburne. A time when you could walk up a flight of stairs to the Seven Gables Bookshop and come down carrying three Grolier bindings, or if you happened to be dithering about paying five thousand pounds for a wonderful sixteenth-century illuminated Missal, the bookseller would pull out a 1494 book of hours with a velvet binding and say he could throw that in as well for the same price.

A bibliophile will take deep pleasure in it, but a bookseller will feel a closer kinship and resonance with Franklin's accurate, precise and stylish recollection of transactions between dealer and collector. I was charmed by Franklin's diffidence – can a rare book dealer even afford to be as diffident and shy today? Did his diffidence belong to that time – *those* days – or does it stem from him being a scholar-book dealer?

The minutiae of bookselling made him awkward. He was often embarrassed about selling, asking prices or quoting them; even thinking of referring to someone as customer made him uncomfortable. Franklin thinks catalogues are self-advertisements and after doing about eight of them, he stopped, noting that they felt like 'an infinitely vulgar form of self-offering'. Instead, he exhibited at international antiquarian book fairs and talks of how they were composed of invariably painful moments, inescapable boredom, some discoveries and surprises – best of all, at end of day, dining out with other booksellers and gossiping.

He was a collector too and found it difficult to part with his collection. But then he remembers what book dealer Philip Duschnes had said once, 'you must be prepared to sell your best books'. But Franklin was not without an awareness of how 'no bookseller is free of the fear that he will never sell another book'. He fondly remembers what booksellers and customers ritually say to each other, from 'May I look around?'; 'Of course, let me know if I can be of assistance' to 'Look around, make yourself at home'; or 'he very kindly allowed me to buy from his private collection'. One bookseller would say, lifting the phone, 'Lyon, bookseller here'. He records different styles of bookselling and trying to fit into one of them, but while he admired other booksellers, he couldn't easily bring himself to offer his wares, delectable as they were.

Once, on a visit to millionaire collector Paul Getty, he brought along with him quite proudly, all nicely wrapped-up, a *Hyakumanto Dharani*, a Japanese wooden pagoda with a little block-printed scroll inside from the year 770; one of the earliest examples of printing in the world ('except possibly something quite unobtainable from China'). It was charmingly housed in a painted lacquer Meiji-period box. Getty didn't seem to notice the bubblewrapped item. Talk drifted, the afternoon flitted away, and finally Franklin asked, 'And what shall I do about this?' Getty said, 'If I were you, I should just take it away. Exit, miserably.'

Imagine not thrusting something like that onto a collector – one of the *earliest* examples of printing in the world; a museum-quality piece like that today would be brandished around, and auctioned to death. He remembers a visit to wealthy collector Paul Mellon's house, where 'precious books were casually housed.' Mellon came out asking 'Want to see the Caxtons?' and opened a corner cupboard in the breakfast room and there they were, the first printed books in England. Mellon also brought out, just as casually, the manuscript of Blake's *Songs of Innocence and of Experience,* tall format with wide margins, probably done by the Linell boys in the studio, who Blake was teaching at that time.

In the early days when Franklin dealt out of his book

barn, he would eagerly await the visits of Hans Kraus, the redoubtable antiquarian dealer (who came especially because London bookshops were shut on Sundays while Franklin's book barn stayed open) who was always hard to please. Franklin wanted to impress him – he had no expectation of sales, only wishing to entertain Kraus, not bore him. One Sunday, Franklin laid out for him such choice items as a papal bull on vellum ex-communicating Queen Elizabeth and the splendid two-volume Bible printed by Schoffer in Mainz, 1468. 'But these', Kraus said in quiet dismay, 'are all printed books, I am interested only in manuscript.'

And so it was that one fine Sunday that Franklin drew out from his safe an opulent Armenian manuscript from the seventeenth century, amply illuminated with gold, and handed it to Kraus, who said, 'What are *you* doing with *this thing*?'

'It was the nearest thing,' Franklin writes, 'I ever came to a compliment.'

THE LURE OF THE HUNT

A box of truffles for the bibliophilic sweet tooth: Fifty-two scrumptious tales of rare book finds at bargain prices, by collectors, dealers and bibliomaniacs. In a box under his bed, a man finds a five-hundred-year-old book; an eBay auction purchase could possibly contain annotations in Shakespeare's own hand; a first edition of *To Kill a Mockingbird* still in an unsoiled dust wrapper in a flea market for five dollars, and a collection of vintage comics with an estimated value of $3.5 million discovered in a closet – these are just a few of the exciting true accounts of book-hunting in *Rare Books Uncovered* (Voyageur Press, 2015) by Rebecca Rego Barry, the editor of *Fine Books and Collections*, a premier magazine for collectors.

Barry interviewed several collectors and dealers to shape her absorbing narrative, entertainingly glossing it along the way. As editor of *Fine Books*, she is perfectly placed to access bibliophiles of all persuasions with stories about hunting for rare book treasures and snagging them at bargain prices. *Rare Books Uncovered* fills the gap in the books-on-books genre for titles dealing with contemporary accounts of book-collecting, especially collecting done on a small purse, with modest resources at one's disposal. There are ample accounts – in books, pamphlets and catalogues – about institutional acquisitions of rare books and large rare book collections assembled by wealthy collectors, but there's precious little about the serendipitous rare book finds made by the common bibliophile trawling for bargains in all kinds of likely – and unlikely – places.

Barry's book is also a timely and much-needed update to the 'Tamerlane mythology' embedded in book-collecting circles: the deeply held belief of treasure hunters that 'anything can be anywhere', that is, one can never predict what rarity will be lurking where, and today could be the day one hits the jackpot; that dream of making a sensational rare book find at a ridiculously good price. The first account herein, involving that legendary book runner Martin Stone, is probably the most gratifying story any book hunter can ever hope to hear. Here was a book dealer who had seen it all, every conceivable rarity, and had made a habit of turning up books of the 'only known copy' variety. But then he finds himself in a moment that fulfils even his great bibliophilic dream of a phenomenal find – one that even he admits will probably never happen again. Stone gets shown an entire floor packed with scarce, sought-after out-of-print editions in near-mint condition! It is the excellent condition of these century-old books that shakes up even this veteran book hunter.

My personal favourite tale is of a private press treasure found by Philip Bishop, bibliographer, dealer and collector of the typographically sensible limited editions of Thomas Bird Mosher. I – as well as several modern collectors – will relate to his moment of discovery: pouncing on a book dealer's bibliographic mistake. In the early '90s, thumbing through an *AB Bookman's Weekly*, Bishop came across an advertisement for a Mosher press book. He was at once alert and tingling with excitement.

Even the scant description for the book was enough to tell him that it may be the famed edition he had been hunting for many years. A vellum copy of *The Germ*, of which only four copies were printed in 1898 by Thomas Bird Mosher, done up in a dazzling exhibition binding. Bishop told Barry: 'It's the black orchid of Mosher's publications. It's one of the finest specimens of his book production... There are only four copies in existence, and I just wanted *that book*!' But what filled him with trepidation (and wonder) was that this copy was being advertised by what looked like a remote trading post out West, rather than a proper antiquarian bookshop. Could it all be a terrible mistake?

Nevertheless, he decided to go for it: phoned them, bought it and asked for it to be shipped overnight, paying heavily for priority mailing. When it arrived the next day, Bishop locked his bookshop to examine the parcel undisturbed, and unwrapping it, got a glimpse of a mint green slipcase – the first sign that it could be the very thing he had been looking for. Barry writes: 'he was trembling with excitement... One look at the spine pretty well sealed it. "Oh my God! I'm looking at this book, and I am seeing the onlays, the incredible tooling, and all edges gold, bright, shimmering."' Barry neatly captures the moment – and the excitement – still present in his voice, twenty years later.

When I asked Rebecca Barry if there were any surprises while researching for her book, she offered this: 'I was ecstatic to receive a letter from Pulitzer Prize winner Larry McMurtry early on in the process. I refer to him as a "spiritual leader" for bibliophiles, and I was hopeful that he might share a story from his scouting days. So I posted a letter to his bookshop in Texas. Within a week or so, a typed reply arrived. I was amazed. It's not insignificant that several of my interviewees quote the author-bookseller, and having his story in the book means the world to me.' Barry herself made a nice find early on in her book-collecting days (something Indian bibliophiles will find interesting): tucked inside a first edition of *Death of A Salesman* was a ticket that turned out to be a press pass for the 1931 Indian Round Table Conference.

I will let you discover its provenance for yourself when you read the book, along with the other fifty-odd rare book discoveries uncovered inside its covers! Nick Basbanes, in his sparkling foreword to the book, sums up the lure of the bargain hunt: 'One of the many beauties of book collecting is that it is an activity that can be enjoyed, and mastered, at any level. We can all admire private libraries that are assembled with the backing of small fortunes, but just as impressive in my eyes are the collections that emerge from connoisseurship and perception deployed in the field, nudged along by serendipity and good old-fashioned luck.' I can easily see a second volume of *Rare Books Uncovered*, bringing us more appetizing tales of book-hunting conquests.

GRAHAM GREENE, BOOK COLLECTOR

Graham Greene once went on record to say that if had not been a writer, he would like to have owned and run a second-hand bookshop. He was a keen (and pretty sharp) book collector. He made sure that books presented to him were always inscribed and signed by the author. Even as a teenager, he sought first editions and signed copies. He knew the value of a book signed by him. He did the book crawl whenever he could, wandering from auction rooms to antiquarian bookshops to flea markets in England, picking up what felt valuable and beautiful to him. He was constantly swapping his collection, selling or trading an edition for another edition he desired more. And so the number of rare or first editions in his collection never remained the same, often dipping and swelling.

At the time of his death, it numbered nearly 3,000, with as many as 500 editions signed or inscribed by the greats of modern literature. When his nephew opened a second-hand bookstore, Greene was the inspiration behind it. He often wrote in the margins of books (a rough estimate is as much as 30,000 margin linings).

We learn of Greene, the collector, from books that even his most keen readers don't look to: *With All Faults* (1973), the autobiography of David Low, a bookseller Greene befriended and often bought books from. Greene wrote the introduction to the book, reminiscing about their book-collecting friendship, and it is here that he offers his confession of what he would like to have become if hadn't become a writer. *The Annotated Library of Graham Greene* (1993) catalogues his books and letters. The most revealing is *Dear David, Dear Graham: A Bibliophilic Correspondence* (1989).

He writes to Low after stumbling on a rare find in Clapham: '... a bookshop near the church on the edge of the common. I bought there for two shillings an Order of Holy Week, date 1668 with plates by Hollar, in a beautiful red Morocco contemporary binding. It was dedicated to the Queen... I have still got it and I wonder how much it is worth.' He often scribbled the sale details of a book. With his lover, Dorothy, who illustrated several of his children's books, he collected Victorian detective fiction. Another love affair is recorded through the book inscriptions Greene and Catherine Walston made for each other through the years. While still married to Vivien Greene, he dedicated *The End of An Affair* to 'C'. Several of the books she gave him are boldly inscribed, such as in the flyleaf of a fourth impression Augustine's *Confessions*: 'To Graham on Capri May-June 1950 with a Red Cross on the Bottom. With love from Catherine'.

In the last years spent in Antibes with his last lover, Yvonne Cloretta, he kept a house filled with books, specially several first and limited editions of his own books. He would often frequent a restaurant here, and once wrote in a copy of *Martin Chuzzlewit* he happened to be reading while dining: 'Two women having dinner at Felix – one has been left by her husband. The other is bored by her husband.' Most of his books and letters are in libraries now. And of course, in the hands of some intrepid collectors.

In *A Pound of Paper: Confessions of a Book Addict*, film critic and biographer John Baxter records how he became an obsessive book collector because of Graham Greene. While browsing in a London flea market, Baxter noticed an unusually thin-looking book dealer in a beret with nicotine-stained fingers ('a morning fag guttered in the moist morning air'), who quickly sensed Baxter's keenness for Greene. It was Martin Stone, the legendary London book runner, who proffered not one but three rare Greene editions to Baxter, one of them a British first edition of *Our Man In Havana*. And he was asking just five pounds for each. The instant he bought the lot, Baxter realized he had gone from being a reader to a collector.

Greene was notorious for not signing books. However, if you surprised him on the street with a fine edition of one of his books, he was known not only to sign it but even leave a long inscription in his spidery handwriting. Baxter would leave his Greene editions with a bookseller whose bookshop the author frequented, and in this way, managed to get some of them signed. Greene was apparently so embarrassed by his first published book, *Babbling Brook*, a slim volume, that he bought up all existing copies to destroy them – and this well may have been possible since the print run was as small as three hundred copies. Few copies exist today in the rare book market, and if one ever turns up, it sells for upwards of £5,000.

Many of his earlier books (*Stamboul Train, The Confidential Agent*) had small first print runs. Baxter recalls making a find quite unexpectedly at the famous antiquarian bookstore, Maggs. They had only a few Greene editions of note. One in particular caught Baxter's attention: an inscribed first edition of *The Lawless Roads* without a dust jacket for 150 pounds. It wasn't a very collectible item and without the dust jacket, worth even less. But Baxter, now fully into Greene, spotted something the bookshop had missed. It was dedicated, in that spidery Greene hand to the Jesuit priest the author had dedicated *The Power and The Glory* to, making it at once precious. Baxter snapped it up.

Baxter's fanatical Greene obsession ends on a strange note. Years later, he sold his Greene collection to Swann's book auction gallery for a two hundred percent profit. Now his shelves were bare, but he says this only proved an enticement to begin collecting again. 'The incomplete is always alluring,' he writes. Greene, the collector, would have understood. In his introduction to *With All Faults*, Greene himself wrote: 'The value of a collection to the collector lies less in its importance, surely, than in the excitement of the hunt, and the strange places to which the hunt sometimes leads.'

THE MYSTERIOUS BOOKSHOP

I first visited The Mysterious Bookshop in 1989, when it was a dark, cozy little bookshop in mid-town Manhattan. I was quite tickled by the idea that there could be a bookstore entirely devoted to just mystery and crime titles. I wasn't aware then of the shop's rich history which draws from its famous owner, Otto Penzler. Later, after I had left the bookshop, I discovered that Mr Penzler was one of the most celebrated figures in mystery fiction publishing and that he owned one of the finest collections of rare first editions in detective fiction – most of which are inscribed to him by the genre's most famous authors, whom he knew personally as either publisher, friend or as the field's most knowledgeable bibliographer-anthologist.

The Mysterious Bookshop in New York City is one of the last bookstores in the world specializing in mystery and detective fiction. It is also one of the oldest and biggest. (Murder Ink, the city's first mystery bookstore once located in uptown Manhattan, sadly closed its doors in 2006, as did Partners and Crime, the other specialist mystery store in Greenwich Village).

The second time I dropped into The Mysterious Bookshop was some months later, the same year, in the hope that I could meet Mr Penzler briefly and have him sign my Mysterious Press copy of Vincent Starrett's *The Private Life of Sherlock*

Holmes. Starrett, a great bookman who had once assembled, in the '30s, the greatest collection of Sherlockiana, had been the inspiration behind the Baker Street Irregulars. *The Private Life of Sherlock Holmes* was the first scholarly study of the world's first consulting detective.

Owing to Otto Penzler's deep interest in Sherlockiana, The Mysterious Bookshop also specializes in Conan Doyle material. If you want more than just reading copies of mystery, crime and detective titles, this bookstore is a good place to be: its shelves are filled with collectibles for reasonable prices, in the range of $15 to $50 – not a bad price to pay for a collectible when copies can start at $100 and go up to $500.

Though it had been a busy day, Mr Penzler very graciously agreed to see me for a few minutes. I told him I had come all the way from India to his bookstore in the manner not unlike that of a mystery fan making a pilgrimage to a shrine. He was suitably impressed but also a little bemused that The Mysterious Bookshop should figure so largely in the life of an Indian bibliophile. We spoke very briefly, perhaps a minute or two after that, and he readily signed *The Private Life of Sherlock Holmes*.

When I visited The Mysterious Bookshop next, it was a decade later at its spacious new Tribeca location in Lower Manhattan. This time, I was carrying with me several titles from The Mysterious Press but he was unavailable. I spent a good part of the day browsing and talking to the staff, asking them for recommendations. One set of publications from The Mysterious Press that I have pursued are their Christmas keepsakes. For the past eighteen years or so, Mr Penzler has kept a tradition going, of issuing little keepsakes from the press and the bookshop as Christmas gifts for customers. He would commission an original crime story from a bestselling mystery author and produce them in a limited-run pamphlet edition of a thousand copies.

There was, however, one plot rule or condition the authors had to include when setting these stories (and a delightful condition it was too, and the reason why I collected them): some of the action in each story had to take place in The Mysterious Bookshop! The best of the keepsakes were collected in *Christmas at The Mysterious Bookshop* (2010). It's a marvellous anthology, unique for containing a range of bookish stories featuring a real mystery bookshop and its real proprietor, whose bespoke collection of rare and first editions of mystery and detective fiction totals at least 50,000.

One story here revolves around the hunt for a lost Dashiell Hammett manuscript; in another, Lawrence Block's hero, Chip Harrison, has to investigate the disappearance of an unpublished Cornell Woolrich manuscript from Penzler's private library at his office. It happens during a Christmas Eve party at the bookshop, and all the guests – several of them famous figures from the New York publishing world – become suspects. What is singular and charming about this anthology is that it is the bookshop that is often the *femme fatale* in these stories!

The best book, to my mind, that Mr Penzler has ever done, is his most recent, *Mysterious Obsession: Memoirs of a Compulsive Collector* (2019). This is his own story of how he collected first and signed editions of the high spots of mystery and detective fiction. Each chapter deals with an acquisition; the tale of how he found and bought these rarities is told crisply and enjoyably. It has since become one of my favourite books on collecting to dip into again and again.

PART FIVE

GUILTY BIBLIOPHILIC PLEASURES

DR R OR THE SNUBBED COLLECTOR

My affection for A.S.W. Rosenbach stems not from his reputation as a renowned rare book dealer (on that score, he was needlessly flamboyant, boastful and given to exaggeration) but rather for something he's mostly forgotten for, something Dr R – Rosy, that is – was himself embarrassed about: *The Unpublishable Memoirs* (Mitchell Kennerley 1917), a collection of biblio fables he authored. Rosy apparently often wished they *had* remained unpublished!

I am really rather very fond of this book. I've read it many times, and I'm bound to keep reading it many more times. It is so utterly entertaining for its clipped, terse narrative – a stripped-down style – and the emotion and details and the engrossing plots each tale is invested with. If Jeffrey Archer wrote stories about bibliophily, this is how they would read. Except Rosenbach came before Archer, so he is a true original for the way he plots and tells these tales. The hero of most of these stories, you strongly suspect, is but an alter ego of the future impresario of rare book dealing.

The stories concern a young collector called Robert Hooker, who goes about pilfering the rarest books and art objects because he feels they belong with him, in his private museum. Hooker is cast in the light of a bibliophile pirate, the Robin Hood of bibliomaniacs, taking from rich collectors and giving to himself, the poor collector. He thinks up of clever, devious and fun ways to steal what's impossible to steal – even the objects with the tightest security are no match for his wits.

Honestly, it is this book that Rosenbach should have been proud of, not his better-known accounts of book dealing in *The Book Hunter's Holiday* and *Books and Bidders*, all of which pale before this intensely felt, blazingly honest bibliophile fantasy. Rosenbach always craved for distinction and how ironic that he never achieved that in his memoirs, but managed just that so effortlessly with biblio-fiction. How I wish he had gone on to write many more such tales of Hooker, the snubbed bibliophile who gets even.

One can so easily (knowing Rosy's excitable, grandiose feeling for rare books) see in these stories of a covetous bibliophile, the dark fantasies of Rosenbach, the collector, the man who wanted to gather for himself all the rare treasures of the rare book world. We know from so many accounts of colleagues and friends, and indeed, even his bibliographers, that Rosy surreptitiously took away the best books in his stock – at least the things he *coveted* – and put them away in his private library, there to fondle and caress all these unholy loves privately.

To give you a sense of the kind of tasty bibliophilic plots Rosenbach imagines for Hooker's adventures, I'll outline one or two without giving anything away. In the first tale, a rare book that Hooker had saved up to buy is snatched from under his nose by a rich collector:

> 'After years of dithering, Robert Hooker has finally walked into a rare bookshop to buy an exceedingly rare volume, one of only two copies known. He has finally accepted that he has to pay the asking price, and towards this he has scrimped and saved. The dealer lays it before him. At that very moment, a wealthy and famous

collector stomps in, and without ceremony snatches the book saying he'll buy it right away.

At home, among his books, his anger increased. It was the old, old case of the rich collector gobbling up the small one. It was outrageous! He would get even—if it cost him everything. He dwelt long and bitterly upon his experience. A thought struck him. Why not prey upon the fancies of the wealthy! He would enter the lists with them; he would match his skill against their money, his knowledge against their purse.'

Hooker works out a scheme to trick the rich collector into parting with the elusive book, and thus begin the adventures of Rosenbach's anti-hero, and it is a lot of bibliophilic fun. Not all stories feature Hooker. One that I am especially fond of from the non-Hooker stories is called 'The Great Discovery'. A young man loses his fortune overnight and is now forced to pawn his belongings for money. Engaged to a woman, he breaks it off as the honorable thing to do. A day comes when he has nothing left to pawn except a few rare books that he treasures, and though he has gone hungry the last few days, he has kept himself from taking them to the pawn shop. Finally, he is left with no choice, and takes the 1817 Keats volume – the first edition of the first published book by this poet – to the pawn broker. Does he go through with it? Does the bibliophile goddess smile on him, and bring about a book-collecting miracle? (You can easily find out what happens next *right now* since *The Unpublishable Memoirs*, being out of copyright, is in the public domain, available to read or download online.)

My absolute favourite in the collection is 'The Lady of the Breviary'. It concerns an illuminated manuscript, the Abelard

Missal, depicting the love story of Heloise and Abelard. The missal is in the possession of the Blaythwaite family, and Hooker has fond memories of being shown this volume again and again by its owner, Richard Blaythwaite, who is now, alas, dead, leaving everything to his beautiful daughter who has never had the slightest interest in rare books or collecting. Hooker is aghast to learn she might give the Missal away to some museum. Hooker visits often, in the hope that he can persuade Miss Blaythwaite (we never learn her first name) to give it to him.

Rosenbach describes the Missal through Hooker's eyes:

> 'It was a marvelous manuscript dating from the sixteenth century, and contained at the end the beautiful and tragic story of those medieval lovers, Abelard and Heloise. The pictures that decorated the missal, however, were its chief glory... They were the work of Giulio Clovio, and executed by the great miniaturist for Philip the Second of Spain. The full-page illuminations, with the exquisite colours, heightened with gold, were worth a king's ransom, or a queen's reputation. The binding was in keeping with the superb quality of the breviary, being in old purple Morocco, the royal arms of Castile impressed in gold upon the sides.'

Miss Blaythwaite is clearly fond of Robert, but the book collector only has eyes for the book. Will he come to his senses and realize he has been coming so often to her house not to see the Missal alone... and is there a chance that Miss Blaythwaite, under Robert's tutelage, will blossom into a bibliophile? The last line of the text, spoken with aching tenderness by Miss Blaythwaite, will bring tears of joy to both lovers and collectors.

FOR PLEASURE AND PROFIT

The cutting up of illuminated manuscripts for pleasure and profit has a long and fascinating history, with one character in particular called Otto E. Ege (pronounced 'eggy'), emerging as its most 'endearing arch-villain'. No less than Christopher de Hamel, once Sotheby's famed manuscripts auctioneer and revered palaeographer, thought of Ege that way. De Hamel viewed this whole business of cutting up or cutting out with some empathy, and had a soft spot for someone like Ege who supplied those single illuminated leaves as well as those lovers of medieval illumination (like me) who bought them.

In his monograph *Cutting up Manuscripts for Pleasure and Profit* (Book Arts Press, 1996), de Hamel says Ege took complete or near-complete manuscripts 'and broke them up to sell as individual leaves. He began the market for single illuminated leaves, thus making it possible for middle class connoisseurs to own a fragment from an illuminated manuscript. He was a book breaker, a biblioclast, and yet he is seen quite sympathetically as a man who wanted to promote the book arts, bring beauty into people's lives.'

De Hamel admits he bought one of those leaves himself! He had, even as a young man, bought fragments and leaves from English manuscript dealer Alan G. Thomas. De Hamel points out in his monograph that an illuminated manuscript book that was bought for $12,000 and broken up and sold for $190,000 in just a few months, is the kind of profit few dealers can resist getting involved in, whatever the ethics of it.

The breaking up of medieval manuscripts still flourishes, he notes, but no one will admit to it. It is always the previous owner who did it, or the customer who came after, or just a shrug of the shoulders to dismiss it and say, no idea how it came to be separated from the book. A bookseller – de Hamel does not say who – apparently always stated in his catalogue in bold letters, 'WE DO NOT BREAK UP MANUSCRIPTS'; but frequently did. Alan Thomas would insert this line in his catalogues offering leaves: 'Cut up by some damn fool' and most devastating of all, H.P. Kraus, who said he is a firm believer of not breaking up manuscripts, let Sotheby's break one up for him, and saw his profit go up by 600 per cent.

De Hamel wants to be clear that it is vandalism, though he has been sympathetic to Ege and other dealers – he implicates himself knowingly, and is honest about his own desire to have these beautiful leaves at a price he can afford, or put another way, he could never have afforded to own one if it had not been separated from the book.

Otto E. Ege, a professor of art history, became so smitten by illuminated manuscripts that he started out collecting as many as he could buy on a college teacher's salary and then, convinced of their beauty and glory, felt it was his task to put them in the hands of middle-class people in order 'to bring beauty into their lives'. So, he broke up complete or near-complete manuscripts and sold each leaf individually.

What started out as an evangelical mission turned into a nifty business when he realized pricing each leaf individually (prices varying with how much or how little decoration there was, whether with miniatures, gilded letters, historiated initials, etc.) from the same manuscript meant he could make anything from three to five times more than what he had paid for the whole thing.

He began selling the leaves mounted and, by the 1940s, had even made portfolios with several leaves that sold as a set. He teamed up with dealer Philip Duschnes to get them out to collectors. His grand portfolio sets (assembled perhaps in 1950) consisted of about forty portfolios with fifty beautiful illuminated leaves from individual manuscripts at $750 a set. (A steal! Even a *single* leaf from this portfolio would sell for more than that today.) But the sets never reached the open market because he died in 1951, and his wife disposed of most of them to institutions.

And now in the present, the prices single leaves fetch on eBay and other major online auctions is astonishing. The price of a single illuminated leaf containing a tiny miniature or a historiated initial done in colours and gold, will reach a hammer price of $1,600 to $2,800. This is for an *average* leaf from an anonymous book of hours (or a Psalter or a Breviary). If the leaf in question has brilliant decorative work in it or a particularly fine and large miniature, then the opening bid will begin at $ 5,500 and go up to $12,500.

De Hamel dates the cutting up of illuminated initials and miniatures in some instances to as far back as the fourteenth and fifteenth centuries – this was not done for profit but to make a contemporary manuscript look more pretty. And shockingly, it would usually be nuns in a convent who would enhance unadorned manuscripts this way. He has seen two manuscripts where this was in evidence: one was a fourteenth-century manuscript with fifty or so illuminated initials stuck to it that had been cut out from a thirteenth-century manuscript in the possession of a convent. Similarly, he has seen a fifteenth-century manuscript with pasted-on illumination culled from a fourteenth-century manuscript.

There are several medieval manuscripts in the Oxford libraries missing miniatures and initials – and several of these were mutilated not to beautify another plain manuscript but just for sheer amusement or to pass the time; in one case, says de Hamel, the children of one of the Oxford dons would cut out miniatures from their father's library on wet afternoons, as if it was like stamp collecting. In another instance, around the nineteenth century, children removed all the illuminated initials from their father's missal and pasted them in scrapbooks to spell out their names in fancy ways!

Another form of cutting up or cutting out was libraries giving these away to distinguished guests visiting them! As recently as 1820, points out de Hamel, a historiated initial was cut out from the magnificent Winchester Bible from the twelfth century and given to a guest of the Winchester Cathedral. He points to another case from 1927, where a guest writes to the canon librarian of the Cathedral, thanking him for 'the illuminated initial "S"', saying how it is the most beautiful thing in his possession, and quickly adding that he would, of course, remain mum about it. In other words, hush it up.

So, as far back as the medieval period, scribes and owners of books themselves were cutting out miniatures and initials to re-use in other books. This was followed by clerics and members of royal families cutting up miniatures as relics of the past (in the way we would try to preserve or acquire old photos). At this same time, visitors to libraries with manuscripts wandered the stacks with penknives in their pocket.

With Ruskin and later, Sydney Cockerell (both known for their manuscript collection), a different kind of cutting up happens – not mutilation of illuminated manuscripts but the gifting of bifolium leaves (a group of leaves running together) to close friends and family as birthday gifts, or to honour them. Ruskin notes in his diary: 'Cut up Missal in the evening – hard work.' De Hamel feels Ruskin is unjustified in being the hero of manuscript breakers; he only gave friends leaves from broken manuscripts in his collection, which were apparently only four out of some 100 manuscripts he owned. He just liked to tick off the establishment.

Cockerell was known to give away detached leaves from manuscripts, usually whole leaves or a bifolia. Even a great manuscript collector like Chester Beatty would gift detached leaves from the numerous manuscripts in his collection. Ruskin is often invoked by dealers who break up manuscripts, and de Hamel has to always correct them that Ruskin did not tear out leaves and was not a snipper of miniatures.

Sharply, at the start of the twentieth century, cutting leaves becomes a business, a trade: there was a huge profit to be made from these beautiful leaves. De Hamel gives more spectacular instances: 'You buy a manuscript for a thousand dollars, you break it in two and each half is worth $900. You tear it in half again and each quarter is worth $800; you split it again and each eighth is worth $750; and so on'. He offers another stunning example from an actual auction sale in 1980, where a manuscript book that sold for $12,000 at Christie's, was broken up quickly and 'sold' out to the tune of $190,000 – the single text leaves retailed from $350 to illuminated initials at $800 to $1,750 for those with historiated initials.

He then goes on to make the most absurd – though pleasurable – case in defence of those stray leaves already broken up from a whole book; he is not serious, he says, but would like to entertain the notion and see where it goes. He offers several points that are very compelling and persuasive indeed, making me feel less bad about the leaves I've bought.

Many thirteenth-century Bibles and fifteenth-century choir books have no textual value today; apparently whatever we can learn about them, we can learn just as well from one leaf as the whole manuscript. Single leaves are easy to display, shockingly some of the most beautiful manuscripts in the world, he says, have been taken apart as leaves in museums so they can be displayed. Quite a few of these single leaves for sale come from manuscripts that are imperfect and, as a Sotheby's auctioneer, he can swear to the difficulty of selling a whole imperfect book, while leaves sell easily. A miniature or a bifolio is a whole unit, complete in itself, so it's not so terrible that the whole book is not present. Eventually, in the long cosmic view, all things, including manuscripts, will be destroyed, so some breaking up for the enjoyment of connoisseurs can be forgiven. Our ancestors, he concludes, have been cutting up manuscripts for centuries, and we'll probably continue to do so, even though we should not. Such is the irresistible beauty of an illuminated manuscript that even its fragments will do.

BLOSSOMING BIBLIOPHILIA

In the Suicide's Library

One of the luckiest biblio-finds I made recently was chancing on a copy of Tim Bowling's *In the Suicide's Library*, a true and thrilling account of modern-day bibliomania, poetry and disappearing artists. 'I'm a poor man with an expensive taste for rare books, a gentleman of lean purse... and a bibliophile rapidly on the path to bibliomania and moral decay.' With these opening lines, you are instantly captivated – it could be your story, after all. *In the Suicide's Library* (finely printed and published by Gaspereau Press, 2010) is gripping, suspenseful, edgy and fun.

To begin with, what happens in the book is this: one day, Tim Bowling, an accomplished Canadian poet, stumbles on a signed copy of a book of poetry on the shelves of a university library. The signature, Tim notes, is 'ornate... in rich, black ink beautifully showing off against an off white page... A beautiful calligraphic wave in a polar sea.' This signed copy takes firm hold of his bibliophilic heart: he must have it. But it is the only copy of its kind. No other exists. And Bowling, a book collector who instinctively understands and realizes how this copy must be cherished, protected and honoured, begins contemplating ways to possess it.

The book in question is *Ideas of Order* by the poet Wallace Stevens. There is nothing extraordinary about the copy except for the ownership signature on the endpaper, denoting the copy belonged to Weldon Kees. This is what gives the copy such aura; Bowling has become fascinated by this underrated, forgotten artist who vanished one day without a trace. Kees was many things: poet, artist, jazz musician, experimental filmmaker and 'most dramatically, mysterious suicide'. His disappearance has become legend; his car was found parked near the Golden Gate Bridge – Kees had talked of vanishing to Mexico. Had he vanished or had he killed himself?

Tim's blossoming bibliophilia flowers into bibliomania: yes, he must find a way to safeguard this copy from some teenager who might deface the signature, or a bibliophagist who might tear that page out, or some borrower who might one day casually lose it. He meditates on ways to rescue the copy and, just when he's figured out a way to do it, he learns that someone has borrowed the copy and has failed to return it, though it is well past the due date. I won't spoil it further by telling you what happens, but the whole absorbing account – graphically chalked out as you turn the pages feverishly to find out – is full of a kind of suspense that is at once moral, visceral and existential.

There are three criss-crossing narratives here: the first – the one that I enjoyed the most and the one that forms the major part – is Tim's account of his book-hunting transactions via online rare book dealers. Spending hours browsing through the stock of antiquarian booksellers, finding what you want but not buying it right away, instead letting a few days go by until your desire for that copy is uncontainable. Calling up the bookseller with a pounding heart hoping no one else has bought it and then, with trembling hands, rushing through the checkout process on your computer to complete purchase. And then a few weeks later, you hear 'the lovely chuck of the mail box'. The book is in the house.

Another story here is the author's quest to tease out the details of Kees's disappearance, and the third intertwined narrative is the poet's dilemma over his discovery of Kees's own copy of the Wallace Stevens book sitting coolly on the library's bookshelf. *In the Suicide's Library* is one of a handful of book-collecting tales that unfold on the Internet. Much of the ritual of desiring and pursuing and collecting happens here with online antiquarian bookshops. This is exactly how much of collecting happens around the world today; indeed, this is how I collect. There aren't too many non-fiction accounts of bibliomania that are literary, illuminating and poetic to boot, and that's what *In the Suicide's Library* is.

Tim Bowling is the author of many volumes of prize-winning poetry, and one fetching aspect of his poems is how bibliophily turns up as a theme. In the volume called *The Book Collector*, he has a moving poem on Harry Elkins Widener, the young collector who died on the *Titanic* soon after a spell of book hunting in London. Another intimate pleasure offered by *In the Suicide's Library* is the chain of reading on books about books that mirrors (and enlarges) your own reading: as the author browses and buys, he recalls what other bookmen have said about collecting – from Wilmarth Lewis's *Collector's Progress* to Edward Newton to Rosenbach.

And then there are Bowling's own seductive sentences: 'True collectors, I had come to believe, live not in the text but in the margins and the front flyleaves.' 'Reading is one kind of pleasure; association is a deepening and enhancing of that pleasure.' 'Then I lay back on the black sheets of the bibliomaniac's unending bachelorhood.'

It won't be long, I suspect, before *In the Suicide's Library* becomes a modern cult classic in the field of bibliophily.

THE X-ACTO KNIFE IN E. FORBES SMILEY'S POCKET

The Map Thief

When E. Forbes Smiley III, one of New York's top dealers in rare maps, walked into Yale's Beinecke Rare Book and Manuscript Library on 8 June 2005, no one suspected he was there to steal some of their most valued maps. Smiley wasn't feeling well that morning and when he pulled out his handkerchief to cough into, he didn't notice that the X-acto knife he had brought along to razor out the maps had slipped out and was now lying on the floor. A little later, he stepped out for a coffee, pondering his plans. The London Map Fair was about to begin and, ill as he was, he needed to be there: map collectors from all over gather there to buy and sell and trade in antiquarian maps.

While he had been away, the atmosphere at the library had suddenly altered: one of the librarians had discovered the X-acto knife and now the library had summoned a police detective to watch Smiley on his return. Watching the map dealer on the security camera, the detective noticed Smiley fidgeting with his blazer pocket. Why was he even wearing a jacket on this warm summer morning? Smiley was oblivious to all this, and simply kept requesting more antiquarian books that had valuable maps bound or inserted in them. When he finally left the library, the detective let him walk a little distance before he asked to look inside his briefcase. It contained several maps. 'I'm a collector,' Smiley explained. 'These maps are mine.'

But the librarians were unable to say with certainty if these maps had come from their collection. It was only when the detective asked him to empty his blazer pocket that they found the tiny map identified at once by the staff: a map from a 1631 book with the only known portrait of explorer John Smith, who had been the first to depict the coastline of New England with some accuracy. Rarely does this map surface in the market, and when it does, it can sell for anything from $50,000 to $100,000. When Smiley had examined the book earlier that morning, he had noticed the tiny map had already come loose from the book, its 400-year-old glue having given way. And when he felt sure no was watching, he had quickly slipped the map into his blazer pocket.

Michael Blanding's *The Map Thief* (Gotham Books, 2014) tells the full story of Forbes Smiley's exploits, introducing us to the subculture of rare map dealers and collectors. He also lays out for us cartographic stories of these map makers and explorers with notes on the origins of the first maps of the New World. When Smiley finally confessed, it was to stealing 97 rare maps, amounting to 3 million dollars. This, however, as Blanding points out, is not the whole story: several libraries are still missing some 250 maps. Was Smiley not telling the court everything or was this the work of other rare map thieves?

Forbes Smiley's passion for maps had enabled him to become an expert; being able to recognize different versions of the same map from subtle variations had been his way of getting some edge in the field. Even though he had made a lot of money, and had become a successful (though controversial) antiquarian dealer, he had also spent lavishly, overextending himself, and was now in a financial hole. He told Blanding that it was probably in 2002 that he began stealing maps, and found he could not stop because of a desperate need for funds to pay for his luxury home in Martha's Vineyard.

How could this have happened? How is it that dealers and collectors failed to recognize stolen material? Blanding says that the world of rare map dealing and collecting is not like the art world where there are no copies or few copies; in the map world, copies of the same rare maps are plenty, with tiny variations making it difficult to establish provenance. People can bring in a rare map to a dealer or collector and claim that it belonged to their grandfather or that it had been in their family for generations.

Map collectors, at least a good majority of them, don't want to ask too many questions about where a rare map came from if they were getting it for something lower than the market price, or if the competition to possess a rare map is intense and this suspicious copy becomes their only chance to own one. Another questionable tradition (the ethics of which are still debated) in the antiquarian market is breaking up an atlas (or a rare book) and selling individual maps to make more money.

The Map Thief is a diverting tale when it deals with Forbes Smiley and the map dealer's rarefied world, but when it backgrounds, and in some detail too, the cartographic history of maps dealing in Americana, it is not as gripping (as the publisher's rather blurby title claims): not every reader wants to know so much about rare American maps and the collectors who obsessively pursue them.

RARE BOOK RING

Thieves of Book Row

I have been eagerly waiting for the next grand tale of biblio-thievery and biblio-detectives from Travis McDade, rare book curator and author of *The Book Thief* (Praeger, 2006). In *Thieves of Book Row: New York's Most Notorious Rare Book Ring and the Man Who Stopped It* (Oxford University Press, 2013), McDade uncovers a thrilling true story about Manhattan's fabled block of second-hand bookshops, that has never been told before. Known as Book Row, it was packed with booksellers from the 1890s to the 1960s, and stretched as long as six blocks up of Fourth Avenue. The bookshops and booksellers here have been justly celebrated in several accounts, the fullest to be found in *Book Row: An Anecdotal and Pictorial Account of the Antiquarian Book Trade.* But we've heard little about the nefarious practices (ranging from the unethical to the criminal) that some book dealers resorted to on Book Row and McDade's finely researched account – 'pieced together from hundreds of parts' – tells the whole story.

In particular, it concerns a rare book-theft ring run by a crooked book dealer, a stolen copy of Edgar Allan Poe's rarest book and the biblio-detective who determinedly pursued the book thieves and their rare book loot. The opening half of the book is a rich and detailed evocation of Book Row: the books were everywhere, from the disordered piles of volumes stacked up to the doorway and the windows (making passage inside impassable) to overflowing from rickety tables displayed on sidewalks, and 'in the very air people breathed: the dusty tomes of old books exhaled from each open door'. Some of them were 'notoriously scruffy book caves where occasional worthwhile first editions and elusive titles awaited searching and patient eyes', while others were 'specialised, antiquarian enterprises operated by highly knowledgeable bookmen'.

In those days, rare books in libraries were casually found on open stacks, giving any patron access to handling them and even walking off with them. This trust that libraries showed began to be abused and exploited by several book theft rings, chief among them run by two men, Charles Romm and Harry Gold. They would recruit book thieves from among the homeless and unemployed in New York and Boston – the bums on Bowery, the homeless in Central Park sitting around fires in the winter nights, the drunks sprawled outside taverns. The training was simple: they had to memorize a list of the most wanted and desired rare books held in libraries, case the joint, and pull off the heist. The top men in the ring were trained for more intricate jobs post heist: removing all traces of library markings.

This was a fairly delicate, even sophisticated, operation, and often Gold did not trust anyone else but himself with it, especially where a high-spot item was concerned. They had to remove stamps, ink and embossing (or perforation), and the Romm and Gold biblio-klept gang found all sorts of ways to erase such markings, from using bleach, hot iron and a painstaking process of filling back the holes in perforations.

Gold would then fence the books to various dealers and collectors. McDade points out that though many dealers on Book Row did not join the ring, they turned a blind eye to what was happening; some colluded by buying these copies, even though they could spot faint traces of library markings.

Gold has his eye on a few highly desirable rare books from the New York Public Library, one of the few libraries that had wised up to the rare book ring and had started to hold rare books in supervised closed stacks. Gold now ropes in a new man, much younger than his old hands, to plan a heist at NYPL's rare book room. Samuel Raynor Dupree is a desperate young man eager to impress Gold, and his first job is to make himself a familiar, trustworthy patron to the rare book librarians guarding these treasures, so that they would leave him alone, even just for a few minutes, so he can dash off with Poe's slim volume of poetry, *Al Aaraaf* (1829), which had become scarcer than the anonymously published *Tamerlane*. Gold and his gang, after much planning, were poised to pull off the job: on a 'cold Saturday in January 1931' Dupree walks up to the librarian and requests the book.

How the rest of the tale unfolds and how the library detective, William Bergquist, gave them chase, should be discovered in McDade's own intricate narrative as the item makes its way up and down Manhattan's rare book world, drawing in dealers, librarians and collectors. McDade's primary interest in researching and writing up these cases of biblio thieves – whether in *The Book Thief*, or his blog posts or in this new work – is to survey and record the security and legal aspects of rare book theft.

His first book spent considerable time on following the legal trial of a notorious book thief and his court sentencing, the first instance of a weighty and serious verdict handed to a book thief. In *Thieves of Book Row*, he devotes a large part of the book to tracing the various security measures libraries began devising after repeated rare book thefts. In the figure of the biblio-detective, Bergquist, and the rare book librarians who aided him, he investigates the methods library detectives employ to outwit and nab the wiliest of book thieves.

RAZORING OUT BIRD-BOOKS

Torn from Their Bindings

In the 1980s, a failed art print dealer named Robert Kindred raided several university libraries and stole hundreds of rare, often beautiful, lithographic plates. They would be carefully ripped out of these highly valued journals and plate books, many of them hand-coloured, and then Kindred would sell them to other print dealers and collectors. One hot summer day, Kindred, along with his partner Green, got into a car loaded with book theft tools such as razor blades, glass cutters and flashlights, and began a spree of looting from American libraries across several states as though they were the Bonnie and Clyde of rare book thieving. They had a map with college libraries circled, a list of books and journals they were targeting, and the criminal greed to mutilate and deface beautiful books for their profit.

Torn from Their Bindings (University Press of Kansas, 2018) I feel, is Travis McDade's best book. Here investigation, research and narrative are nimbly balanced, making for crisp, provocative reading. Kindred and Green's first hit was at Texas A&M library. In the '80s, it was not unusual for libraries to have even valuable books on open stacks (rather than being locked up in Special Collections) and this allowed both of them to comfortably choose a table, stack the journals and books they had targeted, and leisurely razor out the plates from their bindings. The plates, at least at the start, were mainly from what's known in the trade as 'bird-books'.

The first journal, *Ibis*, had been bound so tightly, it was difficult for Kindred to get to the gutter, and he found himself several times coming close to cutting into a plate. Once, when he thought he nearly had it, he realized cutting more would mean chopping off the beak of the bird in the plate, so he let that go. The amount of detail about what Kindred cut out and what he left in is amazing, because McDade, after all these decades, is able to tell us which plates he took, why he took them, and which ones he spared. At their second stop, Rice University, they got fed up of using the blades which had blunted and began just tearing out the plates. When Kindred spotted a book where the plates were all highly saleable, he simply ripped off the covers and put the whole book into his bag to steal away.

As usual with McDade, the tale is very well told with a focus on the ethical and legal consequences of such wanton pillaging of heritage art. One of his aims in writing about several rare book thefts is to inform us of how often such book crimes occur, as well as make a plea for book preservation, the tightening and updating of library security, and raising the bar on punishment for these crimes that in the past used to be treated with a light court sentence, either of community service or minor fines. But it occurs to me that quite outside of all these concerns, an ironic moral dilemma may confront the writer of such true accounts of rare book theft, as well as me, the reader of such accounts: how outraged can we be about the exploits of rare book thieves if we are also enthralled by them?

The authors of books about true rare book crimes – whether it is McDade in *Torn from Their Bindings,* Allison Bartlett in *The Man Who Loved Books Too Much* or Michael Blanding in *The Map Thief* – shape their narratives to hook us into the exploits of these thieves, making us feel the tension, excitement and desire that the thief feels, much in the same way Hitchcock made us sweat along with the murderer as he went about planning his crime. Having enjoyed the narrative, partly relishing the blow-by-blow account of a book theft in progress, how to make a sudden switch and cry foul, and express just outrage at such pillaging?

That's the shared quandary for the reader of such accounts as well – how to be censorious of something you've just enjoyed reading about? There's actually a blurb on the jacket of *Torn from Their Bindings* that says it reads 'like an Elmore Leonard novel'. What about all those heist movies – don't we cheer the thieves on, even though they are clearly the bad guys in the story, making us unwitting (or perhaps not all that unwitting) co-conspirators? Book collectors, book dealers and rare book librarians will, in a flash, condemn rare book thieves and forgers but still enjoy reading about their notorious exploits, in both fiction and non-fiction.

I wonder if the authors who research and document these real-life book crime stories should not at some point in their writings say something about how we all get caught up in this vicariously – as appalling as it is – and that it can't just be moral outrage we feel at the end of it, since we seem to be a bit guilty of enjoying it; or at least deriving some pleasure from it. Or else, why write it that way? And why expect us to be absorbed and entertained by it?

PART SIX

A TYPOGRAPHICAL ADVENTURE

[OR MORE ADVENTURES IN COLLECTING]

CHASING HANDMADE PAPER

Collecting fine press books – that is, finely printed letterpress books – the first thing a collector looks for is the kind of paper they are printed on. It does sometimes feel like the ultimate resting place for a bibliophile's interest in the printed book is handmade paper, and other fine papers: mould-made, marbled or decorated. All the things that first engaged you about the arts of the book – type, typography, and letterpress printing – seem just the tasty crumbs leading to that deep dish: beautiful paper. At least it has been so for me, as I doggedly pursue books, broadsides, pamphlets and keepsakes printed on handmade and mould-made paper: Amalfi, Barcham Green, Arches, Twinrocker, Tovil, Frankfurt, Fabriano, Rives, Umbria, Roma, Magnani, Ingress, Kelmscott handmade, Natsume, Goyu, Kochi and Hosho. And just as seductive are those marbled, decorated and paste papers used as endpapers and covers for books and keepsakes.

Why, sometimes I think I may even reach a point when I could forsake type and just let my fingertips and eyes revel in an unprinted sheet of a handmade Hosho or a dampened mould-made Johannot. Or find great pleasure in various samples of marbled paper. Take the example of Sidney Berger and his wife Michèle Cloonan, bibliophiles and paper historians so fascinated by decorated paper that they have assembled thousands of lovely examples from all over the world, making it the richest collection of beautiful papers in private hands.

Collecting fine press books, the papers they are printed on is the first thing to look for. Or at least that's what I do. I know for a lot of fine press collectors, those smooth Zerkall wove or Basingwork parchment papers are just as acceptable as letterpress printing surfaces, but I require a laid or textured paper, whether handmade or mould-made. Some mould-made papers, particularly from Europe, when dampened for printing, are lovely to the touch: Rives, Johannot, Hahnemühle, Fabriano, Arches and Frankfurt. The kind of decorated/marbled papers I am fond of, are also those done from papers with some texture and character to them.

One of my favourite things to collect for my book arts collection are specimen or sample books and folders of handmade papers issued over the years by the great paper companies and mills. Specimens of various handmade papers from a paper distribution company or a paper mill will be gathered into a book or a folder, and either sold or given away to printers, typographers and rare book institutions. The most bespoke of these paper sample books have risen in price in the rare book market, both for the beauty of the famed papers contained in them, and their rarity.

The best stuff, though, as far as paper specimens go, is from the Japan Paper Company, issued mainly as folders or swatch books. My greatest find is about thirty paper specimens from the Japan Paper Company containing the most beautiful handmade papers designed and printed by celebrated printers and typographers such as Bruce Rogers, Goudy, John Fass – well, name a fine printer from that time, and he's there. I had managed, over the years, to get various swatch books from

Japan Paper Company, put out between 1910 to 1940. One of the most prized is a swatch book of the best Oriental papers, showing a range of Japanese handmade paper for printing and decoration.

The folders the Japan Paper Company put out contained between eight to ten to twelve broadside sheets inside. However, there were just a few that contained as many as forty. That's the one I wanted, and after years of looking for it, and giving up on ever finding it, it suddenly surfaced one day. These broadsides on these beautiful papers, printed in many colours, were more ephemeral than most other ephemera, such as keepsakes or pamphlets. They were, for the most part, given away to their clients and their survival depended on printers, designers and bibliophiles recognizing their value and preserving them.

The more generous folders have become scarce in the market. While you can, on occasion, spot in the rare book market a few folders issued much later, after the Japan Paper Company became the Stevens Nelson Paper Company, it is hard to come by even one from those good old Japan Paper Company days. The Japan Paper Company was one of the leading importers of handmade papers for fine press editions. When Harrison G. Elliott became the company's manager, he greatly expanded the firm's scope, distributing papers from fifteen European and Asian countries.

I was astonished then, and very excited, to see a listing on Biblio for what looked like the original Japan Paper Company folder, containing up to thirty specimens. There were images posted of some of the specimens, and they had my pulse racing. The opening specimen was beautiful indeed, printed in orange and black and designed by Frederic Goudy on

Kelmscott paper. Another specimen on Tuscany handmade was even more gorgeous, done by Bruce Rogers, using the same vermillion red borders that frame his famous title page for the *Fra Luca*-Grolier book. Others mentioned in the description (though without images) had been done by John S. Fass.

I called the bookseller directly, did not get him and left a message. An hour later, he called back. After I'd said I was calling about the Japan Paper Company papers, he expressed surprise: 'Oh! That's something I just listed not even like an hour ago'. I asked for more details, which he was pleased to give, fetching the folder of specimens and going over them with me. I could not resist asking how he'd come by it. 'A couple of weeks ago, a book scout who brings me some nice and unusual things now and then, brought this in saying he's not seen one of these in a long time. I gave him a good price for it, because it did look like an uncommon item.'

He'd priced it at $300, and gave it to me for $275. Honestly, it was a good price. The same thing would have been at least $800–$900 with more prominent book arts dealers. Since I bought this a couple of years ago, I have never seen another one of them again, not even with a smaller number of samples. Spotting it as quickly as I did was sheer luck. Some of the 'handmades' that I did not have before, were present here: Invicta, Arnold unbleached, Crown and Sceptre, Van Gelder, Papier de rives, Hayle, Eltham, Highclere and Whitchurch.

There is one extraordinary paper sample book, however, that is not scarce, is fairly inexpensive and is a veritable treasure trove – a must-have if you're a collector just getting started with fine printing. *Specimens: A Stevens-Nelson Paper Catalogue* produced in 1953 is a collection of more than hundred beautiful handmade and mould-made papers in the world. The paper specimens are not blank, but are all printed and illustrated by many noted printers and designers. The papers were supplied by different paper mills from Europe and Japan.

Several copies of *Specimens* are always listed online on ABE, eBay, Biblio and even Amazon. The prices range from $75 to $350, with the lesser-priced copies usually lacking the price list or the slipcase, or with wear to the binding. But they are all the same edition, and as long as all the papers are present (they are numbered, so you can tell if specimens have been removed) and are in fine condition inside, you can buy the lower-priced copies. The book is a one-of-a-kind opportunity to own some of the most beautiful papers in the world, designed and printed by some truly fine printers and presses. Many of these papers are not available anymore because the mills have closed or they don't make them anymore, making this book a precious record of what were once the finest paper specimens.

Stevens-Nelson, formerly the Japan Paper Company, had, since 1903, supplied printers with fine papers from European and Japanese mills. For this project, *Specimens,* they roped in some of the world's most accomplished fine printers and designers to make use of their handmade and mould-made papers. Behind each printed specimen is a colophon with the name of the paper, its colour, weight, size and the designer and printer involved in printing the specimen.

The foreword, beautifully designed by Bruce Rogers and printed in red and black, says, 'This is a catalogue of the finest printing and art papers in the world. They are made by hand, or by hand in conjunction with the mould machine, in a tradition that is centuries old—not because hand work is quaint or romantic, but simply because man has not been able to devise any other means of manufacture that will produce such superlative qualities.'

I have to admit I don't like about half the designing and printing in it – too much colour for me, with an emphasis on the graphic arts in printing than the typographic, and much of it for commercial purposes. It was meant to be a trade sample for printing houses, and the concept behind such a book was to show what the Stevens-Nelson Paper corporation had in stock, or could make available from Europe and Japan. Everyone who has a copy of *Specimens*, I'm sure have their own favourites among the samples. What I enjoy most in the book are the specimens with just lettering and ornament: the handsome opening pages designed by Bruce Rogers in red and black on Tuscany handmade paper, declaring that these are the finest printing papers in the world, is quite the favourite.

The most interesting 'paper specimen' book in my collection actually qualifies also as a unique, one-of-a-kind copy – an Englishman named Jim Terzies, who was a school teacher and a calligrapher with a deep interest in handmade papers, created a personal book of Barcham Green papers. A history of the famous papermaking mill, F.J. Head (that later became Barcham Green) was published as a pamphlet in 1975. Terzies wanted to put a fine binding on it, but it proved too slight for such casing. He then got the idea to bind in with the pamphlet numerous samples of F.J. Head/Barcham Green papers in his collection – and that's exactly what he did, with a quarter-vellum spine and decorated boards. He had the instantly recognizable watermark of F.J. Head papers tooled in gilt on the spine, and a calligraphic paper label written out by him announced the title.

Apart from the paper samples, many of which are not in

production today, the most attractive aspect of this book is a two-page handwritten note by Terzies, that is tipped-in at the front. It's lovely for being entirely done in an elegant calligraphic hand. I acquired this from Frederic Shearer of Entropy Books, who was himself extremely fond of this book. He was loath to let it go, and has told me more than once how he'd love to have it back.

A NOTE ON PRIVATE PRESSES AND FINE PRINTING

When William Morris began the Kelmscott Press in 1891, he revived the art of fine printing, and began the modern fine press movement. He took for his model and inspiration the earliest printed books, incunables, printed by the master printers of the fifteenth century, and made books superior to anything anyone had ever produced. He designed his own typeface (what would come to be called a proprietary typeface, which is a design belonging solely to the press for its use), ordered a paper handmade to his exacting specifications, imported a black ink that would have the glossy depth seen only in incunables, and designed rich, elaborate ornamental borders to frame the pages of text. The type was handset and printed on an Albion iron hand press.

The books from the Kelmscott Press are some of the highest achievements in modern fine printing; as collectors and book dealers and typophiles have pointed out: by focusing so fiercely, wholeheartedly and sumptuously on making the printing of a single book as fine as it could ever be, William Morris produced books that were superior to anything printed before, including the books of the great master printers of the past he so admired!

For over a century and a half before Morris decided to

make books this way, books had stopped being printed by hand. Printing had become commercial and mechanized, foundry typefaces were few and very worn, there was little impression of type into the paper, the machine-made paper had no character or quality, the paper was printed dry, the ink was substandard – in short, poor material and lacking fine craftmanship.

One day, in 1888, when attending a lantern slide talk given by typographic scholar Emery Walker at an Arts and Crafts meeting, Morris felt galvanized by what he was looking at: Walker had photographed letters – more precisely – type fonts from the books of early printers such as Nicolas Jenson, and had blown them up in proportion to better reveal the proportions, elegance and beauty of these founts.

Something clinched for Morris here, in this moment, and a project that had been brewing in his mind and heart for a long time, came to the fore: the idea of starting a private press that would once again print such beautiful books from fine type, fine paper and fine presswork, embellished by ornamental decoration. Emery Walker turned out to be his neighbour in Hammersmith, and Morris urged Emery to walk back home with him that evening.

On the way, without wasting time, Morris broached the subject of designing a new typeface modelled perhaps on the Jenson roman letter and Walker, an enthusiast of fine printing, was spurred into action. And soon, the two were poring over examples of typography, design and letterforms in the early-printed books they both had in their possession as collectors.

Morris's deeply held notion about what would make all the difference to making a fine book has proven correct till today: the key was using superior materials to make a book, to not compromise on what went into bookmaking. By this, he primarily had in mind the handmade paper, the ink, the type, the hand press and the binding. Morris had the firm of Joseph Batchelor make a handmade paper exactly to his specifications; after trying out various inks, he settled for one imported from Germany; next, sturdy Albion iron hand presses were bought and his final touch was perhaps the element that was key to the revival of modern fine printing: a proprietary typeface – that is, designing his own type, and having it cut in metal for the use of his press, which he now named Kelmscott after the manor he lived in by the Thames river.

Morris named his first proprietary type Golden; the punches for the type were cut by Edward Prince, a master of that craft. The masterwork from the press was the *Chaucer*, which Burne-Jones, the artist who made the wood engravings for the book, called 'a pocket cathedral', for so magnificent it was in appearance and feeling. Morris died in 1896, so six years was all he had at his press, yet more than fifty fine books were printed at the Kelmscott Press, some of which were richly decorative.

You can imagine the excitement, joy and admiration the Kelmscott books must have created among bibliophiles and typophiles then – it inspired many in England, Europe and America to begin their own private presses. While the Kelmscott Press is arguably the most celebrated private press in the history of fine printing, two other English fine presses fairly contemporaneous to it, are just as admired and collected: the Doves Press and the Ashendene Press. These three are often known as the Triple Crown among private presses.

T.J. Cobden-Sanderson, the founder and printer of the Doves Press, turned Morris's notion of the Ideal Book into his own deeply personal notion of what the Book Beautiful should be. It would not be decorative, it would not have colour; what would speak for his books was just fine paper, fine type and fine presswork. Bare. Austere. Pure. It is amazing, in retrospect, given Morris's decorative influence in fine printing, that Cobden-Sanderson should have dreamt of such simplicity to create his Book Beautiful.

He took from Morris the importance of superior material, fine design and impeccable presswork, but his vision of how a fine book should look typographically was the opposite of Morris's. Cobden-Sanderson, also a fellow resident of Hammersmith (what a hotbed of hot metal type Hammersmith was, as John Dreyfus once pointed out), had flirted with many professions, including being a lawyer, and finally in his forties, became a master bookbinder.

And though his work was admired widely and greatly, he felt his true calling lay elsewhere. A mystic at heart, he found it really lay in being a fine press printer. He had already demonstrated that within just a year, he could become the finest bookbinder in England, and in a huge leap and a brief apprenticeship later, he became a master printer. Partnering with typographer Emery Walker, Cobden-Sanderson founded his Doves Press in 1900. Eschewing decoration, colour, ornamentation and illustration, Cobden-Sanderson printed his books with only the proportion and arrangement of fine type on fine paper to make them beautiful.

And stunningly, he accomplished it, in book after book. At times, there was a hint of red in the minimally used rubricated calligraphic initials (by master lettering artist Edward Johnston) or paragraph marks; otherwise, it was just black type on paper with impeccable presswork.

The key to the beauty of the unadorned Doves Press books is attributed to the typeface designed by Emery Walker and Cobden-Sanderson, based on a typeface used by Nicolas Jenson. After a close study of this roman face, Cobden-Sanderson and Walker again had Edward Prince cut the punches for their type. It was called, simply, the Doves type. Now, a lot of credit has been given to Emery Walker for the success of the Doves type, but as fine press scholars have pointed out, the credit should also go to the types used by the early printers, the drawings of the type by Percy Tiffin, and the punches cut by the hand of Prince.

It is important to note this because later in the life of the Doves Press, there erupted the now infamous feud between Walker and Cobden-Sanderson over the ownership of the Doves type. Initially, the agreement was that the type and matrices would revert to Walker after Cobden-Sanderson closed the press, but as he felt more and more frustrated with Walker's slim involvement in the day-to-day workings of the press, as well as having to endure constant criticism of his design and presswork, the printer decided secretly to not give it to Walker.

But how to keep it from Walker (or his family) after he was dead and gone? One night, it came to him: destroy all the Doves type and matrices by chucking them into the Thames river. And so he did, years later, night after night, throw them from the Hammersmith bridge into the river below. Walker and his family were furious when they found out, and well, it got nasty from there on.

Because of this, the Doves type is sui generis – you can never find anything printed from this type in any other book except a Doves Press book! Cobden-Sanderson's reasoning was not as petty as not letting Walker have it because he found him indifferent to the chores at the press (such as going over proofs) but that he wanted to prevent the use of the Doves type in the hands of a printer or press that would not have the ideals of the Doves Press at heart, and would use the type poorly or in ways that would violate the purity of a Doves Press book.

Fascinated by this feud, this controversy, I read many accounts of this, as well as letters that flowed back and forth between all parties concerned, which by now were Sydney Cockerell and St. John Hornby. I think it is in Marianne Tidcombe's definitive book on the Doves Press that a clear picture emerges, allowing you to take a side. For most of fine press history, bibliophiles sided with Walker, and initially, so did I – nobody tires of pointing out how instrumental Emery Walker was in the design of proprietary typefaces for the Kelmscott Press, the Doves Press, the Ashendene Press and the Cranach Press.

But once the press had got going, and the books were being printed by Cobden-Sanderson with the help of a few pressman, including J.H. Mason, the gifted compositor, it does look more and more like it was the genius of Cobden-Sanderson that sustained the integrity and beauty of the Doves books. Walker would look over the shoulder of the printer and dismiss the layout as 'Just won't do'. But there's ample evidence that Walker was often wrong – in fact, the things that he rejected in the Doves books are the very things today we celebrate them for. One instance will do: the famous long calligraphic initial in red by Edward Johnston that opens the Doves Bible, 'In the Beginning...', where the I extends all the way down the whole page – if E.W. had had his way, that would have been nicked.

When Edward Johnston, the lettering artist, sent Cobden-Sanderson that page, the I was in red and perhaps five-lines long – Mason then drew the initial a little further down, and Cobden-Sanderson, standing next to him, in a flash saw it all, and drew the initial all the way down the page, and both of them felt it worked wonderfully. Walker looking at it later, dismissed it. Luckily for us, Cobden-Sanderson did not listen to him.

At the height of the feud, Sydney Cockerell, respected bookman, former secretary of the Kelmscott Press and a friend to both men, tried to mediate. In a note to Cobden-Sanderson, Cockerell condescendingly reminded him how much the private press community owed Walker for his printing expertise. Cobden-Sanderson wrote back a marvellous reply that gets to the truth of all this: he points out that *this* is exactly the problem; that while Walker was resourceful with printing equipment and full of typographic knowledge, he was *not a fine printer*.

He goes on to remark that Walker's expertise at the Doves was mostly traditional, working with and passing on what he had known from his study of the early master printers and their typographic ideas. While he, Cobden-Sanderson, designed and printed a page in a way that he felt was typographically sound and excellent – he experimented, but Walker, who had no actual experience in fine printing – went by the book. I don't know if Cockerell was suitably chastened, but I hope he was. Like every fine press enthusiast, I admire and like Walker, but as Colin Franklin once observed, 'Walker has suffered from a good reputation', so perhaps casting some doubt on his behaviour during the controversy (such as suing Cobden-Sanderson's wife, Anne) may not be such a bad thing for his reputation. Add to this the story Brooke Crutchely, university printer at Cambridge, heard from J.H. Mason (but dismissed it as uncharacteristic of the man): that Walker's breakfast consisted only of a large onion, and his reputation can only fare better.

Among all the classic private presses, it is the printing style and aesthetic of the Doves Press that would become an influential model for future modern fine presses who felt more empathy for Cobden-Sanderson's purely typographic books, for his idea of the Book Beautiful as being a finely proportioned page from a beautiful, legible type on a fine, crisp handmade paper.

The Ashendene Press is perhaps my favourite press among the classic British private presses. The books from this press were neither very austere nor very decorative. They had a nice balance of beautiful type, calligraphy, colour, illustrations and gilding. C.H. St. John Hornby, a fairly well-to-do bibliophile, began his press in 1895. He printed (with the help of a pressman) on an Albion hand press, on handmade paper from a lovely typeface designed and cut for his press that he named Subiaco, because it was based on a type from the fifteenth-century printers, Pannartz and Sweynheym, in the monastery at Subiaco. (In this, Emery Walker and Sydney Cockerel also helped.)

Here again was a private printer, an amateur with an unerring eye for design, typography and fine printing. The fact that each book from the press became more sought-after, becoming quickly oversubscribed on just being announced, should tell us Hornby was a born printer.

What I liked about the Ashendene books right away, is Hornby's use of many splendid calligraphic initials hand-coloured in red, blue, green and gold, that brings, as Colin Franklin said, 'gaiety' to the printing. The calligraphy, hand-colouring and gilding is the work of Graily Hewitt, another gifted lettering artist. The last book from the Ashendene Press (the fairly expensive purchase I made) was the bibliography. It has since become the go-to model for fine presses in constructing press bibliographies.

A second favourite from the classic English private presses for me is the Eragny Press. In fact, if I were asked to point to one press that truly fulfills the ideals of a private press, it would be this press of Lucien and Esther Pissarro. The Eragny Press is also more deeply personal than the Triple Crown presses. Lucien and Esther Pissarro were poor, struggling artists in London when they began their little press in 1894.

They printed books in small editions on handmade paper with fine type from a hand press, surrounding the text with initials and ornaments they designed, with illustrations Lucien engraved from wood blocks in five colours and gold. He had taught himself wood engraving, and then printing from a hand press. Esther, who helped with both, would later do most of the hand printing herself, even printing the initials, ornaments and wood blocks with meticulous craftmanship.

Through a long process of trial and error, rejecting hundreds of proof sheets, they figured out how to design, engrave and finely print their books. What's worth noting quickly here is that merely being an amateur printer doesn't make you a fine press printer, especially one that is enshrined in the history of fine printing as the Eragny Press is, as one of the most charming of the arts and crafts presses. Lucien took his craftmanship and artistry one step further when he and Esther mastered the use of gold leaf for their initials and wood engravings.

The papers were dampened for printing, and this made it particularly difficult to use gold as it stuck to the wet paper, but in the end, Esther and Lucien were such perfectionists, they mastered it. It is true, as Franklin points out in his *Private Presses*, that Lucien did not pioneer this technique of gold leaf on wood blocks; that the Japanese had been doing it for over a century. However, the books of the Pissarros at the Eragny Press were very different from those Japanese books – they were rooted in the ideals of the arts and crafts movement in England: handmade paper, hand-set metal type, initials and ornaments and borders, all of it printed on a hand press in two or more colours with wood-engraved illustrations printed directly from the block.

Another fetching quality of the Eragny Press is that it probably never made any profit, and just broke even, keeping them afloat while they worked on their next book. It was largely supported by Lucien's father, the impressionist painter Camille Pissarro, who didn't have much himself but gave what he could so the couple could go on printing their beautiful books. The proprietors of the Triple Crown presses, William Morris, John Hornby, and T.J. Cobden-Sanderson, were all well-to-do and did not look to the work of the press to financially support them.

But though these three presses began and ended as hobby presses where one prints for pleasure, they grew to be large presses, using the aid of pressmen, compositors and staff to produce impressive, stately fine press books which were often oversubscribed before publication, and usually turned a small profit. The Eragny Press, from the start, did not have the luxury of being a hobby press, and Lucien and Esther laboured at the press, hoping their books would turn in an income.

Marcella D. Genz, in her finely written and researched biography of the press, *A History of the Eragny Press,* reveals how while the couple accounted for what each book brought in, itemizing the expenses, what they never put in there was the cost of their artistry and labour – it was always just the cost of the materials and the expenses paid to binders. And thus, ironically, the hobby presses like Kelmscott and Ashendene became commercial in their output while the Eragny, which meant to be commercial, became the most private of private presses. Except for making their own paper and doing the binding, Lucien and Esther did every little scrap of work at the press.

The way the Eragny Press operated is one cherished notion of what a private press is; prior to them, another couple – actually, a family – was printing in this personal way at the Daniel Press. FAO Daniel, a dean of Oxford College, was printing in this private, personal press, many years before Morris. His wife and children joined him in printing charming little books from their home! Again, I have to emphasize: the Daniel Press has a place in the history of fine printing because they printed well, and are not reckoned with simply because they were amateurs.

The Eragny Press was only one private press among several from the 1850s to 1920s in Britain and America, that were part of an arts and crafts movement that had caught fire because of William Morris and his Kelmscott Press. Apart from Kelmscott, Doves, Ashendene and Eragny, there were other marvellous private presses in this period: the Vale Press, the Essex House Press, and just a little later, the Gregynog Press (which can count among its output some of the most beautiful books ever printed) and the Golden Cockerell Press, known for its fine use of wood-engraved illustrations.

Together, they raised the arts and crafts movement to glorious heights, taking you away from the mechanical to the handmade. A question that often comes up is if these books (which have become expensive to buy for no fault of their own, except that they were so finely crafted that their worth in the market has shot up) is whether they are meant to be just looked at and fondled and put away without being read. The artist-printers behind these books, every one of them, would be appalled and saddened if their books were meant only to be collected and not read. They made their books to be read. Well, I can tell you from experience that I do read my fine press books (with great care, of course), some of them several times over, and can also personally testify that these books, because of their physical *fineness*, intensify your pleasure of reading.

For the bibliophile, there is nothing quite like the experience of reading a favourite piece of text – whether poem, story, essay, or as in my case, something on the arts of the book – from a finely printed book. The pleasure doubles and reading in this way involves your senses as well.

William Morris loved reading, and it is with the hope that his books would be read with greater pleasure for also being beautiful in appearance and feeling, that he put so much into them. Cobden-Sanderson turned to printing only to make books in which the printing would be so fine, it would seduce you into reading. Hornby's books look so inviting, that one takes deep pleasure and satisfaction in reading a text printed by him.

How do these classic private presses fair in the market today? The Kelmscott Press books are probably the most expensive; the least expensive of Morris's books are still somewhere around $900–$1,200. The Kelmscott *Chaucer* is still the most prized private press book, the last copy on paper (not vellum) selling for $70,000. The big productions from the Ashendene are never less than $2,000 and go up to $12,000. The few pamphlets Hornby did for the press, like the *Chronological Handlist,* can be gotten for $200. The Eragny Press, for the colour wood engraving and elaborate borders, are all the rage, as well as growing increasingly scarce, and can range from $500 to $15,000. The Doves Press, no doubt for the simplicity and severity of its purely typographical book, all done in one type, mostly black and white, with limp vellum covers, are $200 to $2,000, with the great book from the press, the Doves Bible in five folio volumes, worth $22,000.

Vale and Essex House books can all begin at $75 and go up to $500. The Gregynog Press books, however, for their sumptuous productions with wood engravings, hand-coloured and gilded initials, and bound finely at the press, have varying prices, depending on the kind of fine binding (from the press's own bindery, or custom-bound or a commissioned binding from a designer binder) that each copy comes with.

One other element, apart from fine typefaces, in these English private presses that developed into a fine art form, was wood engraving, which these presses used a lot in their productions. Many accomplished wood engravers emerged in this period and took engraving on a boxwood to new and great heights. Among them were Gwen Reverat, Joan Hassall, Blair Hughes Stanton, Eric Gill, Reynolds Stone, Eric Ravilious, Agnes Miller Parker and Tirzah Garwood, to name just a few.

Master lettering artist and calligrapher Edward Johnston revived calligraphy and lettering; his students Graily Hewitt, Alfred Fairbanks and Florence Kingsford further embellished the craft.

Bibliophile societies like the Roxburghe Club, the Grolier Club, the Caxton Club, The Typophiles and The Book Club of California, promoted the study of books as artistic and historical objects, and encouraged fine bookmaking by commissioning fine press printers and hosting exhibitions of fine books.

The next wave of arts and crafts printing happened in America between the 1890s and 1920s, when many small presses inspired by Morris and his books produced highly decorated handcrafted books. The better presses from this period made some exquisite books and added an element that even Morris had just stopped short of using in his books: hand illumination. Morris loved illumination, and perhaps if he had lived longer, may have introduced illumination to the Kelmscott books. (Then again, perhaps not!) The illumination and hand-colouring in the Cranbrook Press and the Philosopher Press is enchanting, while a press like the Elston Press made typographically sound books.

Around the same period, but going further than the 1920s, several giants of typography, design, calligraphy and papermaking emerged in America: Bruce Rogers, Dard Hunter, Frederic Goudy, and W.A. Dwiggins. Each in their own way, took fine bookmaking to exalted heights. A singular achievement here, a watershed moment for fine printing, is Bruce Roger's creation of his Centaur type, perhaps the most stately and legible typeface yet designed. The other significant development was the revival of hand papermaking by Dard Hunter.

Soon, across the Atlantic, in England, Stanley Morison would be instrumental in getting the English Monotype company to revive classic typefaces (that were getting more and more worn) and cast them anew, while creating more new and modern typefaces, such as Eric Gill's Perpetua.

In Europe, too, there were accomplished printers, presses and type designers. The Cranach Press and the Bremmer Press in Germany, the Officina Bodoni in Italy, the renowned hand press operated by the scholar-printer Giovanni Mardersteig, the exquisite calligraphic metal typefaces of Jan Van Krimpen in Holland, and Hermann Zapf in Germany, who would go on to design some of the finest types of the twentieth century.

SPECIMEN LEAVES

One of the first tips an accomplished collector of fine press books will offer a collector just starting out is, 'if you can't afford the books from the great private presses, collect whatever ephemera you can from these presses because they are priced modestly'. This can range from prospectuses, announcements and keepsakes to trial pages, proofs and specimen leaves from a press you admire or want to have examples of in your collection. Often, as fellow fine press collectors who've gotten ahead of you are eager to point out, a prospectus or announcement from a private press will be printed on the same fine paper the book is printed on, and may even contain an original wood engraving printed directly from the block.

I took this to heart and began scouring for ephemera from the fine presses and printers I was beginning to be so captivated by. I didn't dare begin with the classic presses (Kelmscott, Doves, Ashendene, Eragny, Gregynog, Essex House, Vale) and focused instead on mid-twentieth-century and contemporary presses.

I remember well the first prospectus I bought for $25: from the Bird and Bull Press, a fine press I had become keen on because its printer, Henry Morris, had a special affinity for the book arts (which you'll recall is my collecting focus within fine press books) and would stubbornly print only unpublished manuscripts dealing with the arts of the book. The prospectus I bought was slightly special (and so priced a little more than most Bird and Bull prospectuses I was seeing on ABE): it was inscribed and signed by Morris to a standing order customer.

As a fan from India, I could hardly believe that I would so soon have a signed Bird and Bull item in my collection. As far as I could make out, none of the B&B prospectuses on sale had been signed by Henry. The prospectus was for *Nicolas Louis Robert and His Endless Papermaking Machine*, printed in red and black on Frankfurt mould-made paper. It had a title page, two pages of text, and the B&B printer's device. I ordered it, and when it arrived, I was a little aghast to see the lovely sheet had been folded once in the middle and mailed, leaving a sharp crease in the paper right down the centre.

I was incensed; it even took away the pleasure of seeing HM's long, half-page, handwritten inscription. I wrote to the bookshop, saying an antiquarian bookshop should know better than to fold a fine press prospectus just to make it fit into a smaller cover. They wrote back a patient note that they hadn't folded it, that it was the printer himself who had done that when he mailed it to his standing order client – most prospectuses, they went on to say, when first sent from the press, are folded to fit an envelope. They'd even said so in their ABE description.

I looked at the little ordering slip antiquarian booksellers include with your purchase, and there it was: 'folded once in the original mailing envelope'. I was somewhat mollified, though I failed to understand why a printer would go to the trouble of printing a fine prospectus only to crease it with a half fold. Later on, as I bought more fine press prospectuses, the fold became a common sight I got used to. I even began noticing how almost every bookseller description for a prospectus on sale noted a fold or a crease.

Many bookshops specializing in fine press stock, I discovered, would typically bundle a set of prospectuses from one press (or even from different fine presses) and sell them as one lot, and I found this a wonderful opportunity to acquire them in one go at attractive prices. A little bookshop in Wales had a clutch of Fleece Press prospectuses, and when I called the shop from Bengaluru one evening, the owner sounded pleased that someone had taken interest in them. When I finalized the sale, sending off a PayPal payment, she expressed delight that it would go to someone who seemed to really want them.

From Provan, I bought a dozen catalogues of the Whittington Press, a major contemporary private press from Britain that has continuously produced some of the most substantial private press books, with important text and illustrations, in a host of finely bound deluxe editions. From Colin Neville, a folder full of ephemera from the Incline Press, with the prospectus for *Harvesting Colour,* their celebrated book on Ann Muir's marbling skills, with an original tipped-in sample of a Muir marbled paper.

A small coup from my earliest forays into collecting was coming upon twelve very elaborate Gehenna Press prospectuses for $50. Usually just a single prospectus from this press can be listed for $25 because of the fine paper, type, printing aesthetic and original colour illustrations employed by this highly esteemed press of artist Leonard Baskin, and his revered pressman, Harold McGrath.

David Butcher has been such a thorough and scholarly collector of press books that he did an entire book on the pleasures of collecting private press prospectuses (titled *British Private Press Prospectuses, 1891-2001*) fittingly printed by the Whittingon Press in 2001, with the deluxe copies containing a portfolio of original prospectuses from many British private presses. In his introduction, Butcher points out that, 'the catalogues and prospectuses issued by private presses over the last century are not only beautiful examples of the work of each press, but also offer clues to the development of the titles they promote. Many are printed on handmade paper with illustrations from the original blocks and some are set in a proprietary typeface unique to the press... such prospectuses have become popular with collectors... because they can be a satisfying substitute for a book which is rare, difficult to obtain and often priced beyond the reach of most people...'

Butcher notes that prospectuses were another place for printers to use their range of type, otherwise seldom used for their books. Another reason to acquire them is to have something printed from the classic presses with their specimens of their famous proprietary type, such as Kelmscott's Golden or Troy type, Ashendene's Subiaco, Eragny's Brooks and of course, the most celebrated, the Doves type of T.J. Cobden-Sanderson and Emery Walker.

If wood engravings are your thing, some presses which specialized in engravings can offer a treasure trove in the form of their catalogues. Right from Gregynog to Golden Cockerel to Whittington, you can come across one fine engraving after another from the masters. Butcher points out that collectors look out especially for prospectuses that feature engravings that were done for the prospectus, and never appeared in the book itself.

From Butcher, I was pleased to find out that the first chronicler of the modern fine press movement, Will Ransom, had to be content with collecting prospectuses in place of books because he was really poor, and a struggling writer. He tried his best to make a living from what he loved doing, and it was a daily battle as his letters to the paper historian, Dard Hunter, reveal.

After I'd had my fill of prospectuses from contemporary private presses, the desire grew to acquire prospectuses from the four great arts and crafts British presses that began the modern fine press movement. But not one, not a single example, of a prospectus was I able to find from Kelmscott, Doves, Ashendene, and Eragny. Over the years, they had all been picked clean off the market. Any mention of a prospectus now from these presses on the antiquarian market was only in listings of books from these presses – that is, the original prospectus for the book laid into it.

And that was scarce, too: to find a Kelmscott or Doves or Eragny Press book with the published prospectus or announcement for the book as issued originally from the press. At that time, when I was making a start with collecting, books from these highly sought-after and collected presses were (and still are) expensive, and well out of my buying range. If the book included the prospectus, dealers charged even more for such a 'complete' copy.

It turned out, though, that not finding (or being able to afford) prospectuses from these famous private presses turned me on to something else that excited me more: original specimen pages from these presses. Once in a while, a rare book dealer will come across a disbound or damaged copy of a book from, say, the Kelmscott Press. The pages or leaves are then sold separately as specimen pages to give collectors a chance to acquire printing samples from this coveted press that cost only a tiny fraction of what the book would have sold for. (From such disbound leaves also came another fascinating kind of fine press book: the leaf book.)

These specimen leaves are priced variously, ranging from $50 to $500, depending on how attractive a particular leaf is – if ornamented with Morris designs or a whole signature than just a single leaf, it would cost a pretty penny. Remarkably enough, for a price, you can even acquire leaves from the Kelmscott *Chaucer* if you were willing to pay $500 for a leaf. I was able to very quickly acquire some loose specimen leaves from the Ashendene Press's *Don Quixote*, and the famous fine press *Hamlet* edition done by the Cranach Press with woodcuts by Edward Gordon Craig from William Reese Company. They had priced them according to the richness of the E. Gordon Craig woodcuts and the famous portions of the text. They started at $150 and went up from there.

The only press I have had difficulty finding original leaves or even some small ephemera samples from is the Eragny Press. Day by day, books from this once-underrated press grow in popularity and command higher and higher prices at auctions, book fairs and in catalogues. Collectors now find them the most charming and attractive of the great presses, and the one with the most colour and joy. The scholar-collector David Chambers has repeatedly noted how Lucien and Esther Pissarro's work is the only classic British press he was drawn to, and that to his mind, Eragny was the press to be collected assiduously. He himself had been lucky once, as a young collector, to have come upon a small 'pile' of them in a London bookshop and had been able to buy them cheaply since Eragny was not as highly collected then as the Triple Crown presses – Kelmscott, Doves and Ashendene.

I regret, then, that I didn't buy something from a stash of Eragny Press Christmas and New Year cards that Sophie Schneideman Rare Books and Prints had on sale in 2018. The prices were admittedly steep for ephemeral items, but such things done by hand from Lucien and Esther are scarce, though by the time I came around to thinking I would be better off getting at least one of them, they were all gone.

I still have the listing I had marked out from Sophie's catalogue: 'New Year card from Esther, Orovida and Lucien Pissarro, 1928. Eragny Press. Wood engraving by Lucien Pissarro Nativity in Cave with "All Best wishes for the New Year" from Esther, Orovida and Lucien Pissarro and addressed from The Brook. Hand printed in Brook type. 14 x 9 cms, wood engraving 6.5 x 7 cms. Printed on japon vellum. Very clean and crisp. A good impression of Lucien Pissarro's last wood engraving. Fern 275 notes that it was printed in an edition of twenty.'

Coming back to the leaves, I found something exciting from the Doves Press that later turned out to be not so exciting, after all! The bookseller I bought it from has to take a bit of the blame for this. I bought a four-page signature from that Cobden-Sanderson masterwork, the Doves Press Bible. This was temptation enough, but adding to the attraction of getting a piece of the most celebrated work from the Doves Press, was the bookseller's description informing you that the margins had notes in green ink either in the hand of the printer, Cobden-Sanderson, or the calligrapher, Edward Johnston.

The Doves Press of T.J. Cobden-Sanderson, an extraordinary craftsman, is noted for its austere beauty and immaculate presswork. When the books of every other arts and crafts press at that time – Kelmscott, Ashendene, Vale, etc. – had been highly decorative in nature, or had substantial colour, Cobden-Sanderson believed the ideal book was just fine typography, printed in black against white, with only a touch of red here and there from a very fine type cut for the press on dampened handmade paper with careful, harmonious composition and presswork.

The typographic scholar John Dreyfus famously remarked that the printing at the Doves Press was 'dangerously approaching perfection'. The red ink in the Doves Bible was employed for calligraphic initials done by the modern master and teacher of calligraphy, Edward Johnston, who revived the Lettering Arts in the twentieth century. And the four-leaf signature I bought, even had a few calligraphic initials. The description for this item noted that in the margin of the leaves were tiny handwritten inscriptions that resembled a marked-up copy of a trial page, possibly from the hand of the printer or the calligrapher.

This made me jump at the leaf, and after speaking to the dealer on the phone to confirm all this, I bought it, even though it cost twice what a Doves leaf would usually sell for. I was very pleased with it; first of all, there was the pure typographic beauty of the Doves printing, the renowned type to admire and study, and the elegant calligraphic initials to slowly take in and savour over the next few weeks. Much later too, whenever I would take it out to look at it again, I would feel a small thrill at possessing what was possibly a trial page or a proof from the famous Doves Bible, carrying in it the manuscript hand of the calligrapher or the printer.

A year later, I found out by chance what those hand-scribbled inscriptions were, when a pair of fine press printers did some sleuthing of their own when they bought a disbound copy of the Doves Bible and noticed red and green ink notations on several pages. John Randle, the printer at Whittington Press, and David Butcher (a frequent contributor to the press) were preparing their next big book from the press, *Pages From Presses*, an ambitious leaf book, with essays by Butcher on the five classic British private presses, each copy of the book to carry an original specimen leaf from each of the presses.

Randle and Butcher had been tipped off about a disbound copy of the Doves Bible, and they had bought the lot to be able to use it in *Pages from Presses*. When they noticed the red and green inscriptions, they were a bit baffled but it didn't take them long to realize what these notations were: this copy of the Doves Bible, this masterpiece of fine printing, the apple of every collector's eye, had once been used as a lectionary for daily service use in a church! The tiny inscriptions were abbreviations of chapter and verse to be read each Sunday. I was amused but also miffed that I had ended up paying a lot for my Doves leaf, and disappointed that the notations were not after all in the hand of either Cobden-Sanderson or Johnston. Quite recently, in early 2019, a collector and book dealer in the UK noticed the same marks in a Doves leaf that he had won in an auction, with a note from the auctioneer hazarding that 'this is most likely the hand of Cobden-Sanderson'.

Stanbrook Abbey prospectuses are some of the best to collect, in my opinion, because they can frequently stand in for the book. They are usually four pages or rather one sheet folded into two to make four sides, and contain the book's title page, a sample page from the book, sometimes a colour calligraphic initial or illustration, and the colophon. What more do you need? The early prospectuses were mostly on handmade papers (English mostly, and Japanese whenever the book called for it) and the typefaces used were always a joy to behold, usually being Romanee or Cancellaresca Bastarda, the beautiful faces of Jan Van Krimpen.

The Allen Press used European handmade papers or fine mould-made papers, and printed them damp. If you are lucky, there will be a small hand-coloured decoration, usually a leaf, done by Dorothy Allen. After hankering after two of their scarcest prospectuses – *Printing on a Handpress* and the *Allen Press Bibliography* – I found two copies of each, and couldn't resist acquiring both! Who knows when they'll surface again?

More worthwhile and more fun to collect are holiday greetings from fine press printers. I recently acquired four such lovely sets from a dealer, of Christmas and New Year greetings from Carol Blinn of Warwick Press, Jerry Kelly of Kelly Winterton Press, Kay and Virginia Kramer of the Printery, and Leonard Bahr of the Adagio Press. Plenty of colour in them, in the inks and the ornaments, and even in the papers. Several of them have a handwritten note or inscription in the cards.

One of the two prospectuses I am most proud of owning in my collection is the fairly scarce prospectus designed by Bruce Rogers for *Fra Luca de Pacioli*, printed in red and black on the same lovely Batchelor handmade paper the book was printed on. The prospectus shows Bruce Rogers's first setting of its famous, stunning decorative title page. The other prospectus is for *By His Own Labour*, the biography of papermaker Dard Hunter by Cathleen Baker, printed by Steve Miller of the Red Hydra Press. It's beautifully designed and impeccably printed in red and black on dampened Twinrocker handmade paper.

CHASING THE KELMSCOTT ALBION HAND PRESSES

The lure, the spell of the Kelmscott Press clung to me after I stumbled on fine press books, and I soon became steeped in its lore. One of the thrilling things I found out in the process is that after the press closed, the three Albion iron hand presses that Morris had used to print the Kelmscott books had been acquired by other printers who had then gone on to print books using these very same presses. I just had to have these books.

Somehow, the Albion hand press that had been used to print its finest book, the *Chaucer*, had travelled all the way to America from England, and the Goudys, Frederic and Bertha Goudy of the Village Press, who, like many fine printers of the day, had been galvanized by Morris and his press, had gone to the trouble of acquiring his press after Kelmscott ceased.

One of the very first books they printed on this Albion was *Three Essays* (1924), a book done on commission for the Grolier Club, a bibliophile society. Luckily, it was a copy I could afford. The book's colophon read: 'One of three hundred copies, printed on handmade paper at the Village Press by Frederic and Bertha Goudy, utilizing William Morris's Albion hand press.' This, for me, was electrifying: the same press that William Morris had used to print his Kelmscott Press books?

A single specimen leaf from the Kelmscott *Chaucer* in the market today, can range between $500 and $1,600. The way I saw it: I could, at $40, possess at least a book printed from one of the presses Morris had used (the actual operating and pulling of the hand presses was done by two skilled pressmen) by acquiring a copy of *Three Essays*, and to boot, pages designed and printed by Frederic Goudy, a Morris disciple and a master printer himself.

I ran my hands gently over the pages of *Three Essays*, taking in the press of letters into the handmade paper, mindful that the printing press these pages had flowed out of had also printed some of the most celebrated finely printed books in the annals of fine bookmaking more than a century ago. In a flash, I had, through this scruffy copy, been connected to a typographic tradition and aesthetic that went back to Goudy and his Village Press, Morris and his Kelmscott Press, and all the way to the earliest master printers Aldus, Ratdolt, Jenson, Schoeffer, Gutenberg and the first major book printed in Europe from movable metal type on a hand press, the 42 Line Bible.

It got me wondering, though, how the Albion, standing seven feet tall and weighing at least two thousand pounds, had made its way from England to the Goudys in 1924? Was there a story to this? What I found unexpectedly spurred me on a chase to collect the oddest of fine press books: those printed from the three different Kelmscott Albions *after* they had left the premises of Hammersmith, England; the home of William Morris. After the Kelmscott Press closed, the three Albions, one of them a smaller proofing press that Morris only used to play around with, were sold to other private press printers.

Sydney Cockerell, Kelmscott's secretary and a fascinating

scholar-collector, remarked at the selling of the press's equipment, 'we had three Albion Presses at the Kelmscott Press, they were just like any other Albion Presses, without any magical attributes.' He was more possessive of the types, and let the press equipment go to fellow British private presses.

None of them were particularly in awe of these iron hand presses just because they had once belonged to the Kelmscott Press, and didn't mind parting with them. American fine press printers felt differently; they had worshipped Morris and his books, and were eager to acquire them if they could, almost as if they were talismans that could transform their printing art. And when they got hold of these Albions, they eagerly printed books and keepsakes with colophons that noted with pride that they had been done on one of the Kelmscott Albion hand presses.

I had already secured one of them, but were there other books with similar colophons, and done from the other Morris Albion presses? I was awestruck, as you can see, with the great private presses, and felt a deep desire to connect to that time, to those ideals of fine bookmaking, to these tributes and salaams from one great fine printer to another, and this made collecting these books irresistible to me. I also saw an opportunity to assemble a complete collection of books and keepsakes done from these Kelmscott Albions – such a thing is another tradition among collectors: a large collecting focus that opens up other smaller collecting paths that bring you more excitement and delight, and keep you in the game, sustain the chase, and fuel the book hunt.

A factor that probably played a part in pursing this little collecting path is realizing that these books, price-wise, would probably be within my grasp. At first, it wasn't easy to locate them; no one I knew had collected them and no one had done a catalogue on them or written something on books printed from the William Morris presses. And then I found the most beautiful of them, and that's the one I'd recommend buying if someone reading this feels their interest piquing : *The Liberty Bell on the Kelmscott-Goudy Press*. It's printed by a fine press that would go on to become my favourite: the Yellow Barn Press. I'll tell you in a moment why it became the modern fine press I admired and enjoyed the most, but first about the fascinating text contained in this press book.

The Liberty Bell on the Kelmscott-Goudy Press is actually the story of the same Morris-Goudy Press used in *Three Essays*, and what happened to it after Goudy closes the Village Press. Who did it go to next, and its whereabouts today; it even told the pre-story of how Goudy acquired it in the first place. As the bookdealer I bought it from had described it, 'the journey of Albion No. 6551 – the press that helped to print the Kelmscott *Chaucer* – through 100 years, eight owners, and two continents.'

I won't spoil the story by telling it all, but at the heart of it is a printer enthralled by the rich association of a hand press used by Morris and Goudy (the very machine, Albion No. 6551, on which the Kelmscott *Chaucer* had been printed) and his quest to rescue it from neglect, restore it, and reestablish its pride of place in fine printing history.

The Liberty Bell on the Kelmscott-Goudy Press satisfied me in every single way, intensifying my desire to collect more press books, as well as sharpening my collecting focus: from hereon, the hunt was going to be for private press books on the book arts. The quarter cloth and pattered paper covers are after a William Morris design, the paper is Rives, a lovely mould-made paper from France, dampened for printing, the type has a nice bite into the paper, two colours are used, red and black, and there are floriated initials in the Kelmscott style. The highlight is a finely detailed full-page wood engraving of the Morris-Goudy Albion Press, printed directly from the original woodblock.

Neil Shaver at the Yellow Barn Press printed *The Liberty Bell on the Kelmscott-Goudy Press*, and the wood engravings are by John DePol. Shaver and DePol did a lot of books together, and I chased and acquired all of them. One wood engraving in *The Liberty Bell* central to the narrative is the engraving of the Albion: the way Shaver printed DePol's original woodblock of the Morris-Goudy Albion was to deeply impress it into the paper, so that you can see – even without having to run your fingers over it – how deeply tactile the impression is. I had never seen anything like it before; the illustrations in the offset books we are more accustomed to are flat and smooth on the page. Here I could see the ridges of the lines in the dampened, textured paper, and when feeling the engraving, it comes alive in your hand, warm and immediate, as if it was done just for you, something personal and intimate. It's difficult to print woodblocks this way, especially on dampened paper, and Shaver was a master at it.

Wood engraving is the ideal form of illustrating fine press books because they are, like letterpress, a relief process: they are 'type high', raised from the surface in the same way metal type is, and together both can be printed with a nice bite to the paper.

Just after *Three Essays* (1924) and just before *Liberty Bell* (1996), another printer, Melbert Cary of the Woolly Whale Press, who had acquired the Albion, felt fired up enough about owning this hand press to print a keepsake on it in 1934, that stated it in the title: *Some Thoughts on the Ornamented MSS of the Middle Ages, by William Morris; printed on his Albion hand press (1934)*. It gives an account of the *Chaucer* Albion's travels from the closing of the Kelmscott Press to the present day. Issued on the 100th anniversary of William Morris's birth, 24 March 1934, Cary printed this on handmade paper in red and black with Morrisian borders and ornaments. It's handsomely printed, and I was pleased to have found it.

As for the things printed on the two remaining Kelmscott hand presses, one of the accounts is picked up in a little pamphlet called *A William Morris Press Goes West*. The pamphlet, though, is not printed on the Morris hand press, but you find out here that the first book printed on this little proofing press was *Two Consolations*, a lovely book in every way. Printed in 1940 on watermarked Kelmscott handmade paper by Theodore Linenthal of the Quercus Press in 250 copies, this slim quarto is two poems written by Robinson Jeffers based on a visit his family made in 1929 to Kelmscott Manor, once the home of William Morris, and now preserved the way it was. His wife, Una Jeffers, had made a few journal entries on the visit, and excerpts are included from the journal.

Of the three hand presses, only one remained in England. And fortunately, the William Morris Society realized it was just sitting there in Kelmscott Manor, waiting to be used, and decided to do something about restoring it. It left Kelmscott when the press closed, and after it had wandered among a few intermediate owners, Basil Blackwell of the Shakespeare Head Press gave it to the William Morris Society. The keepsake they printed in 1983 was called *William Morris's Printing Press*. I discovered its existence only a couple of years after I had found the first two – the title of the keepsake should have led me to it sooner or quicker, but it never surfaced in my searches.

Perhaps there was something to this timing, to the delay: when I spotted it, I couldn't believe my luck. Of the five or so copies listed on ABE, the lowest-priced copy was the deluxe edition. In fact, it was the *only* special copy on the market. It was one of only fifty copies (out of a 300 limitation) to be printed on handmade paper, and signed by the author and artist. It contained a couple of short essays with a wood engraving. Blackwell writes on the history of this Albion hand press, and part of the colophon reads, 'printed on the Albion Press at Kelmscott House, once used by Morris...'

A last note on the permanent resting place of the Albion hand presses today. The small proofing press is at the Huntington Library, the second press continues to be in Kelmscott House, while the third, the one that most likely printed the *Chaucer* in 1896, is at the RIT Cary Graphic Arts Collection Library. The untold conclusion to the story in *The Liberty Bell of the Kelmscott-Goudy Press* is that its last owner put it up for auction at Christie's, and on 6 December 2013, it went to the highest bidder for $233,000, which happened to be RIT.

It could not have found a better home; the Cary Collection is rich in printing and typographical material. Its then curator said after the acquisition of Albion No.6551: 'The Kelmscott/Goudy Press will have an active life at RIT, not simply as a museum artifact, but as a working press accessible to students, scholars and printers.' When RIT celebrated 150 years of Goudy, they invited various contemporary fine press printers to contribute a keepsake with Goudy in focus; the keepsake from RIT itself was printed on the Kelmscott-Goudy Press, making it possible for me to acquire one of the possibly last things to be printed on the *Chaucer* Albion.

It's thanks to the printers who were in awe of Morris and his accomplishment at his private press, and their desire to preserve the legacy of the iron hand presses that achieved the typographic and decorative beauty of the Kelmscott books, that the presses – unlike the many wooden and iron presses of other master printers that were turned into scrap or discarded – that we are fortunate to still have the Kelmscott presses with us.

RARE BOOK SWAPPING

After a few years of buying material related to fine printing and the book arts in trade – not fine – editions, and thus inexpensively priced, I began in 2013 to cautiously buy a few fine press pamphlets, broadsides and keepsakes (and the occasional book), in the price range of $50 to $75, something that still felt high to me as an Indian collector going up against the dollar and the pound. I had realized by now, though, that where fine press books are concerned, these were starting prices – if you weren't prepared to pay this, there was no point in looking at fine bookmaking as a collecting focus.

So when I got started, almost all the fine things in this price range that beckoned me, that seized my attention as I browsed the stock of dealers in private press and the book arts on ABE, seemed to be conveniently available in the inventory of one book dealer who traded under the name of Entropy Books. (Information for the dealer on ABE said the proprietor's name was Frederic Shearer, with a Michigan address.)

For about a year I ordered regularly from Entropy via ABE, until one item in Frederic Shearer's stock gave me pause, and had me writing to him. Finally, I had come upon a fine press book I wanted that was well out of my buying range. Priced at $125, this was the Alembic Press bibliography, with several tipped-in specimens from the press. Alembic Press in

England was owned and operated by Claire Bolton, and the press specialized in the book arts, having printed books on papermaking, marbling, paste papers, wood engraving, and so on. I thought that with just one book, this bibliography with specimens from the work of the press, I would learn so much more about Alembic and would get a deep taste of this press.

Hence the move to consider spending more than I had spent before on a press book. But this was not the only reason – in fact, there were two huge reasons for wanting to grab Entropy's copy, price be damned! One: the next copy of the Alembic bibliography was $350. Two: laid into this copy I was considering, were about twenty pieces of ephemera related to the press! (Another dealer would have listed just the ephemera alone for $50.) This, plus the copy being so much lower than the next copy, made getting this copy urgent.

THE ALEMBIC PRESS BIBLIOGRAPHY 1978-1988

Quarter cloth with marbled-paper covered boards, small 4to., 58 pages. Eleven tipped-in specimens and numerous ornaments and engravings in-text. Number 9 of 100 copies printed and bound by Claire Bolton on Hahnemuhle paper. Laid in are the prospectus for the present book, with annotations by Bolton; three handwritten notes, two signed by Bolton, on Alembic letter-headed paper; a prospectus for *Dear David, Dear Graham;* and four eight-page lists of available books, two of which are subtly different, one with an annotation and one with an order form; a two-page, photocopied statement and list for 1988; and other ephemera. Tiny booksellers label at rear pastedown, else a fine copy in archival mylar.

I began: 'Dear Mr. Shearer' – and the rest as you will see was sheer idiocy – 'I am very keen on buying your copy of the Alembic Press bibliography, and am writing to ask if you could perhaps offer a discount on the price?' He wrote back quickly: 'Thank you for your enquiry. As the price of my copy is already about half the cost of others on the market, I do not care to go any lower by offering a discount. With the wealth of ephemeral material offered with it, I am more inclined to raise the price in future. Thanks again for your interest. Best regards, Frederic Shearer.'

I had been put in place, and learnt never again to haggle on a price that was clearly more than fair. I put the order through on ABE before Frederic raised the price, and he graciously threw in priority shipping. After this shaky start, transactions got better and richer. I bought many fine things from him over the years, and at one point, my bibliomania for press books peaking, I bought several of his more expensive books – even so, as it always is with this dealer – they were still bargains when you put them next to the prices of other specialist fine press dealers.

Some of the nicest things in my collection have come from Frederic's stock. In December of 2015, I bought several books I had had my eye on for a long time that I had been saving up for, hoping they wouldn't get sold. Carolyn and Victor Hammer's *Chapters on Writing and Printing*, printed on my favourite handmade paper, Japanese Hosho paper. Before making the purchase, I asked Frederic to give me his impressions of the book since I knew he, too, was a fan of the way Victor and Carolyn Reading Hammer printed books.

Frederic responded by saying that he has always thought this book from the Hammers was 'a perfect storm of paper, text and presswork'. Another one-of-a-kind beauty was a matted and framed set of eight calligraphic bookplates in four colours by Leo Wyatt, that he had won at a recent auction. In my opinion, Frederic had underpriced this, and I now wish I had bought the other calligraphic set as well. When I realized how much I wanted the second matted plate, I called him hurriedly to order it, but it had sold. I got three of my most attractive Gehenna Press items from Entropy, including a very scarce piece of Gehenna ephemera, a broadside with a wood engraving of William Morris by Baskin, with a quotation on the Kelmscott Press beneath the engraving, printed on a delicate, thin Japanese handmade paper. This William Morris broadside is the one item, I felt, had been perhaps a bit overpriced, but rarity commands its own prices, and collectors usually have to bow to it. Still, I am glad I did get it – apart from how scarce it is (I have never seen it listed as yet on the market) the aura around this fragile piece of engraved printing is that it brings two giants of fine bookmaking together, Morris and Baskin, creating one of the richest associations in a piece of printing.

For the past several years, I have been acquiring books from Frederic in an entirely different way – one that eminently suits me, though I don't know if he feels this way. But he has not said no – yet. From time to time, I would select interesting fine press items from my collection that I feel I could let go of and offer them to Frederic for trade credit. In turn, he would price them accordingly and allow me to pick from his inventory for that sum. I think we've had fun doing this and it has been in Frederic's own words, 'to our mutual satisfaction'.

Typically, some of his letters to me during the swap would be like the ones below:

> 'Nice to hear that you received and approve of the books. The Hammer "Testament" finally arrived to my

satisfaction. If you can find any more books you'd like to trade and I have any more for you, let's do it again. Best – Frederic'

'I received your parcel yesterday, and am very happy with what it contained. The miscellaneous items you included are perfect for my tastes, encompassing areas I have actively pursued: Victor Hammer, Saul Marks, Duensing.'

'Received your parcel yesterday with the usual satisfaction. Hope you receive mine tomorrow – Frederic'

'This is to confirm credit for the following 8 books:

1. Unless the Grain Die - Stanbrook
2. Printers Flowers, Types - Arman
3. Portraits from Presses - Whittington
4. The Types, Borders, Rules - Overbrook
5. I Will Eat a Piece - Midnight Sales
6. Nothing or the Bookplate - Craig
7. Memory and Her Nine Daughters - Hammer
8. John DePol From Dark to Light

Best – Frederic'

Through such trading, I acquired several high-end fine press items I would not have been able to otherwise afford easily.

Another common factor in the way I collected and the way Frederic acquired books for stock, is looking for rare book bargains. 'As to buying on the internet,' he told me once, sounding almost like an echo of me, 'I admit that I have always been a bottom-feeder. The allure of finding a book I want at $20 when the rest are going for $100 is irresistible. I know this is counter to the dictum of only buying the best copy available. The dictum holds true and is valid over time, but it applies only to those who have the means to sustain it.

'A few years ago I started to become aware of the possibility of buying books at auction. It had always been my experience that books at auction always reached high prices, that bargains could never be found there. This is still generally true. I started putting out fairly low-ball bids here and there never won anything for quite a while. While I never had any success with the big auction houses with their rarefied books, I started to win a very few lots at the smaller auction houses. I always research the books I might bid on as to their availability and prices on the market, decide on the highest price I might pay and then submit a bid in advance. I very seldom bid during the live auction. The last thing I want to do is get into a bidding war. I either get them fairly cheaply or let them go. One example of a successful auction took place at a smaller California house that sold mainly antiques, art work, etc. They did have a number of book lots, of which I won two. One was a complete set of *The Colophon*, which I won for $100 and soon sold for $1,500; the other was a collection of six or seven Dard Hunter Books, along with ephemera consisting of prospectuses and letters. This, I just won with the bidding going right up to my bid of $2,200. I have sold some of the books and ephemera, bringing in well over my investment, and still most of the books and ephemera, with one of the books (*Papermaking in Southern Siam*) listed at $5,500.'

JERRY KELLY'S ZAPF

I was thrilled to finally find myself inside the private library of Jerry Kelly, the accomplished calligrapher and book designer. I had dreamt of this day for years, and on a Saturday afternoon in September 2018, I found my way to his house, which was snuggled inside a thickly wooded neighbourhood in Connecticut. The sprawling house was, wall to wall, lined with bookcases of all sizes, containing illuminated manuscripts, incunabular books from the fifteenth century and masterpieces of modern fine printing. However, I was there primarily to look at something only Kelly's collection could offer: the calligraphic and typographic work of Hermann Zapf, that giant of type design whose calling was 'to create beautiful letters'.

It was indeed Jerry Kelly, Zapf's long-time student whom I was now standing before. A renowned book designer, fine press printer, calligrapher and typographic scholar, he is deeply invested in the life and work of Zapf. No one I can think of today has done more to bring Zapf's work to the world than Jerry, having organized pioneering exhibitions of Zapf's calligraphic work, lectured extensively on his work in type design, written several books on various aspects of this German master's lettering art, and collaborated with Zapf on some stellar letterpress productions, notably *Poetry Through Typography*. His latest triumph is *Hermann Zapf and the World*

He Designed, the widely acclaimed biography of the lettering master.

'My biography,' Kelly told me, as he showed me an advance copy of the manuscript, 'is enriched by decades of conversations with Zapf and fifty of his associates. It features rarities and never-before-seen works and photos, it will include definitive lists of Zapf's type designs and major calligraphic works. The book has more than 400 illustrations, over ninety of which have never been reproduced in a book before.'

After Jerry put away his Zapf manuscript, we got to the highlight of my visit: a tour of his prodigious collection, with an emphasis on Zapf's original calligraphic work in his collection. The calligraphic and lettering work I saw that afternoon took my breath away – I had only seen these exquisite examples of lettering in images reproduced in books, and seeing the original, mounted and framed, is not unlike the difference between seeing a reproduction of an iconic painting and then encountering the real thing: you are struck down by its beauty, grace and power. Along with the many calligraphic Zapf pieces Kelly had bought from private collections and auctions, paying steep prices, there were also on the wall, hung proudly, original calligraphic broadsides from Zapf gifted to Kelly, inscribed and signed to him personally with a calligraphic flourish.

Now, Jerry fished out for me Zapf's three typographic jewels: the Triple Crown among Zapf's books: *Pen and Graver, Manuale Typographicum* 1 and 2 (which Kelly feels is not only Zapf's masterwork, but perhaps the greatest purely typographic book ever designed and printed) and *Typographic Variations*. *Pen and Graver* is especially fascinating for being printed from letters cut in metal by August Rosenberg of Zapf's

Palatino, and printed perfectly on Japanese handmade paper. 'Many collectors and booksellers mistakenly describe the subsequent editions of *Pen and Graver* as being printed from punchcutter Rosenberg's metal letters, but they were printed from electrotype matrices. Only the edition on Japanese paper was printed directly from the engraved metal letters,' he told me. Jerry is possibly one of the few people in the world who has a copy of this Japanese-paper edition, which has become not just scarce, but extremely rare.

As I prepared to leave, Jerry's wife, Nancy, a senior designer at Penguin, handed me their guest book to leave a comment in. And as an instance or model of what previous guests had written for me to follow, she pointed to a page. I looked down at it, gasped, and then looked up to see Nancy and Jerry grinning. The page had been filled by Herman Zapf, who had been their weekend guest once, and his entry was written with his familiar and masterly calligraphic strokes: a calligraphic alphabet design followed by an inscription that spoke of the pleasure of being in a house filled with the warmth of true bibliophiles and fine books.

It was Jerry Kelly's many books on modern fine printing that first made me want to collect fine press books, and it was his devotion to Hermann Zapf that made me a devotee of this modern master of type design.

The first-ever biography of calligrapher and type designer Hermann Zapf is a handsome book, designed by Kelly himself. His overarching personal collection of Zapf material is virtually an archive, prompting even Zapf to say once, 'You know my work better than I do'. Kelly demurred modestly, but his *Hermann Zapf and the World He Designed* shows how spot-on Zapf was. This heavily illustrated biography explores Zapf's work intimately, while warmly evoking his life.

Kelly first met this towering lettering artist in July 1979, when he signed up for a summer course in calligraphy that Zapf had initiated at the Rochester Institute of Technology. Reflecting on this in the biography, Kelly comments that if you had told him then, as he waited outside that first day of class for an early glimpse of the Master, that he would go on one day to become Zapf's friend, colleague and finally his biographer, he 'would have thought you truly mad'.

Kelly and his wife, Nancy, would become lifelong friends with Zapf and his wife, Gudrun, who is also a fine calligrapher, type designer and bookbinder. One of my favourite illustrations in the book is a personal holiday card of the Zapfs: the greeting is printed in Gudrun's Ariadne initials and Diotima italic (which Kelly feels is 'one of the most beautiful italic typefaces' out there) and typographically arranged by Zapf. It was their own personal favourite among the things they designed.

Zapf's stellar career in type design began when he was just in his 20s, for the Stempel type foundry in Frankfurt. One of them was Palatino, a widely used and admired typeface today. Kelly says Zapf loved arranging specimens of type in inventive ways, and in 1954 came his masterpiece, *Manuale Typographicum*, a gorgeous display of the complete alphabet in various typographic arrangements. Published as an oblong 12 x 9 inches folio, it was an entirely new kind of type specimen book, says Kelly.

Typophiles, and even Zapf scholars, will find the biography of immense value for the intricate details Kelly provides for every form of lettering and bookmaking created by him: several key Zapf typefaces, for instance (whether metal, photo-set or digital), get a blow-by-blow account of how they were accomplished, from trial drawings to their commercial release.

He designed more than two hundred exceptional typefaces, and everyone has their favourites; mine are Zapf Civilite, an enchanting calligraphic typeface cut in metal, and Zapf Renaissance, a digital face with flourished swash characters.

The biography also devotes chapters to the great companionship and working life Zapf and Gudrun shared in their marriage. Over the decades, Kelly and Nancy often made trips to their beautiful book-lined home in Darmstadt, Germany, right up to a few months before Zapf's death in 2015. (Gudrun passed away in 2019, at the age of 101.) Rather than a dense, overwrought biography, *Hermann Zapf and the World He Designed* is a deft, affectionate and finely drawn portrait of a magnificent, gentle artist who devoted his life to making letterforms as beautiful, useful and legible as they could possibly be.

COLLECTING CALLIGRAPHIC AND TYPOGRAPHIC BOOKPLATES

An engaging, if minor, line of collecting Indian bibliophiles should pay attention to, is the bookplate and the book label. Quite apart from such bibliophilic devices obviously being a nicer way to show ownership of a book (than writing or stamping your name in it), bookplates and book labels are interesting things in themselves to collect. Whenever I meet serious book collectors in India with a significant library, I encourage them to think of getting their own bookplates and book labels made. My interest in bookplates had only been slight until I saw examples of calligraphic and typographic bookplates and labels. This was something entirely different to the armorial plates I would sometimes see in old books, or even specimens of pictorial bookplates stuck in books that put me off completely. The calligraphed bookplate, on the other hand, felt to me like the fine press version of a bookplate, with its beautiful, elegant letterforms and decorative strokes engraved on wood and printed from the block.

Once my interest in calligraphic and typographic bookplates and labels had advanced, I would always be on the lookout for a pleasing, substantial collection of such bookplates that

I could buy, perchance if they were to come on the market. For a long time, I had little luck; just the odd unused original calligraphic bookplate done by Reynolds Stone or Leo Wyatt – two masters of the engraved bookplate – that would turn up in some obscure online auction that would become mine for a price I could afford because no one else happened to bid on them.

And then, when I was least expecting it, something pretty special came up: a whole packet of typographic bookplates designed and printed by that elegant fine press printer John S. Fass. Anything from his Hammer Creek Press is scarce and coveted, and it was sheer luck that I spotted this for sale before anyone else did; it was listed with a dealer who, not quite knowing how to price something ephemeral like this, had ended up underpricing this lot of unused Fass bookplates in mint condition.

'Bookplates have been an endlessly diverse and charming reflection on the history of bookmaking, and provide a beautiful record of book ownership,' says James Gannon, former director of Rare Books at Heritage Auctions in a listing. Bookplate collector, author and historian James M. Goode writes in *Three Centuries of the Bookplate*: 'The earliest bookplates were woodcuts designed and printed for Catholic monasteries in Bavaria, Germany, beginning in the 1480s – only one generation after Johannes Gutenberg invented the printing of books by movable type in Mainz in 1455.'

By the late nineteenth century, bookplate collecting became a serious, avid pursuit, with a society for ex-libris bookplates being formed in London. Alongside, the making of bookplates for collectors was also on the rise. The turning point in bookplate-making – at least as far as I am concerned – happened around the 1950s, when very accomplished and fine wood engravers began accepting commissions from collectors to do typographic and calligraphic bookplates. More important, and charming, is the fact that these artists enjoyed making bookplates!

Two of my favourite bookplate engravers are Reynolds Stone and Leo Wyatt. While there are quite a number of books on Stone's work, there are only two on Wyatt's. And luckily, both of them are fine press books, so that gave me reason enough to buy them. From Simon Lawrence's Fleece Press: *Bookplates and Labels by Leo Wyatt* (1988) and from Graham Williams's Florin Press, *Leo Wyatt's Little Book of Alphabets* (1985). The Fleece Press book shows various calligraphic and typographic bookplates Wyatt engraved on wood and copper, and they are printed directly from the block with a subtle impression by Lawrence. The Florin Press book shows twelve alphabets Wyatt engraved, each printed in a different colour on Barcham Green paper. Both books were printed on a hand press.

Wyatt came to making wood-engraved bookplates only in his late 50s, and admirably, mastered it in a short time. According to *Bookplates and Labels*, Wyatt had felt challenged by the widely held view then that Stone was 'the sole practitioner of the Chancery Cursive letter in engraved form today', and began turning away from cutting in steel and copper to engraving on boxwood. Wyatt instantly felt he could be just as good if not better and proved it even within a small body of work – because, tragically, he died not long after. Many who know the field well say that had Wyatt lived longer, he would have got better than Stone at this.

He began as a copper engraver for firms dealing with engraved invitation cards, etc., and began to enjoy his work only after he turned to boxwood engraving. He had a day job as a lecturer at an art college in Britain, and was popular as a teacher, with students saying his lettering classes approached genius.

But sadly, in Britain itself, he never gained the huge reputation Stone had, and struggled to find work as an engraver. He had to look for commissions for bookplate-making, and found a larger audience for his work in America. Brian North Lee is perhaps the most well-known scholar-collector of bookplates today, as well as the one who has written extensively on the subject. The text in the Fleece Press book, *Bookplates and Labels by Leo Wyatt* is by him.

Lee describes Leo as an intensely private man who was also shy. But he was a perfectionist. 'Few if any surpassed his rendering of the Chancery script,' notes Lee. Wyatt was carrying on a tradition begun by Eric Gill of the 'modern engraved calligraphic book label'. He was often overly critical of himself, but always humble, and cared only for work and not fame. For the modest price of £12, you could get him to make a small and charming book label for you!

Will Carter, fine printer at the Rampant Lions Press, has an introduction in the book where he recalls what a joy and a pleasure it was to use Wyatt's wood blocks; the lines were deep and immaculate, and there was no clogging of the ink when they inked the blocks, the serifs showed as they should. Carter wistfully adds that he misses opening a package and finding a block by Leo.

The next fortunate bookplate acquisition – and the operative word here is 'fortunate' because when I bought it,

I had no idea how prized and precious a bookplate collection it was. I bought it because I liked the look of it, and how attractively it was priced. Below is the original listing from Provan, the dealer in Wales I buy from so often for his excellent prices and the unusual things he finds:

A keepsake from Ron Smith: A Calligraphic Bookplate printed on Japanese handmade paper in an edition of fifty, with a collection of fifteen other book labels and bookplates designed by Ron Smith. The keepsake – small 8vo pamphlet, mounted bookplate, fine condition in sewn paper covers, one of an edition of fifty signed by Ron Smith, with a collection of fifteen other book labels and bookplates designed by Ron Smith, all in fine condition, with a compliment slip bearing a short message from Ron Smith, initialed by him.'

There were a couple of images accompanying the listing, and I was powerfully drawn to Smith's fine calligraphy on what looked like a delicate Japanese paper. It was only later, when I happened to be reading Brian North Lee's little booklet, *My Personal Bookplates*, did I find out the high esteem in which he had been held by bookplate collectors. Lee praises Ron Smith, a melancholic bookplate-maker who never got his due, and knew it.

Apparently, he lost his entire archive in a storm in 1974, and so no record remains of his substantial ex-libris making. Because Lee had written a little tribute about him, he sent this bookplate collector, unasked, an ex-libris in four different colours that Lee prizes. That's one of his gifts he rates highly. He calls Smith's work excellent and notes Leo Wyatt and Ron Smith were both given to melancholia, in part due to them not getting the recognition they deserved.

The final bookplate find, though not calligraphic or even

typographic in nature, is worth noting for being a satisfying bargain find. It was while reading Brian North Lee's *My Personal Bookplates* and getting to the part about commissioning Brett to make him some personal plates, that jogged my memory about a deluxe edition of *Bookplates of Simon Brett* listed at half its market price. *Bookplates of Simon Brett* (1989) is another Fleece Press book with text by Brian North Lee, and comes in two editions, the regular and the deluxe.

I had given away the regular edition of this book in a trade swap, and had begun to miss it, especially for its frontispiece, a lovely wood engraving of an Albion iron hand press. I like wood engravings that are printed with some impression, but except for the Leo Wyatt book that Simon Lawrence did at Fleece Press, all his other books on bookplates (Richard Shirley Smith, Reynolds Stone) though printed directly from the woodblocks on dampened Zerkall paper, feel a bit flat and smooth to the touch, with just the slightest raised effect.

The Fleece Press has specialized in printing wood engravings from the block even more so than Whittington Press (its printer John Randle got Simon Lawrence into fine printing), so the details are finely done. Quite by chance I had, some months earlier, spotted what looked like the deluxe edition of *Bookplates of Simon Brett* with two different prices by the same UK dealer. On ABE, it was £300, and on eBay, the same copy was £170 with a Best Offer option! Even £300 was already well below the price other dealers had listed it for, which went up to £450–£500.

The deluxe edition had my full attention now because tucked into a pocket at the back of the book are four bookplates proofs signed by Brett, and one of them was of that favourite: the Albion Press. The only thing that hinted this could be the deluxe in the bookshop's eBay listing was a single line of description that said 'quarter leather with a slightly worn slipcase'. The regular was bound in cloth and needless to say, did not come with a slipcase.

I thought it might be worth calling the dealers, Maynard and Bradley, and asking them for their best price for a direct purchase – this way they might accept a lower best offer price than they would be able to give me on eBay. They had an open bookshop with a listed landline, so I called and asked for a revised price. And the owner said, 'That would give us more leeway with the price.' I was going to suggest a best offer of £150 plus shipping, but encouraged by the owner, I offered instead, 'how about £130 with shipping?' He hesitated for a second, and said, 'Fine, I think we can do that'.

Why hadn't this copy been snatched already from the low £170 eBay listing? I think it's because they, oddly enough, had not listed it as the deluxe edition, and while the meagre photos of the book did show the quarter leather spine, it had no photos of the pocket with the four signed bookplates. Even in their text description below, they had simply described it as leather with a slightly worn slipcase.

It's by staying alert to such omissions by booksellers that an impecunious collector makes a score in the book-collecting game. And the memory retention for listings and prices and keeping track of copies that once caught your attention, is critical: a mere mention of Fleece's *Bookplates by Simon Brett* in Lee's *My Personal Bookplates* triggered my memory about seeing this half-priced deluxe copy on eBay. I had, somewhere at the back of my mind, stored away the posted image of the quarter-leather binding, but had not followed through because I was skeptical that it would contain the four signed bookplate proofs.

It's not uncommon for deluxe editions lacking the extras to be priced at half the market price. Typically, the bookseller won't emphasize that it's missing the loosely laid plates, or simply won't realize they are not present, or best of all, as in this case, everything was present but the bookseller had not realized what he had. Nothing sums this up more than when I called the bookshop, and asked the young woman who answered the phone to please get the book in hand, and look at the back to see if it had a pocket with the bookplates, and she said after fetching it, 'Oh yes, you mean these loose papers at the back? Yeah, there are four of them.'

THE TYPOPHILES

From the first time I read about the Typophiles, I was charmed. And a little envious. Here was – and still is – a club for typographers, printers, calligraphers, wood engravers, papermakers, collectors, and lovers of fine printing to meet over an informal lunch to drink, eat and talk to their hearts' content about fine bookmaking.

The pleasure and joy I feel at any mention of the Typophiles is also for its wonderful and brilliant early years, from the 1930s to the 1970s, when so many of my fine press heroes – Bruce Rogers, Frederic Goudy, W.A. Dwiggins, John Fass, Valenti Angelo, Paul Standard and John DePol – formed close working relationships as well as friendships; influencing and changing the landscape of modern fine printing for decades.

And as a book collector, there's another exciting reason to venerate the Typophiles – for those five early and scarce Typophile pre-chap books that every collector covets: *Spinach From Many Gardens*, *Barnacles From Many Bottoms*, *Diggings from Many Ampersand Hogs*, *Left to Their Own Devices* and the two portfolios – not just scarce but rare: unbound tributes to Beatrice Warde and Fritz Kredel.

What in the world, you might ask, are these strangely named books, and why are they so hotly pursued by collectors?

They were tributes to the typographic masters among themselves, their gurus, so to say. And though done gratis, with each contributor doing what he did for the honour and thrill of it, and not for a fee, no expense was spared in the use of fine papers, types, labour over design and illustration, and the number of gifted craftsmen involved in the making of each book.

I've managed to get two of these books, and I'll tell you later which ones and how I obtained them after a long, long wait. First, some background to the Typophiles.

In the 1930s, a convivial group of men involved in fine bookmaking in New York would meet for lunch to talk about fine printing and exchange little keepsakes with each other that they had printed, illustrated or calligraphed for the pure pleasure of it. The Typophiles were made of up both, illustrious figures in the graphic arts and unknown enthusiasts of fine printing and bookmaking. They met over the years across various restaurants and clubhouses in Manhattan.

The conversation over lunch would be a mix of shop talk and gossip, and a good deal of it focused on good craftmanship in bookmaking. The members, mostly young, would drag other people they knew in the printing arts to come join the fellowship. In the early days, the keepsakes were done for fun, playing inventively with type, design and illustration, experimenting with various typographical forms – they revelled in typographical whimsicalities.

Some of its most memorable years were between 1933 and 1938, when the Typophiles met weekly in the old Amherst Club on Lexington Avenue and 36th Street. This apparently is the time that Rogers, Goudy, Dwiggins and Ruzicka dropped by frequently and faithfully.

And one man, Paul A. Bennett, was the spirit behind the group; he kept them together, and was the driving force behind the books and ephemera these Typophiles produced. Bennett wrote a jolly little book in 1938, called *The Typophiles Whodunit*, which is a 'private revelation of the hitherto most mysterious origin, development, practices and works of the Typophiles'. This little book is charmingly referred to as 'the Iliad of The Typophiles' and Paul Bennett, their Homer. He notes here, 'We're a type-conscious crew, in the main, who, when a keepsake is planned, pitch in and do it to please ourselves, and only ourselves. Here, we feel, is a job to be done with a free hand.' *Whodunit* has the most detailed description of those early and scarce Typophile books, itemizing every signature from each of those books. There are other amusements in the book, like the Typophile Hound: a photograph showing a little toy dog pissing on those sacred Typophile volumes!

Even as early as 1938, Bennett was able to say in *The Typophiles Whodunit* that the keepsakes were already sought after by collectors: 'And so the hounds – collectors and dealers, bibliographers and librarians – were fiercely on our trail. The keepsakes began in earnest at their annual Christmas luncheons, and the tradition of keeping these typographical whimsicalities going continued with other occasions – farewell dinners, engagements, anniversaries, birthdays.' PAB, as he was fondly called, notes that everyone who attended these gatherings 'left with an armful of keepsakes'.

The first Typophile book (March 1935) 'grew out of a desire to surprise Fred Goudy on his seventieth birthday'. Goudy was a venerated type designer. They called it *Spinach From Many Gardens: Gathered by the Typophiles and fed to Frederic W. Goudy on his Seventieth Anniversary*. It was put together in nineteen days, and 'this spirit of friendship in boards had an edition of sixty copies'. (Jerry Kelly, the scholar-designer and fine press historian, told me he had been looking for this for fifteen years and unexpectedly found it in a book fair for $250, a fraction of what it is usually priced at. I had never seen a copy myself for several years, until 2019, when a copy was listed by Bromer Booksellers for $2,500).

Bennett goes on to say that the experience of making the Goudy tribute 'was so seductive that we repeated it on October 30th, 1935 with *Barnacles from Many Bottoms* to greet Bruce Rogers on his return from England astride his Lectern Bible. We did a hundred copies of this, but they proved all too few. B.R., you see, is collected.'

Barnacles from Many Bottoms: Scraped and Gathered for B.R. by the Typophiles consists of various signatures designed and printed by fine bookmakers as tributes to Bruce Rogers. Rogers had returned from England after a long spell, and the Typophiles wanted to welcome the Master back home. Bennett noted in the introduction that it would be the last book the Typophiles did, little realizing there were many more to follow.

I came to acquire my copy of *Barnacles* in 2018 from a trade-swap with a dealer I had been buying from and swapping with for many years – Frederic Shearer of Entropy Books. Frederic had just won this BR tribute book in an auction, and graciously alerted me to this new acquisition before putting it up on ABE. Going by previous catalogue and auction prices, he had priced it at $1,500. Two previous records showed up: one for $850 and the other for $1,200.

The dealer felt it was only fair that he prices it higher since those listings were quite old, and the book would be worth more today. I agreed, and gave up some really fine books from my collection to trade for it. A week after we concluded the transaction and I had the book in hand (gorgeous book, finally in my possession when I'd given up hope of finding it), a copy was listed on ABE by another dealer for $450.

Such are the vagaries of the rare book market. If I had begun negotiating with Frederic a few weeks later than when I did, he would have had to price it closer to the lower-priced copy. Had this other dealer underpriced it, or had Frederic overpriced it? Anyway, that nicely priced copy is gone now.

In the spring of 1936, the idea was sprung by the Typophiles to do a Christmas book which would, perversely, have nothing in it about Christmas. Thus was born *Diggings From Many Ampersand Hogs*, a year later, which was a disquisition on & – the ampersand, that is – from many Typophile hands, including a small treatise on it by Fred Goudy. In 1937 came two portfolios – unbound signatures from various Typophiles to pay tribute to that ravishing First Lady of Typography, Beatrice Warde, called *The Typophiles Salute Paul Beaujean* (her pseudonym) and to welcome back that marvellous illustrator Fritz Kredel after his sojourn abroad.

Bennett's *Whodunit* book ends at this point, but a postscript describes the next big book in production: *Left to Their Own Devices,* which would come out in 1937. All Typophile hands on deck were called to design and print a mark, a printer's device, that would best capture and spirit of the group and its doings. 'The resulting collection,' writes one Typophile in *Whodunit*, 'garland, garden or *divan* of typographical and calligraphical crotchets, oddments and dingle-dangles is at this time of writing, in the final stages of printing.'

This was the Typophile book I had wanted before anything else, and got it for a reasonable price from Blue Sky Rare Books. I have to single out one magnificent contribution here from Valenti Angelo. The book, in fact, is coveted for this: a beautifully drawn Typophile press device hand illuminated in lapis blue, vermillion and gold.

Some members contributed up to even three devices – Angelo had two. In all, about 156 devices are shown off in various inks on a grey-tinted Alliger paper from about 115 members, a few of whom were from Britain, like Will Carter and Reynolds Stone. Abe Lerner, a typographic scholar, remarked that the book works so well because though so many printers were involved, there was only one designer behind it: the inimitable John S. Fass. Fass was many years away from forming his celebrated Hammer Creek Press, but even here as a young designer at the Harbor Press, he was already showing his natural felicity for arranging type and decoration.

Devices is the last of the scarce, coveted and expensive Typophile books – the chap books that followed from 1940 on are commonly available for mostly modest prices. The first chapbook was *Songs for a Printer's Way Goose*. I've enjoyed – and learnt much – from the subjects these post *Devices* chap books have dealt with, but I've never been tempted to collect them. However, I do like the Typophile monographs in the new series that the group began in 1984. Here, the monograph's subject, its typographic design and the material used to make it are not only more pleasing but superior to the chap books.

Typically, and dishearteningly, in those early years women, however accomplished in the graphic arts, weren't included in the Typophile luncheons, and this changed only in the 1970s. But even back then, contemporaneous to those desirable pre-Typophile chap books, the wives, girlfriends and mistresses of the men in the group formed their own club and imprint called The Distaff Side. And printed some beautiful books, the first of which – *Boomaking on the Distaff Side* – is perhaps the rarest of all the Typophile books we have been discussing.

The Distaff Side was inspired by Bertha Goudy, who composed and hand-set the type for most of the books she and Frederic Goudy printed at their Village Press. Some of the more notable women here were Edna Beilenson, Fanny Duschnes, Evelyn Hatter and Edith Rushmore. Edna Beilenson of the Peter Pauper Press wrote: '*The Distaff Side is a loosely-knit organization of women enlisted from printing-offices, publishing houses, studios and other hiding-places where may be found devotees of the graphic arts. The group was born out of a righteous indignation that sufficient recognition had never been accorded to the place of women in the history of fine printing.*

After Bennett died in 1966, they disbanded but came back to form The Typophiles Inc. in 1967. A few years later, another leader emerged, with that same moving spirit for the graphic arts – Doc Leslie, or Robert Lincoln Leslie; he was eighty years old, but once again kindled typographic fires.

Four other lavish keepsake tribute packets concerning The Typophiles need to be noted – all of which I pursued and managed to acquire. The first was the *Paul A. Bennett 1897-1966: A Memorial Keepsake*. Sixty separate contributions, loosely laid into slipcase with printed wraparound label, a marvellous gathering of keepsakes from luminaries in the graphic arts from around the world. It can be got for varying prices – from $150 to $500, depending on condition and number of inserts present. Usually, the wraparound label is browned and dirtied.

The next set of tribute keepsakes are fairly uncommon. For Doc Leslie's 100th birthday, a tribute folder was issued in 1985, with many printed inserts from various people in the book arts honouring Leslie. And while Paul Bennett was still alive, he had been celebrated and toasted at a birthday dinner bash at the Statler Hotel, New York, circa 1950, and a folder of keepsakes came out of this called *PAB, A Dinner Tribute.*

The keepsakes and broadsides can be the most elusive – I wouldn't quite label them as 'rare' because we don't know how many copies were made of these things or how often they turn up (or not turn up) on the market. It's possible they are there, not correctly described or listed or catalogued, but collectors keep missing them because we don't even have a checklist for these early typographical whimsicalities, let alone a bibliography. (The chap books have their bibliography, *Bibliography of the Typophile Chap Books, 1935-1992.*)

Over the years, I've traced a few of the more elusive broadsides. The best of these is something quite extraordinary – an oblong calligraphic broadside by Dwiggins in coloured inks on handmade paper, printed in 1937. I got it for a steal at $35 from a dealer who didn't fully appreciate how special it was, and sure enough, perhaps a year after I got the only listed copy, a second copy turned up priced at $350.

It is titled *Typophiles Salutem Vobis Dico* (I salute you Typophiles) and addressed to sixteen of the most famous Typophile members, starting with Bruce Rogers. This broadside is a reproduction of a calligraphic manuscript written out by Dwiggins. To honour him on his birthday, some of the most esteemed Typophile members had sent Dwiggins a signed birthday greeting but they had got the date wrong, sending it seventy-eight days early. To thank them in return, Dwiggins calligraphically wrote out a rather tongue-in-cheek appreciation using various coloured inks on Worthy handmade paper, signing off at the end as '*GUILELMUS DWIGGINIDES*'.

The Typophiles, one and all, appreciated the handsomely produced joke and framed the broadside, but before doing so, they printed a facsimile of the calligraphed manuscript in a small number of copies on handmade paper and issued it as a keepsake.

A HOT METAL MASTERPIECE

The most ravishing type specimen book I have in my collection is *Lead, Tin and Antimony*, printed by Jason Dewinetz from his Greenboathouse Press. It is printed from hot metal type (many cast just for the book!) on handmade paper. It was well beyond what I could easily afford, but I couldn't resist getting it. And now that I own it, I feel privileged and lucky because *Lead, Tin and Antimony: A Sampling of Types Held in Cases or Cast Fresh at the Greenboathouse Press* (2017) is one of the finest handmade letterpress productions in recent years, and for me personally, a kind of culmination of a certain kind of typographic book I had been in search of.

It should be obvious to any typophile what the visceral thrill and satisfaction of a book printed letterpress is – the bite of metal type into textured paper, where you can run your hand over the pages to feel the letters sculpted on to the paper almost in three-dimensional fashion. But of all such finely printed letterpress books, the most ravishingly tactile is the one printed from hot metal type into handmade paper, while the most typographically engaging is a book showcasing or displaying the types of a private press. And in *Lead, Tin and Antimony* both come together in an exquisitely printed fine press book. What Dewinetz, typecaster, typographer, designer and fine press printer from British Columbia, had done here is to choose twenty-four of his favourite metal typefaces that he had long been drawn to or wanted to use in a book, and then, after trying out various arrangements of each type with different short texts (some just a few lines, others running to a page) went on to using his unerring eye for type design, immaculately printing these hot metal types *into* deliciously textured handmade papers (made by Timothy Barrett, a master papermaker) in more than twenty-five colours, to showcase the typographic beauty of all these masterful typefaces on several pages.

The title of the book (comprising the metal alloys used in typefounding) is such a fit and evocative title for this specimen book of type which demanded new typefaces be cast and printed to illuminate a particular text. Only fifty-five copies of the book were printed (another reason to count myself fortunate to possess one). In the prospectus for the book, Dewinetz notes, 'As such, *Lead, Tin and Antimony* serves not so much as a specimen book, but an eclectic and playful tour through some of the cabinets and matrix cases here at the Greenboathouse Press.'

The moment I first set my eyes on the book, I knew I had found the typographic/type specimen book I had been longing for. I had by now managed to gather some really wonderful books produced in a similar vein – a display of various texts in a variety of metal faces. While all of them satisfied me in one aspect or another, none of the completely or deeply fulfilled me. If they used metal types, they used machine-made paper, if they used handmade paper, the texts weren't attractive, if the texts were arresting, they used only two colours – usually black and red – to print, and if all the elements I most wanted in a typographic book were present, the presswork would be lacking or – the biggest turn-off for me – the impression of type on paper would not be deep but slight. *Lead, Tin and Antimony* immediately and fully aroused my typographic imagination. Everything I had dreamed about, was present in the book: for me this was the full flowering of the beautiful type specimen book which has had such a bracing, lovely and long tradition in the modern fine press movement. I guess what lay underneath this is what all fine press enthusiasts realize about themselves: a love for or of *letterforms.*

The showing of Centaur Alphabets in colour is the most beautiful of its kind I have seen. The display of Duensing's Chancery Italic is exquisite, Zapf's Civilite is gem-like, Rimmer's Medieval Nephi is a revelation, and of course, there's the rich title page. I'll probably have to single out every display, because they all hit the mark. The book felt like a culmination or coming together of the best books in this tradition I have been following, the zenith of a type specimen book from a contemporary private press. What a luxurious and sumptuous book it is, making for a sensuous typographical experience. Jason Dewinetz's *Lead, Tin and Antimony* is a typographic gem, a hot metal masterpiece.

HAND-ILLUMINED

As I went about collecting modern fine press books, I would come across a kind of hand-decorated book that I found deeply appealing, even though it looked and felt medieval! While they fell into the typographic tradition of private press books – printed letterpress on handmade paper from metal type – they also brought to the finely printed book another layer of hand craftmanship: colour and illumination by hand. These highly ornamented and illumined books, I soon learnt, were a throwback to the arts and crafts movement. Inspired by William Morris and his Kelmscott Press, small presses around the turn of the century in America began designing, printing and decorating books in this manner.

Many fine printers as well as press book collectors don't take these books seriously, and usually dismiss them as being overdone with little typographic merit to them. When I asked Jerry Kelly, one of the most knowledgeable collectors of fine press books, what his favourite arts and crafts presses were, he told me he didn't care much for them since they had brought nothing new to typography and fine bookmaking. Except for a few arts and crafts presses such as the Elston Press, this is probably true of many of these books. (If you are already familiar with such books, you're probably already thinking of the Roycrofter books – but they shouldn't be so easily dismissed either.)

However, the main appeal of the arts and crafts book, at least to a collector like me who is quite charmed by them, is not their typographic design or presswork, but how their pages are awash with colour and illumination. Admittedly, some of these presses were amateur bookmakers, with the hand-colouring and illumination done in a half-baked fashion, but there are a sufficient number of examples of colour and illumination intelligently, accurately and tastefully used in these books to make you gasp in wonderment at how they look and feel like pages from a medieval illuminated manuscript. Now, here is why I think illumination and colouring in these books cast such a spell: the extra hand-colouring and gilding are usually on the surface of thick, textured paper, often handmade and even watermarked.

As opposed to the thick, smooth, card stock-like paper used for the nineteenth-century chromolithographed book, that also had brilliant hand-colouring and illumination. In the arts and crafts illumined book, you can even *see*, let alone feel, the raised surface that comes from hand applied water colours and gold leaf to the ornaments in the book, whether initials or borders or illustrations. I can't describe to you what a treat it is to see such painted gilding on a laid handmade paper. The flat surface of colours and gold, however radiant, in the chromolithographed books make you feel you are looking at a photographic reproduction of a medieval illuminated page, while the tactility of the arts and crafts books feels like the early fifteenth- and sixteenth-century books that had used handmade paper to decorate and illuminate on.

When I began my chase of these arts and crafts books, trawling for them through the online antiquarian market, I made a delicious breakthrough as a collector, that helped me net some gorgeous books that other collectors and dealers seemed to have missed knowing about. Before I get into what this bibliographical secret I stumbled on was, I should talk about a catalogue that came out a few years ago that was a game-changer where collecting in this field was concerned.

One day in 2016, the accomplished and talented Mosher Press scholar-collector, Philip R. Bishop, alerted me via email to a just-published catalogue that he felt would be of strong interest to me. Phil was, as always, absolutely bang-on: the beautifully designed catalogue (by Jerry Kelly) called 'Colour in American Fine and Private Press Books 1890-2015' was just the guide or tool I had been searching for to aid my newfound collecting focus of books with hand-applied colour and gilding in or onto them.

I went through the catalogue in wide-eyed excitement: there were so many beautiful examples listed – as well as shown – here, and I could not wait to jump on to the antiquarian and rare book market to see what titles from here were available; and if they were, whether I could afford them at all. The collection in the catalogue belonged to Jean Francoise Villain, a collector who had stumbled on these arts and crafts books by chance and had become, over several decades, a fervent collector of this style of fine bookmaking, putting together a truly splendid collection of books from the various arts and crafts presses and printers from the 1890s to the 1930s.

The catalogue, as Bishop had astutely realized, was just the kind of resource and reference I had been seeking – because before I got hold of it, I had, in my own flailing way, managed to track down and buy some fetching examples of hand-coloured and illuminated books, and then had hit a wall. How to look for these arts and crafts presses? What were their names, who were the printers and illuminators, what period were they from, and most important of all, which were the most accomplished?

There was only scattered information on these arts and crafts books, and now suddenly along comes Villain's catalogue with bibliographical details for stunning examples of individual arts and crafts books as well as background information on the presses and the printers. Best of all, the catalogue photographically reproduces page spreads, title pages and striking examples of decoration, colour and illumination from Villain's copies to go with the catalogue descriptions.

When Villain began intensifying his pursuit of the arts and crafts presses (after hearing Susan Otis Thompson, the authority in this field, speak on the subject; later, she would write a magnificent book on this whole movement, which has since become the definitive study of this field), he found that most dealers and collectors were bibliographically a bit in the dark about these books since they had not been collected or stocked in any completist way. He adventured on, foraging for them everywhere, picking up whatever he could. In the process, he was able to illuminate this field, and make a pathway for others who might be drawn to such handcrafted books.

Overnight, the catalogue became a collector's resource for chasing the books and presses he showcased here. Many of these titles or special editions within these titles became the target of collectors, but more significantly, dealers who already had these titles realized they had underpriced them and raised the prices. Dealers began to look out for arts and crafts books at auctions and rare book fairs, and snapped them up to later offer them in their catalogues at higher prices.

Phil Bishop and Jean Francois Villain have been fellow collectors, friends and collaborates for many years, and when Phil sent me that email alerting me, he had thoughtfully, with Jean Francois's permission, attached a PDF of the catalogue before it could be published. That gave me first crack at many of these books before the prices shot up. I didn't stand a chance with the more famous and fabulous arts and crafts books – Susan Thompson's seminal book on these presses, *William Morris and American Book Design*, had already got the bigger antiquarian dealers in the book arts to acquire copies of these titles and put high prices on them. However, as I went on to discover, several titles that are in the catalogue could be found in the online inventory of many regular secondhand bookshops at reasonable prices (though not – especially with my rupee against their dollar – by any means cheaply priced).

And it was here that I found some delectable bargains, and accidentally found out many of them had no clue about how special their copies were, and how they had priced them the same as the regular copies. It happened this way: in Villain's catalogue I had been particularly drawn to some titles which had just the kind of hand-illuminated initials I am very drawn to. One was from a book by the Philosopher Press, and the catalogue had a photo of it. It was a book of poems by Daniel Gabriel Rossetti titled *Jenny*, and the opening chapter had an exquisite floriated five-line initial in three colours, modelled after a famous initial from an illuminated manuscript. And it was printed on handmade paper.

The catalogue said all the initials in *Jenny*, though smaller in size, were similarly hand-coloured. Checking for copies on ABE showed three were available, the prices ranging from $35 to $85 to and $150. My impecuniousness leapt forth, and I decided to grab the lowest-priced copy. The description from the bookseller listing this copy noted that only a few of the initials in the first few pages had colour to them, and the rest were in black and white, and the low price was because this seemed to be an incomplete copy. I was primarily wanting this book for that first decorated initial, and called the bookseller to look at his copy and tell me if that opening initial was in three colours.

He assured me it was, and said about six initials after that were also in colour, but alas, the rest were all black and white. Did I still want it? 'Yes, I'd like to buy it', I replied. When the book arrived, that beautiful initial looked even more lovely on the page. I ran the tips of my fingers over it and felt, to my satisfaction, the slightly raised, coarseness of the hand painted colours in it, made even more palpable because of the handmade paper. The other initials were lovely too, and had retained their bright colours of blue and green and purple.

My desire grew for more books from the Philosopher Press – who knew what beautiful examples of illumination lay in the other books? ABE showed about ten titles from this press from various dealers, priced anything from $55 to $850. And there seemed to be at least three to four copies available of each title available in the rare book market. I picked the next lowest-priced copy to explore – *Sermon on the Mount* – at $55 from a bookseller I had bought before and like very much, Robert Brooks. His description said the slipcase was worn and cracked, but the book itself was near fine.

Of the same title, there was another copy at $65, indicating it had a fine copy where the slipcase was intact. There was a third copy, also apparently fine from a dealer in Toronto, and it was priced $125. I first called Brooks, and asked him to get the copy in hand and tell me if it had any colour to it.

I did not want to use terms like hand-coloured or illuminated because even the common bookseller knows such copies are special. He came back on the phone with the book and said, 'Yes, the title page has elaborate borders in several bright colours surrounding the text, and flipping through the pages, there's colour on almost every page with designs that remind you of stained glass windows.' This felt most promising, and my excitement grew. I had already been feeling that I should have got a full hand-coloured copy of *Jenny*, so for this title I thought it made sense to get the other copy in fine condition even if the price was higher.

But what if that copy had sold and was not available? It would not be the first time I asked about a book to find out it had sold but the dealer had not taken it off his online inventory. I told Mr Brooks to please hold the copy for me for a day, and I would let him know if I wanted it. I tried the other bookseller, and he said he would call back after he had located the book on his shelves. Ten minutes later, he called back with the book in front of him. 'It's a very nice copy,' he said before I could ask him anything. I thanked him and asked him if the colours in the borders or initials still looked bright and vibrant?

'I don't follow', he said. 'What colours?'

'Oh, the title page and borders, I think, have colour to them?

'No; they are all in black and white. Are you sure you aren't thinking of another book?'

I thanked him and rang off quickly, and called the dealer in Canada with pricier copy. Luckily, I got him right away, and he was glad to go find the book for me. I got around to asking about the colour in the book, and he said, 'No, no colour at all. Yes, there are beautiful intricate borders and initials but just black. Why ever did you think it would be in colour?'

It looked like the Philosopher Press, like so many fine presses, had two states of their books, the regular edition and the special edition, which alone was hand-coloured or illuminated. The copy with Robert Brooks was one of the specials. I immediately put the order through on ABE. Had this hand-coloured deluxe copy found its way to one of the specialist book arts dealers or even an ABAA dealer, it would be nothing less than $450.

My copy of *Jenny*! Could that too be one of the specials – and there again, the bookseller had not realized it? There was a simple way to check: I called one after the other the two booksellers who had a copy of *Jenny*. I cut to the chase: were the initials in colour? No, black and white. Ditto for the other copy. Just black and white.

What had happened here, I realized, was that the hand-coloured edition from the Philosopher Press was being listed by booksellers in the same price range as the regular edition. Those with these special copies hadn't realized that the other copies were not illuminated. In fact, both the illuminated editions I had bought had been priced even less than the ordinary edition! This meant there was a good chance the other titles on the market from this press in the special state were probably underpriced as well.

What was showing was only the tip of the output of the press – some forty titles out of more than sixty had been in fine bindings, on Japanese vellum, illuminated elaborately – even the paper copies had all disappeared from the market. Who had run the Philosopher Press? I was now eager to find out more. To my delight, the person responsible for making these books as beautiful as they could possibly be with Kelmscott initials, handmade paper, fine binding, illumination and colour was a woman printer, Helen Van Vechten.

Helen, inspired by Morris and his books which she had collected, began making books with an emphasis on decoration and illumination. After a point, she began working the press herself, and for those books she had been involved in making, the colophon stated the number of copies printed and usually ended like this: 'and the book put through the press by Helen Van Vechten'.

The published prices for *Jenny*, for instance, when it was printed in 1899, was $15 for twenty-five copies on Japanese vellum in full gold-tooled leather, hand-illuminated in water colours and priced, 600 copies on antique Dickinson handmade paper for $2, and with some copies hand-illuminated for $5. These special initials were hand-illuminated by Helen Van Vechten. My incomplete copy is probably one of these specials decorated by the printer.

Sermon in the Mount (for some strange reason 'in' rather than 'on' the Mount) done in 1900, had 'the regulars priced at $2, hand illuminated at $5'. I checked all the other books of the Philosopher Press for sale online and found every copy of every available title was black and white, save for one on eBay – *Mezzotints* – which was doubly attractive for being inscribed by Helen Van Vechten to a friend. This copy of *Mezzotints* had hand-painted Klemscott initials, while the copy of the same title on ABE was the regular black and white. The special on eBay was $40, the regular was $80.

I bought the special, of course, and later realized how scarce anything signed by the printer was. Printed in 1900, printing details for the book states only the cover and title page had been hand-illuminated, so my copy must have been one of very few illuminated personally by Helen – perhaps because it was a presentation copy?

I never got this lucky with the other arts and crafts books I bought – though I did still manage to unearth a few bargains owing to dealers not knowing or understanding the work of these little-known presses. I bought at least a dozen titles from the catalogue, all the while amazed (yet again) at how scarce and beautiful books centuries-old can appear again and again on the antiquarian market, and in such excellent condition. There were plenty of more titles on the market from the catalogue, but they either did not appeal to me or were too expensive (in the $500 to $900 range).

This catalogue of Villain's illuminated and hand-coloured books came out in 2016, the books it features were mostly printed between 1890 and 1920. What were my chances of finding any of these today in the antiquarian market? Villain had been collecting them from the 1970s, and I was just getting started. When I began looking, I was amazed and excited to see that several, if not most of these titles, were still circulating in the rare book market. The choice items were gone or had become too expensive – I never could find, even for a price – a manuscript in vellum calligraphed and illuminated by Bamburg, or Robert Wilson Hyde's *A House Book*.

Or what looked like an arts and crafts book I would have enjoyed owning: *God's Noblest Work*, illuminated by Cora June Cady, a member of the Craftsman's Guild of Boston, that Villain describes as reaching 'a level of sheer decorative exuberance that rivals the best medieval manuscripts'.

I think for me the finest arts and crafts book is the *Cranbrook Papers* from the Cranbrook Press. This is the most impressive arts and crafts book I have seen, a feast as far as colour and illumination are concerned – a superior work, rivalling the work of illuminators from the Middle Ages, and all done on a beautiful handmade paper. I've seen poor to amateurish to timid to cheap work in this field, but George Booth, the proprietor and printer of Cranbrook, spared no expense and effort to produce such dazzling hand-work.

The typography and the presswork are average – Booth never seems to have gotten around to imitating Morris – not at least in the pure sense Conwell and Margaret O'Kane of the Elston Press had. In an another way, too, *Cranbrook Papers* is for me the ideal arts and crafts book: its subject itself is the book arts. Most arts and crafts books – for that matter, most fine press books – have for their subject poetry or literature, so it is rare to find a hand-illuminated book whose text deals with illumination, fine printing, William Morris, the heroes of early printing and other arts of the book.

Each of these 'papers' is really a chapter in the book, several penned by Booth and his friends, and most if not all the 'papers' deal with the book arts. The last book printed by this press was a short history of the press with a checklist, and it was called, simply, *Something About the Cranbrook Press*. Villain's catalogue featured the opening initial from this book – the letter S – that was so beautiful, it arrested me completely.

Now I've seen a lot of illuminated initials in books, but this one was like looking at a great initial from a medieval manuscript.

Villain himself comments on how special it is – I looked everywhere for the book, but there were no copies to be found anywhere. (As of this writing, it is still unavailable.) But even if I found a copy, I knew I would not be able to afford it. But from an old habit of book hunting online in order to while away time in an absorbing fashion, I keyed in Cranbrook Press as a search word for the umpteenth time on viaLibri, and one result, unexpectedly, appeared on eBay for something called *Cranbrook Papers*.

Looking at the listing, there were no photos or images for the book, and the description by the seller did not say much except to note that it was a nice example of an arts and crafts book. It also noted that its full vellum binding had warped, but was internally very fine. I decided to take a chance on it, and bought it. All collectors acquiring their books from online antiquarian platforms experience a sense of anticipation after having put an order through – you just hope your gamble pays off.

When the book or books finally arrive, you get hit with three kinds of expectations: it does not meet your expectation (which is the worst), it does not quite meet your expectations but you could get used to it (not such a bad thing) it meets your expectations (what you'd hoped for) and it exceeds all expectation to leave you stunned (the absolute best thing).

Everything about the *Cranbrook Papers*, as I turned the pages hurriedly, and at times, randomly, made me sit down and catch my breath. There was such masterful and sumptuous use of hand-illumination, and the brilliance of it was that it looked as fresh as the day it was done. The rich water colour paints (of blue and orange and red and green and purple) and the gilding (in various hues of gold from bright to muted), though thickly laid, had absorbed nicely into the fibre of the lovely handmade paper it was all laid out on, so there was no lumpiness or unevenness that you sometimes see with hand-added illumination.

I was expecting to see hand-colouring and illumination here and there, perhaps in a few large initials and several small initials, and perhaps paragraph accents in two colours, but here, Booth had outdone everyone in the making of a grand arts and crafts book: large quarto-sized pages had marginal hand decoration in the style of the best medieval illuminated manuscripts. In addition, on many pages, chapters or paragraphs began with five to ten line initials in colour and gold after initials from famous manuscripts, there were as many as four to six beautiful initials and ornaments to a two-page spread. It felt like Booth and his illuminators may have painstakingly copied the illumination work you see here from actual original medieval illuminated manuscripts. And then made them come alive by applying colours and gold by hand exactly in the manner of those medieval illuminators. The only difference? This was on paper, the originals were on vellum.

And the sweetest surprise in the book for me that I simply chanced upon while turning the pages was, at the start of a chapter, the very same seven-colour S initial that I had seen reproduced in the catalogue! Booth had used it here again – or very possibly this was the first use of it, and then this was borrowed and used again for *Something about the Cranbrook Press,* the last book from the press done in 1902. My luck got better: my copy was one of perhaps five or so that had been bound in full vellum with gilt titles and rules.

Booth, a newspaper editor, had been passionate about fine bookmaking, having bought Kelmscott Press books. He owned the *Chaucer*, and said that every time he ran his fingertips over the pages, he 'felt a tingle'. The desire to print beautifully ornamented books took possession of him – he thought perhaps the Roycrofters would give him some notion of how to make such books. And was disappointed at what he saw there – power presses, rather than hand presses, were being used. He wanted to aspire to the standards of his master, William Morris, and not compromise on material or handcraftsmanship.

Booth visited England, spending time with Cobden-Sanderson and Emery Walker. He was inspired by the socialism of Morris and Sanderson, and brought back some of that to his press workers. He learnt to print on a hand press, and print on dampened handmade paper. He arranged for everything in the manner of Morris, his hero. The watermarked all rag handmade paper, a hand press, black letter type harking back to Gutenberg and illumination after the finest medieval manuscripts. Cranbrook Press operated only for two years, from 1900–1902, and produced nine books and several portfolios of prints and papers.

What happened to illumination after 1920? It continued on for a couple more decades, especially in the work of the Grabhorn Press, where Valenti Angelo hand-coloured and illuminated several books and keepsakes for the press. Angelo himself continued the tradition in his private printing, for his Golden Cross Press, and would continue it even later in the 1970s and '80s, for his The Press of Valenti Angelo. When other presses used colour and illumination post the 1950s, it was not as elaborate or as sumptuous as in the early arts and crafts books. Mid-twentieth century saw two private presses resort to illumination in a controlled, highly artistic fashion: Mason Hill Press and St. Teresa's Press. (In England, of course, there was already the example of the Stanbrook Abbey Press, perhaps the private press best known for its elegant illuminated work.)

In 2019, a fine press book came out of the blue, carrying in it such majestic, wholehearted, elaborate and skilful illumination and hand-colouring as to edge out everything else that came before it in this field. From the hand of Lawrence G. Van Velzer and Peggy Gotthold came *The Travels of Sir John Mandeville*, where the margins of every page contains hand-illumination and colour on a truly spectacular handmade paper dampened for printing. Unlike old arts and crafts books, the presswork by Van Velzer is handsome, and Peggy's illustrations and initials hand-coloured and illuminated by her, are quite breathtaking. The book has been a success with a waitlist for orders.

One other hand-lettering artist, manuscript-maker and illuminator of note must be mentioned: *Maryanne Grebenstein, and her Turn-in-the-Path books. Maryanne is a gifted calligrapher, skilled at hand-decoration and illumination with gold leaf, who writes out a text in a beautiful calligraphic hand and then decorates and illuminates the pages with* gouache *and gold leaf. The books she makes are one-of-a-kind because there is only that one single copy of a manuscript.* 'Annabel Lee', for instance, Poe's well-known poem, is a 'hand-lettered manuscript with calligraphy, gilding and decoration, measuring 9.5 x 12.5 inches, and is written on Pergamenata paper stock with Moon Palace Sumi ink and incorporates 23K gold leaf and gouache in the decoration. It has been bound using marbled paper and book cloth'. Maryanne has calligraphed and gilded several such manuscripts and some of them are still available for sale on her website. You can view her work at www.turninthepath.com.

One of the chief reasons why the earliest makers of arts and crafts books introduced illumination in their books was to make them immediately appealing, in the hope that bibliophiles will be captivated and the edition will sell out. By boldly bringing back medieval-style illumination, colour and decoration, the Foolscap Press as well as Maryanne Grebenstein have shown that there is a market for it. I hope their work will inspire other contemporary printers to revive the tasteful use of colour and illumination in fine press books.

PART SEVEN

MANUSCRIPT HUNTING

MAKING A *MURAQQA*

Collecting Persian and Mughal Manuscript Miniatures

Searching eBay for Western medieval illuminated manuscript leaves that I could afford, I would often see several examples of (what looked like to me) single leaves of Persian or Mughal manuscript miniatures on paper. The miniatures were charming and pretty with brilliant colours and gold illumination. Typically, they had a few lines of calligraphic text in Persian or Arabic at the top and bottom of the page, with the miniature in the centre, showing either a court scene, a harem, a royal procession, or a sage/scholar reading a book. On the other side of the leaf would be a page of calligraphic text. The dealers listing these miniatures were mostly based in Lahore, Delhi or Jaipur.

I found myself very drawn to these leaves but would stop short of buying them because I just couldn't make out if they were actually from old Mughal/Persian manuscripts or if they were just prints or even if they were entirely new paintings created on order, using for their model iconic or historical images from famous Mughal manuscripts. The description for these listings provided by these sellers was hopeless – they confused one even more. They were listed as 'handmade'. But the listing would also say: 'brand-new item', and a little later: 'antique'.

I wrote to two or three dealers and gradually learnt they are not prints (which was good news) and that they were, for the most part, not antique but vintage: they were originally drawn, hand-painted and gilded by various manuscript painters from the 1970s to the 1990s, on manuscript paper that was possibly older: from the eighteenth or nineteenth century. Most of those artists are not alive anymore or have stopped working, while a few continue to make these imitation Mughal-Persian miniatures on order. I finally began buying them, though still cautiously. Compared to European illuminated manuscript leaves, these were attractively priced, from $30 to $150 – even the tiniest, no-frills Western miniature sells for nothing less than $800, going up to $2,200.

How did all this get started? How did these artists learn to make such skillful miniatures (most were done on paper, several on silk or fabric, a few on leather), how did they know what material to use, and how to apply gold? Exploring this vintage world of modern Indian manuscripts a little more in depth, I discovered that they actually had thrilling origins: these artists, their teachers and workshops belonging to various schools of painting go back to the tradition of manuscript production in the Mughal court from the sixteenth century; the tradition of Persian manuscript making even older: the thirteenth century.

After the commissioning and making of illuminated manuscripts at the imperial Mughal court, workshops gradually died out towards the late seventeenth century, the schools of painting that had sprung up continued into the nineteenth century with artists teaching new students the art and craft of manuscript miniature painting. From the time of the East Indian Company itself, there had been a thriving market for these beautifully accomplished modern versions of Persian and Mughal miniatures. Techniques and methods varied, and these differences created different schools of painting, though it all eventually coalesced into the National College of Arts in Lahore.

The artists and workshops eventually scattered, but the skills, technique and the knowledge of materials – pigments, minerals and gold – and where and how to source them, has been passed on from generation to generation, from teacher to student. At some point in the 1970s, dealers in art and antiques in Jaipur began to employ or commission these artisans to revive manuscript miniatures, and a cottage industry of miniature-making sprang up, which continues to this day, since the interest in owning Persian-Mughal miniatures in gold and colours will never entirely fade or die out.

'Gouache and gold on paper' has become an obsession for me: that's how dealers list these miniatures, and I assiduously hunt for them, turning up one stunning example after another. I am creating my '*Muraqqa*', my album of Persian and Mughal miniatures with calligraphic examples. I discovered when digging into the beginnings of this phenomenon, that from as far back as the sixteenth century, two kinds of miniatures were made for the Mughal emperors Akbar, Jahangir and Shah Jahan: miniatures to illustrate a whole manuscript, called 'book-painting', and standalone miniatures made to be mounted in an album, a *Muraqqa*. Once the *muraqqa* was full, with all its leaves mounted with lovely miniatures and masterful calligraphic specimens, it would be bound in finely decorated lacquer boards. The *muraqqa* must not be thought of as simply another scrapbook – some of the finest, such the albums ones owned by Jahangir, were considered more exquisite than most manuscripts, for the quality of calligraphic specimens and miniatures they held.

I have just about completed my first *muraqqa*, and was fortunate to find at an auction two very lovely Persian lacquer album covers from the eighteenth century that must have once contained splendid miniatures. One has become the cover for my just-finished *muraqqa*, and I am already well into gathering for the second album, for which a lacquer binding already awaits.

In the process of looking far and wide for specimens of Islamic miniatures, it hit me that what I should now really be after is the real thing: whole Persian, Ottoman or Mughal manuscripts from the eighteenth and nineteenth centuries that are decorated with *original* miniatures. That is, miniature paintings original to the book, done to illustrate its text or subject, not individual miniatures, and certainly not modern versions of miniatures. It is of course a question of price, of what I can afford. The very reason I had turned to modern Indo-Persian miniatures was because one could buy a decent amount of them without haemorrhaging their savings. But when weighed against a Western illuminated manuscript, even entire, original Persian-Mughal illuminated manuscript can seem temptingly priced. For instance, for the cost of five *single* European miniatures, you can purchase at least two or possibly three *entire* Mughal manuscripts containing several miniatures.

In April 2022, I acquired a sixteenth-century Persian manuscript with five miniatures in gold and colours, and an eighteenth-century Mughal manuscript with five miniatures and three intricately decorated *unwans* (headpiece decorations). I wrote about both acquisitions in *The Book Beautiful*. Between April and August 2023, I acquired three more manuscripts, one of which – *Divan of Hafiz* – is a real Kashmiri beauty from the eighteenth century, with twenty miniatures. But not before losing another fabulous Kashmiri manuscript from the nineteenth century – a *Khamsa of Nizami* with twenty-five miniatures – in a heated auction as the underbidder. This Nizami *Khamsa* had once upon a time been sold by Bernard Quaritch Ltd. Antiquarian Booksellers, London in 1964, to a collector, and had come up on the auction block after more than a century. And even back then, its price had been dear; in the present, the hammer price crossed four figures, pushing it out of my reach.

The *Hafiz-Divan* that I'd managed to find and purchase, and the *Nizami-Khamsa* that I'd failed to get, are later versions of the original manuscripts from the sixteenth century; one contains the poetry of Nizami, the other the poetry of Hafiz. These are perennial texts, favourites through history for calligraphers and artists to write out and illustrate in the way they imagine the manuscript should be written and illustrated. This way, each calligrapher, each artist, is able to create a new manuscript from the original manuscript, a new telling of these classic and beloved poems. Other famous Mughal manuscripts that go through later manuscript re-versions are the *Khamsa of Amir Khusraw* (1598), the *Gulistan of Saadi* (1584), the *Akbarnama* (1596), the *Padshahnama* (1657) and the *Baharistan of Jami* (1595). Sadly, and shamefully, not one of these great manuscripts with their splendid calligraphy and grand miniatures done for the Mughal emperors are in India. The *Khusraw* is at the Walters Art Museum, the *Padshahnama* at Windsor Castle, the *Akbarnama* and the *Hafiz Divan* are with the Chester Beatty Library, while the *Jami Baharistan* is at the Bodleian.

Before I give an account of how I came to acquire the three manuscripts I've mentioned above, a brief note on the history of Persian and Mughal book painting would be of use and interest to outline.

How did the tradition of making illuminated manuscripts begin in India, specifically Mughal India? Its origins lie in Persia. The art of Persian calligraphic manuscripts with miniatures in gold and colours flowered in the fourteenth century; one of the earliest surviving examples of such manuscript-making is the *Shahnameh of Firdausi*, better known as the 'Demotte' *Shahnameh* (after the antiquarian dealer who broke up the manuscript to sell its miniatures individually) done in Tabriz around 1335 and attributed to the miniaturist Shamsuddin, a student of a master of manuscripts, Ahmad Musa. The Demotte *Shanameh* has been praised for its beautiful miniatures, which, while revealing its Chinese and Arabic influence, nevertheless stylistically begins to show a distinctively Persian character with 'rich reds, blues, greens and gold'. Sheila Canby notes in *Persian Painting* (British Museum Press, 1993) that this manuscript 'contains in embryonic form the characteristics of Persian painting of the fourteenth to sixteenth centuries: highly organized, complicated compositions; brilliant colours; mastery of line and sharp contours, and the ability to convey human emotions through gesture, glance and pose.'

The manuscripts were written out, illustrated and illuminated in various ateliers in Isfahan, Herat, Tabriz and Shiraz, under the patronage of various dynasties, rulers and courts. These book studios particularly flourished under the rule of Prince Baysunghur (known as the 'bibliophile prince') and Sultan Bayqara, both of whom maintained several scriptoriums with gifted illuminators, painters, calligraphers and binders. Many of the manuscript paintings were unsigned, but a few artists gained fame in their own time, notably such master miniaturists as Kamal al-din Bizhad, Riza Abbasi, Mirak, Sultan Muhammad, Mahmud Muzahhib, Mir Sayyid Muzzafar and Ali Muhhamad Zaman.

Sometime in 1540, when Humayun took refuge in Tabriz under Safavid Shah Tahmasp (who could boast of the finest atelier in the Islamic world then), he became spellbound by the manuscripts he saw there. Fortunately for him and for the development of book painting in India, the Shah had retreated into religion and had lost interest in manuscripts and allowed two of his finest painters and calligraphers – Mir Sayyid Ali and Abd al-Samad – to accompany Humayun back to India. It is to these two artists from the Persian court that we owe the raising up of the first Imperial Mughal book studio that would eventually grow larger and grander under Akbar, Jahangir and Shah Jahan in the sixteenth and seventeenth centuries.

Though Aurangzeb, who did not care for book painting, brought the ateliers sadly to a close, some of the finest manuscript painting was done during his time; scholars have speculated that it could be because the artists had an inkling he would shut down the imperial workshop, and therefore went to even greater lengths to create paintings that they hoped would persuade Aurangzeb to change his mind. However, painting miniatures for manuscripts and *muraqqa*s did continue in India well into the nineteenth century, under various schools from the Sultanate to the Deccan to the Company School paintings – the latter largely favoured by the British Raj. They were just not as lavish as those from the imperial court.

Scholars estimate that by the time of Shah Jahan, the Mughal library held as many as twenty-two thousand exquisitely illuminated manuscripts.

Akbar's love for manuscripts led to the creation of several imperial ateliers in Agra, Lahore and Allahabad. Each book studio was filled with skilled calligraphers, painters, illuminators and binders. When a manuscript was commissioned by an emperor, several of these artists collaborated to create it. In these collaborative manuscripts, several artists have embedded their signatures, either in the miniatures or in the borders. The painter called Mansur was famous for his skill with painting animals, birds and portraits; Khwaja Jan Shirazi was an accomplished illuminator. What is of much interest is that though the first studios were initiated by Persian teachers, several of the artists in these studios were Hindu and Jain. Some of the most renowned are: Sivadasa, Madhava, Dasavanta, Basavana, Nanda Cela, Govardhan, Bishandas, Miskin, Keshavdas and Manohara. The two most acclaimed calligraphers of their time were Abd al-Rahim, who calligraphed the *Khamsa of Nizami*, and Muhammad Husayn, who wrote out the *Khamsa of Khusraw*; the latter was dubbed *zarrin qalam*, or the golden pen, for the sheer beauty of his writing hand.

To now return to the three Indian manuscripts I succeeded in acquiring: On 7 April 2023, I returned to the 63rd edition of the New York Antiquarian Book Fair, and got lucky again when I ducked into a booth to get out of the way of the crowds crushing the aisles. Staring at me was an attractive nineteenth-century Mughal manuscript that had been opened out to show two full-page miniatures in gold and colours, of a Mughal king and queen holding court. The little card in the glass cabinet describing the manuscript noted that it had ten miniatures.

Before asking to see it, I checked the price and found it very reasonable. The dealer took it out of the case, pulled up a chair for me to sit and look at it comfortably. All the other miniatures in it were just as lovely, and it hit me that it was not just reasonably priced, but a bargain. When I expressed immediate interest in buying it, the dealer even sweetly took 10 per cent off the catalogue price. Though it was the only thing I bought at that rare book fair, the trip was entirely worth it.

On eBay, I bought a gorgeously illuminated eighteenth-century Ottoman prayer book; no miniatures in this one but plenty of decoration in gold and colours in the form of head and tail pieces, and one highly illuminated title page. To describe it more fully: 207 pages; size: 11.2 x 14.6 cm; mainly eleven lines to a page, in clear and handsome *naskhī* script, in black ink; all sentences are separated by small rosettes; all pages are ruled with frames in gold, black and blue. The Arabic text is mainly vocalized throughout. Fifty-nine decorated headings in gold and colours, nine pages of *hilyas.* (A *hilya* or 'adornment' is a calligraphic portrayal of the sacred). The manuscript is bound in full Morocco, with a flap embossed with a central medallion on each cover. Once again, this was priced temptingly; while not a bargain, it was considerably lower than most illuminated manuscripts I have seen in this class.

Probably the rarest and most beautiful manuscript in my collection now is the eighteenth-century *Divan of Hafiz* (or *Diwan of Hafez*), which I acquired in August 2023. After losing the auction for that rather beautiful nineteenth-century *Khamsa of Nizami* in July of the same year, I was scouring the market for a manuscript that could come at least halfway close to the lavishness of that *Khamsa*, and suddenly found myself looking at one. A dealer in Lahore, Pakistan, had a charming Turkish manuscript with five miniatures, and was open to a best offer. It was while we were negotiating a price with offers and counter-offers that he suddenly emailed me a flurry of photos of what looked like a most-promising Kashmiri manuscript with several exquisite miniatures.

The dealer then called me to say he had not shown it to anyone yet – it was the best thing he had or had ever had in all his years of dealing in manuscripts, and then quoted a fantastically high sum as its price. 'A fair price for a manuscript like this, no?' he added. I asked for more details and additional photos. It was, he claimed, a 400-page calligraphic manuscript of the poetry of Hafiz in Persian, with twenty miniatures in colours and gold, finished sometime in the eighteenth century, most likely in Kashmir, where some of the most beautiful Indian manuscripts had been produced.

Using the images I had of the illuminated title page, several text pages and all of the miniatures photographed from various angles and in varied light, I had a Persian manuscript scholar look at it, and she was able to verify that it was indeed the *Divan of Hafiz,* and added that the miniatures were stunning. There was an issue, though: about fourteen of the twenty miniatures were partially rubbed out, with the faces of the people in the illustration faded or wiped out. I had seen this in other old manuscripts too; damage from the manuscript being exposed to constant use, the sweat from a user's fingers, moisture in the air, etc. Even with such defects, the miniatures were the most beautiful I had seen – far superior to that Quaritch *Khamsa* which had eluded me. I could only imagine how spectacular these miniatures must have looked to anyone who had been lucky enough to own or even see the manuscript just after it had been painted and gilded.

The colours in it – especially the oranges, greens and purples, along with the gold that formed the background to most of the illustrations – held your gaze until you soaked in the illustration and became lost in it. Three hundred years or so later, the colours were still overwhelming. The manuscript's ancientness, its palpable antiquity, had an otherworldly quality to it. I was unable to convince the dealer to revise the price – even after pointing to the damaged miniatures: and in the end, in a fit of bibliomania, I bought it.

ACKNOWLEDGEMENTS

My thanks to Philip R. Bishop for generously allowing me to use a photo of a beautiful book in his private collection for the cover of my book. The book is *American Bookbindings in the Library of Henry William Poor* (1903) in a highly decorated fine binding by master binder Alfred William Launder of Bradstreet's bindery.

My gratitude and thanks to Sonali Jindal, commissioning editor at Hachette India, and the team, for nurturing this book.

My thanks as ever to friends and family for their support and affection.

PUBLICATION HISTORY

'Those Glowing Madder-Dyed Reds and Indigo Blues': Richard Kossow's Incomparable Collection of Indian Incunabula

Originally published as 'India's "Incunabula"'. *Fine Books & Collections.* Spring 2019.

Graham Greene, Book Collector

Originally published as 'Writer, collector, hunter of rare books'. *Deccan Herald.* September 2010.

A Bibliophile in Bengaluru.

Bangalore Blue: A Bunch of Nostalgic Tales for and by True-Blue Bangaloreans. (Ed) Stanley Carvalho. 2013. Asian Trading Corporation.

The following appeared in a slightly different form in my columns for *The Hindu*'s *Literary Review* between 2010 and 2019:

- 'Old-type Books Only'
- Biryani Bhai
- Book-collecting Miracles
- 'Own Use Only'
- The Secret Bookshop
- The Bangalore *Alice*
- The Antiquary of Bengaluru
- Kumars

- The Bookwoman of South Ex-II
- A Bibliophile's Bird Books
- An Inky Parade of Tamil Bibliophiles
- Chasing a Rare Indian Type Specimen Book
- Mishaps of a Collector
- (Not) Collecting J.D. Salinger
- 'Windows to the Soul of the Rare Book Trade'
- Ranjitsinhji's 9,000 Elephants Visit Serendipity Books
- The Scruffy Incunabulist
- The Booksellers of San Serriffe and Other Biblio Spoofs and Hoaxes
- Adventures in Minibibliomania
- Philip R. Bishop: Collecting Mosher in Depth
- The Bloodless Bibliomystery
- London's Fabled Book Runners
- Rosy and Lilly
- Colin Franklin, Scholar-collector, Rare Book Dealer
- The Lure of the Hunt
- The Mysterious Bookshop
- Blossoming Bibliophilia: *In the Suicide's Library*
- The X-Acto Knife in E. Forbes Smiley's pocket: *The Map Thief*
- Rare Book Ring: *Thieves of Book Row*
- Razoring Out Bird-Books: *Torn from Their Bindings*
- Rare Book Swapping
- Jerry Kelly's Zapf
- A Hot Metal Masterpiece

APPENDIX

A Further Reading List: Antiquarian Bookselling, Book Collecting, Rare Book Dealers, Book Collectors and Bibliophily

Here is a reading list, in no particular order or preference, that is fairly wide-ranging and comprehensive – though far from exhaustive – made up of my favourite non-fiction books (and pamphlets) about rare book dealing, collecting and bibliophily, every one of which I've enjoyed, learnt from and can recommend.

Contemporary (2001–2023)

- Otto Penzler. *Mysterious Obsession: Memoirs of a Compulsive Collector*
- Stephen Clarke. *Lefty Lewis and the Waldegraves: Collecting, Obsession, Friendship*
- Phillip J. Pirages. *Booked By Fate: A Life of Dealing in the Exotic World of Rare Books*
- Stella Panayotova, (ed.) *Art, Academia and the Trade: Sir Sydney Cockerell (1867–1962)*
- Kurt Zimmerman. *Rare Book Hunting: Essays and Escapades*
- James Fergusson (ed.). *Ian Jackson, 1951–2018*
- Marius Kociejowski. *A Factotum in the Book Trade*
- Nicolas Barker. *At First, All Went Well and Other Brief Lives*

- Denise Gigante. *Book Madness: A Story of Book Collectors in America*
- Nicholas Royle. *White Spines: Confessions of a Book Collector*
- Oliver Darkshire. *Once Upon a Tome: The Misadventures of a Rare Bookseller*
- Margaret Leslie Davis. *The Lost Gutenberg: The Astounding Story of One Book's Five-Hundred-Year Odyssey*
- Christopher de Hamel. *The Posthumous Papers of the Manuscripts Club*
- Richard Landon. *A Long Way from the Armstrong Beer Parlour: A Life in Rare Books*
- Annette Campbell-White. *Beyond Market Value: A Memoir of Book Collecting and the World of Venture Capital*
- Clarence Wolf. *Fifty Years a Bookseller: or, The Wolf at Your Door*
- Ian Jackson. *Bernard M. Rosenthal: A Biographical and Bibliographical Account*
- Peter Murray Jones and Liam Sims (eds.). *Floreat Bibliomania – Great Collectors and their Grand Designs: A centenary celebration of the life and work of ANL Munby. Transactions of the Cambridge Bibliographical Society*
- John Crichton (ed.). *Franklin Gilliam: Texas Bookman*
- Peter Howard. *Martin Stone, Bookscout*
- Stephen Gertz (ed.). *The Remarkable Martin Stone*
- G. Thomas Tanselle. *Books In My Life*
- Richard Wendorf. *The Literature of Collecting & Other Essays*
- John Baxter. *A Pound Of Paper: Confessions Of A Book Addict*
- Ross King. *The Bookseller of Florence: The Story of the Manuscripts That Illuminated the Renaissance*
- Christopher de Hamel. *Sydney Carlyle Cockerell*
- Arthur L. Schwarz. *Dear Mr. Cockerell, Dear Mr Peirce*
- Sidney E. Berger. *The Dictionary of the Book: A Glossary for Book Collectors, Booksellers, Librarians, and Others*

- Joel Silver. *Dr. Rosenbach and Mr. Lilly: Book Collecting in a Golden Age*
- Morrow Linenthal and Noel (eds.). *Medieval Book: Glosses from Friends & Colleagues of Christopher de Hamel*
- Sheila Markham. *A Book of Booksellers and A Second Book of Booksellers: Conversations with the Antiquarian Book Trade*
- Ian Jackson. *The Key to Serendipity: How to Buy Books from Peter B. Howard; The Key to Serendipity: How to Find Books In Spite of Peter B. Howard; Ranjitsinhji's 9,000 Elephants Visit Serendipity Books*
- Larry McMurtry. *Books: A Memoir*
- Colin Franklin. *Obsessions and Confessions of a Book Life*
- Luke Ives Pontifell (ed.). *Roger Eliot Stoddard at Sixty-Five: A Celebration*
- Michael Vinson. *Edward Eberstadt & Sons: Rare Booksellers of Western Americana*
- Michael Vinson. *Bluffing Texas Style: The Arsons, Forgeries, and High-Stakes Poker Capers of Rare Book Dealer Johnny Jenkins*
- Rick Gekoski. *Guarded by Dragons: Encounters with Rare Books and Rare People*
- William Reese. *Collectors, Booksellers, and Libraries: Essays on Americanists and the Rare Book Market*
- Gordon Ray. *Books As A Way of Life*
- Heidi Ardizzone. *An Illuminated Life: Belle da Costa Greene's Journey from Prejudice to Privilege*
- Marvin Mondlin, Roy Meader. *Book Row: An Anecdotal and Pictorial History of the Antiquarian Book Trade*
- Jack Walsdorf. *On Collecting William Morris*
- Viscount Carlow. *On Collecting Books and Printing Them, Too*
- Nicholas A. Basbanes. *Patience and Fortitude: A Roving Chronicle of Book People, Book Places, and Book Culture*

- Nicholas A. Basbanes. *Among the Gently Mad: Strategies and Perspectives for the Book-Hunter in the 21st Century*
- Renato Rabaiotti. *Horae Bibliographicae Cantabrigienses. A Facsimile of Dibdin's Cambridge Notebook 1823;* With Readings from the Library Companion, 1824
- Frans A. Janssen. *Dibdin in Paris*
- Jenni Matz (ed.). *Reminiscences & Remembrances of Herman and Aveve Cohen and the Chiswick Bookshop*
- David Batterham. *Among Booksellers: Tales Told in Letters to Howard Hodgkin*
- Eric White. *Editio Princeps: A History of the Gutenberg Bible*
- Nicolas Barker. *The Roxburghe Club: A Bicentenary History*
- George Ong and Eric Holzenberg. *For Jean Grolier and His Friends. 125 Years of Grolier Club Exhibitions and Publications* 1884–2009
- Mary Eccles. *Mary Hyde Eccles: A Miscellany of Her Essays and Addresses*
- Thomas G. Tanselle. *Other People's Books: Association Copies and the Stories They Tell*
- Alastair Johnston. *Serendipitous Books: A Memoir of Peter B. Howard*
- Carol Porter Grossman. *The History of the Limited Editions Club*
- Thomas G. Tanselle. *The Pleasures of Being a Scholar-collector: The Robert L. Nikirk Lecture, 2005*

Modern (1940–2000)

- Giles Mandelbrote (ed.). *Out of Print and Into Profit: A History of the Rare and Secondhand Book Trade in Britain in the Twentieth Century*
- A.S.G. Edwards (ed.). *The Pleasures of Bibliophily: Fifty Years of 'The Book Collector': An Anthology*

- Wilmarth Sheldon Lewis. *Collector's Progress*
- Lessing J. Rosenwald. *Recollections of a Book Collector*
- Jeff Dykes. *I Had All the Fun: Some Recollections of a Book Collector*
- Ian Jackson. *An Antiquarian ABC*
- O.F. Snelling. *Rare Books and Rarer People: Some Personal Reminiscences of 'the Trade'*
- A.N.L. Munby. *Phillipps Studies*, I to V
- A.N.L. Munby. *Portrait of an Obsession* (condensed version of the *Phillipps Studies* by Nicolas Barker)
- Millicent Sowerby. *Rare People and Rare Books*
- John Schroder. *Collecting Rupert Brooke*
- John Bidwell and Carol R. Briggs (eds.). *A Bibliophile's Los Angeles. Essays for the International Association of Bibliophiles on the Occasion of Its XIVth Congress (30 September–11 October 1985)*
- Hans Peter Kraus. *Hans Peter Kraus: In Memoriam. 1907–1988*
- Jean Peters (ed.). *Book Collecting: A Modern Guide*
- Robert H. Jackson, Carol Rothkopf (eds.). *Book Talk: Essays on Books, Booksellers, Collecting, and Special Collections*
- David Chambers (ed.). *A Modest Collection: Private Libraries Association, 1956-2006.*
- George Fletcher (ed.). *A Miscellany for Bibliophiles*
- Stephen Gertz (ed.). *Book Trade Tributes to Peter B. Howard*
- Drif Field. *Not 84 Charing Cross Road*
- Christopher de Hamel, Richard Linenthal (eds.). *Fine Books and Book Collecting: Books and Manuscripts Acquired from Alan G. Thomas and Described by His Customers on the Occasion of His Seventieth Birthday*
- Nicholas A. Basbanes. *A Gentle Madness: Bibliophiles, Bibliomanes, and the Eternal Passion for Books*
- David Magee. *Infinite Riches: The Adventures of a Rare Book Dealer*

- H.P. Kraus. *A Rare Book Saga*
- David A. Randall. *Dukedom Large Enough: Reminiscences of a Rare Book Dealer, 1929–1956*
- Norman H. Strouse. *How to Build a Poor Man's Morgan Library*
- Norman H. Strouse. *A Collector's Decabiblon*
- Donald Dickinson. *Henry E. Huntington's Library of Libraries*
- Edwin Wolf with John F. Fleming. *Rosenbach: A Biography*
- A.N.L. Munby. *Essays and Papers*
- Kathryn Rickard. *My Adventures in Minibibliomania.*
- John Dickinson. *John Carter: The Taste & Technique of a Bookman*
- John Carter. *ABC for Book Collectors* (Ninth revised edition, updated by Nicolas Barker and Simran Thadani)
- Colin Franklin. *Obsessions and Confessions of a Book Life*
- David Mason. *The Pope's Bookbinder: A Memoir*
- Robert Wilson. *Modern Book Collecting*
- David Low. *With All Faults*
- Sigfred Taubert. *Bibliopola: Pictures and Texts about the Book Trade*, 2 vols.
- Nancy and Lawrence Goldstone. *Used and Rare: Travels in the Book World*
- G.T. Goodspeed. *The Bookseller's Apprentice*
- Seymour De Ricci. *English Collectors of Books and Manuscripts: 1530–1930, and Their Marks of Ownership*
- Robin Waterfield (ed.). *Dear David, Dear Graham: A Bibliophilic Correspondence*
- Percy H. Muir. *Minding My Own Business: An Autobiography*
- Anthony Rota. *Books in the Blood: Memoirs of a Fourth-Generation Bookseller*
- John Sparrow. *Association Copies: An Essay with Examples Drawn from the Author's Own Collection*

- Donald C. Dickinson. *Dictionary of American Book Collectors*
- Donald C. Dickinson. *Dictionary of American Antiquarian Bookdealers*
- Nicolas Barker. *Bibliotheca Lindesiana: The Lives and Collections of Alexander William, 25th Earl of Crawford and 8th Earl of Balcarres, and James Ludovic, 26th Earl of Crawford and 9th Earl of Balcarres*
- Nicholas Barker. *The Book Collector.* A special number to commemorate the 150th Anniversary of Bernard Quaritch Ltd., 1997
- George Sims. *The Rare Book Game/More of the Rare Book Game/Last of the Rare Book Game*
- William W. Clary. *Fifty Years of Book Collecting*
- Henry Wagner. *Sixty Years of Book Collecting*
- E.J. O'Dwyer. *Thomas Frognall Dibdin; Bibliographer & Bibliomaniac Extraordinary 1776–1847*
- Alan G. Thomas. *Great Books and Book Collectors*
- William Alexander Jackson. *Records of a Bibliographer: Selected Papers of William Alexander Jackson*
- Charles P. Everitt. *The Adventures of a Treasure Hunter: A Rare Bookman in Search of American History*
- Seymour Adelman. *The Moving Pageant: A Selection of Essays*
- John Carter. *Taste and Technique in Book-Collecting*
- John F.X. Harriott. *Farewell to True Bookshops*
- John T. Winterich. *Collector's Choice*
- Carl L. Cannon. *American Book Collectors and Collecting from Colonial Times to the Present*
- Wyman Parker. *Henry Stevens of Vermont: American Rare Book Dealer in London, 1845–1886*
- John T. Winterich. *A Primer of Book Collecting*
- Robin Myers and Michael Harris (eds.). *Antiquaries, Book Collectors, and Circles of Learning*

Classic (1809–1939; several, if not all, of these titles are in the public domain and can be read online or downloaded)

- T.F. Dibdin. *Bibliomania*
- T.F. Dibdin. *The Bibliographical Decameron, Or Ten Days Pleasant Discourse Upon Illuminated Manuscripts And Subjects Connected With Early Engraving, Typography And Bibliography*
- Robert Curzon. *Visits to Monasteries in the Levant*
- John Hill Burton. *The Book-Hunter*
- Octave Uzanne. *The Book-Hunter in Paris: Studies Among the Bookstalls and the Quays*
- William Robert. *The Book-Hunter in London*
- P.B.M. Allan. *The Book-Hunter at Home*
- Barton Currie. *Fishers of Books*
- William Loring Andrews. *Jean Grolier de Servier: Viscount D'Aguisy. Some Account of his Life and of his Famous Library*
- William Loring Andrews. *Gossip About Book Collecting*. 2 vols
- William Loring Andrews. *Sextodecimos et infra*
- William Loring Andrews. *The Old Booksellers of New York, and Other Papers*
- William Loring Andrews. *Among My Books*
- Oscar Albert Bierstadt. *The Library of Robert Hoe: A Contribution to the History of Bibliophilism in America*
- Frederic Somner Merryweather. *Bibliomania in the Middle Ages*
- Roux de Lincy. *Researches Concerning Jean Grolier: His Life and His Library*
- A.S.W. Rosenbach. *Books and Bidders: The Adventures of a Bibliophile*
- Leona Rostenberg and Madeleine B Stern. *Old & Rare: Thirty Years in the Book Business*

- William Harris Arnold. *Ventures in Book Collecting*
- William Harris Arnold. *First Report Of A Book-collector: A Brief Answer To The Frequent Question "Why First Editions?"*
- William Hazlitt. *The Confessions of a Collector*
- Edward A. Newton. *The Amenities of Book Collecting and Kindred Affections*
- Henry Stevens. *Recollections of Mr. James Lenox of New York and the Formation of His Library*